A Cultural Dictionary of the Chinese Language

A Cultural Dictionary of the Chinese Language introduces the 500 most important cultural traits of the Chinese as reflected in language use, especially in Chinese idioms (*chengyu*), proverbs and colloquial expressions (*suyu*).

Communicative competence, the ultimate goal of language learning, consists of not only linguistic, but intercultural competence, which enables the language learner to speak with fluency and understanding. The Chinese language is richly imbued with cultural wisdoms and values underlying the appropriateness of idioms in the Chinese language.

The *Dictionary* provides intermediate and B1-C1 level learners as well as scholars of the Chinese language with an essential reference book as well as a useful cultural reader.

Liwei Jiao is Lecturer of Chinese at Brown University, USA. Besides his rich 20-years of experience of teaching Chinese at various levels at Renmin University of China, the University of Durham and the University of Pennsylvania, he publishes extensively in Chinese phraseology, language and culture, and Chinese phonetics. Among his many publications are *500 Common Chinese Idioms* (co-authored, 2010); *500 Common Chinese Proverbs and Colloquial Expressions* (co-authored, 2013); *The Routledge Advanced Chinese Multimedia Course* (co-authored, 2009, 2014); and *A Thematic Dictionary of Contemporary Chinese* (co-authored, 2019). He is a contributor to the *Routledge Encyclopedia of the Chinese Language* (ed. Chan Sin-Wai, 2016) and *Encyclopedia of China* (3rd edition, forthcoming).

A Cultural Dictionary of the Chinese Language

500 Proverbs, Idioms and Maxims
文化五百条

Liwei Jiao

First published 2020
by Routledge
2 Park Square, Milton Park, Abingdon, Oxon OX14 4RN

and by Routledge
52 Vanderbilt Avenue, New York, NY 10017

Routledge is an imprint of the Taylor & Francis Group, an informa business

© 2020 Liwei Jiao

The right of Liwei Jiao to be identified as author of this work has been asserted by him in accordance with sections 77 and 78 of the Copyright, Designs and Patents Act 1988.

All rights reserved. No part of this book may be reprinted or reproduced or utilised in any form or by any electronic, mechanical, or other means, now known or hereafter invented, including photocopying and recording, or in any information storage or retrieval system, without permission in writing from the publishers.

Trademark notice: Product or corporate names may be trademarks or registered trademarks, and are used only for identification and explanation without intent to infringe.

British Library Cataloguing-in-Publication Data
A catalogue record for this book is available from the British Library

Library of Congress Cataloging-in-Publication Data
Names: Jiao, Liwei, author.
Title: 880-01 A cultural dictionary of the Chinese language : 500 proverbs, idioms, and maxims = Wen hua wu bai tiao / Liwei Jiao.
Other titles: 500 proverbs, idioms, and maxims
Description: Abingdon, Oxon ; New York, NY : Routledge, 2020. | Includes bibliographical references and index.
Identifiers: LCCN 2019027771 (print) | LCCN 2019027772 (ebook) | ISBN 9781138907294 (hardback) | ISBN 9781138907300 (paperback) | ISBN 9780429356476 (ebook)
Subjects: LCSH: Chinese language—Dictionaries—English. | Proverbs, Chinese—Dictionaries—English. | Chinese language—Idioms—Dictionaries—English. | Maxims, Chinese—Dictionaries—English.
Classification: LCC PL1455 .J48 2020 (print) | LCC PL1455 (ebook) | DDC 495.1/321—dc23
LC record available at https://lccn.loc.gov/2019027771
LC ebook record available at https://lccn.loc.gov/2019027772

ISBN: 978-1-138-90729-4 (hbk)
ISBN: 978-1-138-90730-0 (pbk)
ISBN: 978-0-429-35647-6 (ebk)

Typeset in Times New Roman
by Apex CoVantage, LLC

For my daughter Kathy.

Contents

Introduction   ix
Acknowledgements   xiii
List of entries   xiv

1   Overall (总论)   1

2   National character (民族性格)   6

3   Religion, philosophy, politics, history (宗教, 哲学, 政治, 历史)   23

4   Life, society, arts, literature (生活, 社会, 艺术, 文学)   43

5   Social relations, family, women, education (社会关系, 家庭, 女人, 教育)   62

6   Nature, animals, language (自然, 动物, 语言)   79

Appendix 1 English index of entries   101
Appendix 2 Alphabetical index of Chinese entries   108
Appendix 3 Alphabetical index of Chinese expressions in footnotes   115
Appendix 4 Index of entries by their cultural value   134
Appendix 5 A brief chronology of Chinese history (to 1912)   141

Introduction

A Cultural Dictionary of the Chinese Language: 500 Proverbs, Idioms, and Maxims (hereafter CDCL) is a concise dictionary for intermediate and advanced learners of Chinese as well as general readers to efficiently grasp the essence of Chinese culture that is embedded in common Chinese proverbs, idioms, maxims and well-known stories.

CDCL is intended to serve as a quick reference guide to Chinese language and culture and hopes to supplement and moreover leverage the comprehension and production of phraseological expressions in *500 Common Chinese Idioms* (by Jiao et al., Routledge 2011) and *500 Common Chinese Proverbs and Colloquial Expressions* (by Jiao et al., Routledge 2014), which were jointly conceived with this book more than ten years ago.

CDCL is not only immensely useful for learners of Chinese at the intermediate level and above, but also invaluable for instructors of Chinese at all levels, as well as a compelling read for general readers who are interested in Chinese culture for its convincing analysis and engaging stories.

Chinese language and culture

Language and culture are inevitably intertwined, especially in civilizations such as that of China, which has a long and rich history and an ancient and highly sophisticated culture. CDCL aims to answer two general yet vital questions on the relationship between Chinese language and culture. One question concerns how basic cultural concepts are reflected in fixed expressions and famous stories; the other is on which aspects of culture are embodied in common Chinese words, structures and expressions. To be more specific, take '爱' and '老虎' (literally 'love' and 'tiger') as an example. 爱 (love) is an abstract human emotion (although many may not agree), and 老虎 (tiger) is a common word in Chinese. CDCL aims to answer questions such as 'How is the concept of 爱 (love) expressed in the Chinese language?' and 'What do 老虎 (tiger) and related expressions reflect in terms of Chinese culture?'

Nowadays it is easy to know and even experience a little bit of Chinese culture as it is easily observed through giant pandas, kungfu, *qipao* (*cheongsam*, mandarin gown), the Great Wall, Chinese cuisine, Chinese herbs, green tea and Confucius etc., but for those who have not studied Chinese culture at an academic institution or experienced it in an authentic cultural environment, it is difficult to comprehend many aspects in depth. For example, Westerners may observe that most Chinese people are rather reserved and speak relatively little in public, but do not fully understand why. In ancient China and even in the contemporary China, 'to speak less' (少说) is a fundamental value in Chinese culture. It is reflected in an array of expressions, such as idioms like 言多语失 (talk-more-speech-err, the more one

x *Introduction*

talks, the more errors he will make) and 谨言慎行 (prudently-speak-cautiously-act, to speak and act cautiously) and proverbs like 病从口入, 祸从口出 (disease-from-mouth-enter, trouble-from-mouth-out, a ready tongue is an evil). If a Chinese child is late in uttering his first words, his grandparents will not worry at all and probably say 贵人语迟 (great-people-speak-delayed) to the child's parents. Chairman Mao (Mao Zedong) had an excellent understanding of Chinese culture. He had two daughters whose first names are 讷 (slow of speech) and 敏 (quick in action), apparently derived from a line by Confucius 君子欲**讷**于言而**敏**于行 (The noble man desires to be hesitant in speech, but sharp in action). If one knows the above-mentioned expressions and story, he would be able to profoundly understand this aspect of Chinese culture and use relevant and authentic expressions to communicate with Chinese people in an accurate way.

How this dictionary is organized

Entries in this book are arranged loosely based on their culture relevance or the thematic system of words. For example, Entry #194 'Teacher and Student, Master and Apprentice' is next to Entry #195 'Respecting Teachers' because of their close connection in Chinese culture, while Entry #289 '73 and 84' is next to Entry #290 'Three hundred' because of their relevance as numbers.

Under each entry, there are up to a dozen or more fixed expressions that expound or denote the cultural implication of the entry. For example, under the entry 'Food and Drink' (#122) are five well-known expressions.

An entry consists of an English term and its Chinese equivalent, as well as a number between 1 to 10, especially the following ones, 1, 2, 3, 5 or 10, which indicates the cultural value of the entry, with 10 being the most important. Judgement is based on the author's experience of previously compiling three dictionaries that are congruous with this book in overall design, conceived more than ten years ago. Readers of this book, either experts on Chinese culture or students on a Chinese course, may not agree with the author on every exact number, but it is the author's good intention to provide an easy index for readers who are not yet well acquainted with Chinese culture. For example, all will agree that 'filial piety' (孝) is one of the most important concepts in Chinese culture, therefore, Entry #168 'Filial' is marked with a number '10.' As another example, Entry #140 is 'Mystic Dragon Cult Leader (神龙教主) 5.' Many readers may not be familiar with this name, but if you have a working understanding of China's general history, some knowledge about the founding emperor of the Song dynasty and the Cultural Revolution, and adequate knowledge of the martial arts novel, *The Deer and the Cauldron* (鹿鼎记) by Louis Cha Leung-yung (金庸), you would agree that the cultural indicator '5' is fairly appropriate, if not exact.

Almost all Chinese expressions are annotated in the footnotes. The format of the footnotes shows 'the expression in simplified Chinese,' 'the expression in traditional Chinese' in brackets, 'the expression in pinyin,' and 'the word-to-word annotation in English' in parentheses. Free translations of expressions are not given in the footnotes because they appear within the text. A hyphen '-' is used to represent a Chinese character or a clause that has no difference in simplified and traditional forms, for example, 不以成败论英雄 [---败論--] bù yǐ chéngbài lùn yīngxióng (not-by-success or failure-measure-hero) and 一蟹不如一蟹 [-] yī xiè bùrú yī xiè.

There are five appendices at the end of the book: (1) English index of entries, (2) Alphabetical index of Chinese entries, (3) Alphabetical index of Chinese expressions, (4) Index of entries by their cultural value, (5) A brief chronology of Chinese history (to 1912).

Introduction   xi

Some notes on the compilation of this dictionary

This book does not answer to all questions relating to Chinese language and culture. According to a classification by *A Thesaurus of Modern Chinese* (现代汉语分类词典, by Su Xinchun et al. 2013), there are 12,659 categories of lexemes, which could reflect differences in culture. Additionally, culture is impossible to be broken down into pieces. This book includes 290 entries, most of which are not expounded elsewhere in this regard, for example, Entry #103 'One man (一人).'

CDCL is not simply massive compilation of proverbs, idioms, slangs, maxims and quotations, which is not difficult owing to advances in modern technology. It is, however, an observation of Chinese language and culture at their meeting point. For example, there are more than 60 fixed expressions with the pattern '金*玉*' (金 meaning 'gold' and 玉 'jade'), although only eight are included in this book. (See Entry #229)

It is a shame that many famous expressions cannot be explained fully in details. For example, '不能极问' (cannot ask in details) appears in entries on 'Teacher and student, master and apprentice' (#194) and 'Education: learning methods' (#192) of this book, but neither is explained. Below is justification for inclusion of this expression:

> Confucius is universally regarded as the greatest educator in the entire history of China. He had unprecedentedly innovative ideas on teaching and learning; however, his teaching methods were not without their flaws. The Eastern Han dynasty philosopher Wang Chong (27–100) criticized Confucius in the 28th Chapter '*Criticisms on Confucius* (问孔篇)' of his book '*Critical Essays*' (or '*Disquisitions,*'论衡): 以学於孔子, 不能极问也. 圣人之言, 不能尽解, which means 'because learning with Confucius, one cannot ask in details. Therefore, Sage Confucius's words cannot be fully understood.' Modern scholar Yi Baisha (易白沙, 1886–1921) held the same opinion in his influential article '孔子平议' (objective review of Confucius) in 1916. The *Classic of Filial Piety* (孝经) is one of the most influential books in Chinese cultural history. The book is records of dialogues between Confucius and his prominent disciple Zengzi (曾子 or 曾参, 505 BCE–435 BCE) and consists of 1,903 characters. In this book, Zengzi only uttered FOUR sentences. The first one represents opening remarks without any substance, and the second flattering words. Only the third and fourth address true questions. It was said that there was a person, 少正卯 who was strongly against Confucius's thoughts, but was put to death for spreading unorthodox ideas only seven days after Confucius had assumed the post of prime minister of the State of Lu.

Chinese culture is unique largely due to its long and profound history. One key clue for understanding Chinese culture is that China was an agricultural society throughout most of its history. This helps to explain why 锅 (wok) carries much cultural significance in the Chinese language. For example, 'to offer all one has' can be expressed with 砸锅卖铁 (smash-wok-sell-iron).

It is the author's sincere wish that users of this book can apply what they gain from this book to analysis of not only traditional Chinese culture, but also of contemporary linguistic phenomena. For example, why is 'One Belt One Road' (the Belt and Road Initiative, BRI, See #114) called '一带一路' not '一路一带' in Chinese? The Road (Silk Road, 丝绸之路) was coined before the Belt (Maritime Silk Road) and is much more well known. A possible explanation is that '路带' (road strip) makes little sense but '带路' (lead the way) makes much more sense because it suits China's ambition (中国梦 Chinese dream) to lead the

xii *Introduction*

world. This being said, some expressions, which were of cultural significance in ancient times but are hardly intelligible at present, are omitted, for example, 穷得穿不起裤子 (too poor to afford a pair of pants).

The author has tried his best to observe and explain the linguistic and cultural phenomena involved in this book from the standpoint of ordinary learners, but due to his educational background and work experience, intellectual influence is inevitable. For example, when 'legacy' (功名) is mentioned, the author's instinct is to refer to the poems by Southern Song dynasty poets and generals Yue Fei (岳飞, 1103–1142), Xin Qiji (辛弃疾, 1140–1207) and Wen Tianxiang (文天祥, 1236–1283).

Acknowledgements

The author wishes to express his appreciation to Ms. Alison McFarland, Ms. Eveline Liu, and Ms. Mae Fullerton who proofread many parts of the draft of this book, and my editors at Routledge: Senior Publisher Andrea Hartill, and Ms. Claire Margerison for their support of this book, the fifth one in a row with Routledge. This book is for my daughter, Katherine Jiao, who has been a major source of happiness for me during the past four years in the compilation of this book.

Liwei Jiao

Entries

Chapter 1: Overall (总论)

1. Chinese language and culture: negative tendency (中国语言的负面倾向) 10
2. Chinese characters and way of thinking (汉字与思维) 5
3. The battle of Chinese character forms: traditional, simplified or pinyin? (汉字之争) 5
4. Auditory impression of the Chinese language (汉语的听觉印象) 10
5. Sound and culture (语音与文化) 2
6. Temporal sequence (时间顺序) 5
7. Idioms with markers of simile (带比喻词的成语) 3
8. Electricity and Chinese idioms (成语中的电) 2
9. Getting rich and building roads (致富与修路) 1
10. Change (化) 3
11. The verse that changed China the most (影响中国最大的一句话) 5

Chapter 2: National character (民族性格)

12. Change (改变) 5
13. Change, in the wrong way (变坏) 3
14. People, the (人民) 10
15. Standpoint (立场) 5
16. Courage (勇气) 5
17. Times and heroes (时势与英雄) 3
18. Tolerant (宽容) 5
19. Oneself and others (人与己) 2
20. Utilitarianism (功利主义) 5
21. Partial and impartial (公与私) 3
22. Speculative (投机) 5
23. Who do you think you are? (你算老几啊?) 1
24. Snobbish (势利眼) 1
25. No principles (无原则) 5
26. Not standing out (不出头) 5
27. Sophistication (灵活) 1
28. Kick someone to the curb (卸磨杀驴) 5
29. Mental balance (心理平衡) 2
30. Success and failure (胜负, 成败) 5
31. Fame and fortune (名利) 10

Entries xv

32. Integrity vs. ability (德与才) 3
33. Benevolence and justice (仁与义) 3
34. Refined and popular (雅俗) 2
35. Humorous (幽默) 2
36. Good or bad (优劣) 5
37. Stress the past, not the present (厚古薄今) 3
38. Vast land and abundant natural resources (地大物博) 3
39. Old or new (新与旧) 10
40. Lu Xun (鲁迅) 5
41. Onlookers (看客) 5
42. Silence (沉默) 2
43. Stay foolish (难得糊涂) 3
44. Shortcuts (捷径) 2
45. Greedy (贪婪) 3
46. Repent (回头) 2
47. Legacy (功名) 5
48. Integrity in one's later years (晚节) 1
49. Nonverbal love (无言的爱) 3
50. Share weal or woe? (同甘还是共苦) 3
51. Life and death (生死)5
52. 'Death penalty' and modesty (死罪死罪) 5
53. To survive by all possible means (活着) 3
54. Men's three treasures (农民的三宝) 3
55. Die, death (死) 5
56. Chinese condolences (节哀顺变) 2
57. Same and different (同与异) 5

Chapter 3: Religion, philosophy, politics, history (宗教, 哲学, 政治, 历史)

58. Heavenly principles (天理) 10
59. Mandate of Heaven, or God's will (天命, 天意) 5
60. Laws (法) 5
61. Auspicious signs and the color white (祥瑞与白色) 3
62. Locations of the four temples in Beijing (北京四坛的方位) 2
63. Fairness (公道) 2
64. Men vs. ghosts (人与鬼) 5
65. Yin and yang (阴阳) 5
66. Retribution, karma (报应) 10
67. Buddhism and emperors with a posthumous title of 武 (佛教与'*武帝') 1
68. Buddha and monks (佛与和尚/僧) 3
69. Buddhist texts and knife (佛经与刀) 1
70. Sharp-witted remarks (机锋) 2
71. 'Go drink tea' (吃茶去) 2
72. Dusts and the human world (尘与世) 2
73. Outstanding statecraft and brilliant military exploits (文治武功) 5
74. The first thing to do after a new emperor ascended the throne in ancient China (新皇继位后做的第一件事) 1
75. What was needed to rule China? (如何治理中国?) 5

xvi *Entries*

76. Prime ministers must be chosen from Confucian scholars (宰相须用读书人) 3
77. Four magnificent characters and the declination of the Northern Song ('丰亨豫大'与北宋的衰败) 3
78. Blessing and the unfortunate Song dynasty (宋朝年号与'祐') 3
79. To take or decline the throne (劝进与固辞) 2
80. The pride of a great empire and the reluctance to lose power (帝国不愿舍弃的荣光) 3
81. Open and aboveboard (光明正大) 2
82. Correctness of names (名正言顺) 5
83. Posthumous titles (谥号) 5
84. Temple names of emperors (庙号) 3
85. Temple names and achievements of emperors (庙号与成就) 3
86. Naming taboo (避讳) 5
87. Given names: taboo and honor (改名) 3
88. Feudal (封建) 2
89. Peaceful and chaotic (治与乱) 2
90. Penitential decrees and letters of self-criticism (罪己诏与检讨书) 2
91. Emperors, kings, generals, ministers (帝王将相) 5
92. Keeping the emperor company (与大人物相处) 2
93. Not even recognize cows and goats (见牛羊亦不识) 3
94. Sages and men of virtue (圣贤) 3
95. Master (*子) 2
96. Model of all Chinese (中国人的楷模) 2
97. Three Immortal Deeds (三不朽) 10
98. Loyal and martial (忠武) 2
99. Ministry of Rites and its importance (礼部的地位) 1
100. Chinese emperors should thank historians. (中国皇帝应该感谢史官) 5
101. The last bit of an emperor's dignity (皇帝最后的尊严) 1
102. Long live (万岁) 3
103. One man (一人) 2
104. Savior (救星) 1
105. Little * (*小*) 2
106. Party, the (党) 5
107. Ignorant young ladies (无知少女) 2
108. Collectivism (集体主义) 3
109. Boldest proclamation of reform (三不足) 2
110. Not flip flop (不折腾) 5
111. Warning inscription on a stone (戒石铭) 2
112. Thoughtcrimes (思想罪) 3
113. Discuss in an open manner (妄议) 3
114. One Belt One Road Initiative (一带一路) 2
115. Japanese era names feature common Chinese characters (日本年号中的汉字) 3
116. North Korea and South Korea (北韩与南朝鲜) 5
117. The history and a young girl (历史与小姑娘) 3

Chapter 4: Life, society, arts, literature (生活, 社会, 艺术, 文学**)**

118. Purpose of life (生活的目的) 10
119. Ordinary Chinese people's dream, now and then (河清海晏与岁月静好) 1
120. Attitude to life (生活态度) 2

121. Custom (风俗) 5
122. Food and drink (饮食) 5
123. Liquor and drinking (酒, 喝酒) 5
124. Bad habits (恶习) 3
125. Gamble (赌) 5
126. Dream (梦) 10
127. Beauty (美女) 10
128. Fondness for children (恋童) 5
129. Rich and powerful (富贵) 5
130. Noble temperament (贵族气质) 1
131. Unrestrained (风流) 5
132. Poor (穷) 10
133. Debt (债) 2
134. Gain extra advantage and suffer losses (占便宜与吃亏) 5
135. Find a happy medium (折中) 5
136. Individual vs. group (一人与一群) 5
137. Mean person (小人) 5
138. Flunky vs. talent (奴才 vs. 人才) 3
139. Louis Cha Leung-yung (金庸, Jin Yong) 5
140. Mystic Dragon Cult Leader (神龙教主) 5
141. Fawn (吹捧) 5
142. Kindness and hatred (恩仇) 3
143. Kindness (恩) 3
144. Hatred (仇) 5
145. To one's face and in his back (当面与背后) 3
146. Gifts to avoid giving (不能送的礼物) 3
147. Mirrors (镜子) 1
148. Face and dignity (脸, 面子) 5
149. Civilities (客套) 5
150. Rumor (流言) 3
151. Find fault (找借口) 3
152. Suspicious (怀疑) 2
153. Seek others for help (求人) 2
154. Deterioration (变差) 1
155. Colors and culture (颜色与文化) 3
156. Representatives of Chinese literature (中国文学的代表) 2
157. Common lengths of forms in Chinese literature (几种中国文学体裁的长度) 2
158. Confucius says (子曰) 1
159. Gifted scholars and beautiful women (才子佳人) 3
160. Chinese literary works with the richest culture (富含中国文化的文艺作品) 3
161. Antithetical couplets (对联) 5
162. Music one gets to kneel down when listening (跪着听的音乐) 1
163. Painting (画画) 2

Chapter 5: Social relations, family, women, education (社会关系, 家庭, 女人, 教育**)**

164. Human relations (人际关系) 5
165. Social hierarchy (等级) 10

xviii   *Entries*

166. Rulers and the ruled, ancient and present (社会的两极) 3
167. Ancestors (祖宗) 5
168. Filial (孝) 10
169. Parents (父母) 10
170. Parents and children (父母与子女) 5
171. Families: exemplary and satisfactory (家庭: 令人羡慕的和令人满意的) 5
172. Rule the roost (当家) 1
173. Husband and wife: good (夫妻: 关系好) 10
174. Husband and wife: bad (夫妻: 关系差) 3
175. Children (孩子) 5
176. Cousins (表亲) 2
177. Women, regarding sex and marriage (忠, 贞, 烈的女人) 5
178. Women, unlucky (倒霉的女人) 5
179. Discrimination of women (女人干坏事) 3
180. Women and their names in ancient China (女人的名字) 3
181. Women and goods (女人与货) 10
182. Prostitutes, other names of (妓女的别称) 2
183. Earthquakes and women (地震与女人) 3
184. Wives, housewives and brooms (妻子, 妇女与扫帚) 5
185. Rosy cheeks (红颜) 5
186. Heroines (女英雄) 2
187. The true... (真 . . .) 1
188. Sub-ministerial level universities (副部级大学) 5
189. Innovation and Chinese college mottos (大学校训与创新) 3
190. Education: importance, content (教育: 重要性和内容) 5
191. Education: learning methods (教育: 学习方法) 3
192. Learning methods (学习方法) 1
193. Value and joy of learning (读书的价值和快乐) 5
194. Teacher and student, master and apprentice (师生, 师徒) 5
195. Respecting teachers (尊师) 5
196. Friends and friendship (朋友, 友谊) 5
197. Soulmates (知己) 5
198. Boss (老板) 2
199. Bo Le (伯乐) 2
200. Middlemen (中间人) 2
201. Experienced and inexperienced (内行与外行) 2
202. Copycatting culture (山寨文化) 2
203. Foreign and rustic (洋与土) 2
204. Foreign and imported goods (洋货) 1

Chapter 6: Nature, animals, language (自然, 动物, 语言)

205. Blue mountains (青山) 1
206. Water (水) 3
207. Water and fire/soil/wind (水火/水土/风水) 2
208. Super 'wind' (超级风) 1
209. Flowers and willows (花柳) 2
210. Flowers, grass, trees (花草木) 1
211. Flowers and unfaithfulness (花与不忠) 2

212. Peonies and prosperous (牡丹和富贵) 2
213. Four Noblemen (四君子) 2
214. Tigers (老虎) 2
215. Dogs (狗) 5
216. Dogs and chicken/pigs (鸡犬/猪狗) 2
217. Cows (牛) 1
218. Symbolism of goats (羊的象征意义) 2
219. Monkeys (猴子) 2
220. Bats (蝙蝠) 2
221. Fish and meat (鱼与肉) 1
222. Eyebrows and urgency (眉毛与紧急) 1
223. Hands and feet (手和脚) 1
224. Wok (锅) 2
225. Chinese cooking methods (中国菜的做法) 2
226. Buns or dumplings (包子) 2
227. Bone (骨头) 1
228. Color and lust (色) 1
229. Gold and jade (金玉) 5
230. Metals, precious and non-precious (金银铜铁) 1
231. More precious than gold (比金子还贵) 2
232. Importance of tools (工具的重要性) 2
233. Needle (针) 1
234. Nails (钉子) 2
235. Wall (墙) 3
236. Boats (舟和船) 1
237. Roads and ways (道和路) 1
238. Quality and rice (质量与大米) 2
239. Medicine (药) 2
240. East . . . west. . . (东/西) 1
241. South . . . north. . . (南/北) 1
242. I was here (到此一游) 1
243. Foreign countries with '国' in their Chinese names (*国) 2
244. Warning, mild (温和的警告) 1
245. The worst curse word (贼) 3
246. Not afraid (不怕) 1
247. More bad guys (坏人多) 5
248. Things (东西不是南北) 2
249. Juxtaposed antonyms meaning 'category' or 'scope' (并列反义词表范围) 5
250. Juxtaposition of male and female (连绵词: 雌雄) 1
251. Spatial-temporal metaphors (时空比喻) 5
252. Modal verb serial (能愿动词的连用) 1
253. 'And' vs. 和 (和与 'and') 3
254. The meaning of yìsi ('意思'的意思) 5
255. I'll think about it (研究研究) 2
256. Chinese equivalent of the English word 'do' (弄) 2
257. Classics (经) 3
258. Heavenly Stems and Earthly Branches to compute time (天干地支纪年) 5
259. Idioms with 'heaven/earth' (带'天/地'的成语) 3
260. Language games (文字游戏) 2

xx *Entries*

261. Language play on internet (网络上的语言游戏) 2
262. Euphemisms for 'to die' ('死'的委婉语) 5
263. Euphemisms for 'sexual intercourse' ('做爱'的委婉语) 5
264. Homophonic puns (谐音双关) 3
265. Fish and 'surplus' (鱼和余) 1
266. Prosperity and prostitution (繁荣'娼'盛) 1
267. Dilution of vulgar words (傻*) 1
268. The most heartbreaking vows (最让人心碎的誓言) 5
269. Choice of Chinese characters for foreign place names (外国地名中的汉字的选择) 2
270. Classical translation of movie titles (电影片名经典翻译) 2
271. Forget-me-not (勿忘我) 1
272. Vegetables introduced to China (传入中国的蔬菜) 1
273. Chinglish, updated (新中式英语) 1
274. Brothers' names and radicals (兄弟人名的汉字与部首) 3
275. Forms of address: respectful, honorific and modest (尊称, 敬称, 谦称) 2
276. Southern Chinese names and 阿* (南方人名中的'阿') 1
277. White Bone Spirit (白骨精) 1
278. Circle of. . . (*坛/界) 2
279. To speak eloquently (能说) 3
280. To talk nonsense (胡说) 1
281. Difficulty levels of Chinese rhyme (韵脚的难易) 2
282. Chinese characters composed of 人 (比, 从, 北, 化) 2
283. Synonyms (近义词) 5
284. Binomal words (连绵词) 3
285. Chinese ordinal numbers (汉语顺序号) 3
286. Three and four (*三*四) 2
287. Lucky numbers (6 和 8) 5
288. Five buttons (五颗扣子) 1
289. 73 and 84 (七十三, 八十四) 1
290. Three hundred (三百) 1

1 Overall (总论)

1. Chinese language and culture: negative tendency
(中国语言的负面倾向) 10

From the perspective of evaluation, the Chinese language is negative overall. Among all the words with evaluative connotation, most being adjectives, there are far more negative ones than positive ones. Chinese idioms (*chengyu*) are considered formal and refined. However, the ratio of the number of positive idioms to negative ones is 50:1 according to the *Contemporary Chinese Dictionary* (*Xiandai Hanyu Cidian*, 2005 edition). Additionally, according to *500 Common Chinese Proverbs and Colloquial Expressions*, the most common word found in the entries is 'bù,' which means 'not' or 'don't.' In contrast, in the *Fact on File Dictionary of Proverbs*, the two most common words are 'good' and 'man.'

- #37 Stress the past, not the present (厚古薄今); #154 Deterioration (变差); #247 More bad guys (坏人多); #267 Dilution of vulgar words (傻*)

2. Chinese characters and way of thinking (汉字与思维) 5

Does this look like a greenhouse with a few steps? The actual meaning of this Chinese character is almost completely contrary to what a Westerner might imagine. The character is 寒

2 Overall (总论)

(hán), which means 'cold.' We can catch a glimpse of the Chinese way of thinking when creating characters by analyzing how the meaning of this character is formed. The bottom two horizontal strokes mean 'ice' (冫 or 仌). The outside portion of the upper part is 宀, which means 'house.' The four (almost) identical cross-like parts stand for 艸, which means grass (hay) clusters, and the remaining part, among the grass (艸), is a curling man. Now the formation of this character is clear: Outside of the house, it is freezing, and inside the house, a man curling up is in some grass/hay for warmth. The character 寒 therefore means 'cold.' Usually, the formation of the meaning of a Chinese character is no more than three-fold. In this example, this character has three elements. The first is ice vs. a house and a man, the second is the house and the man inside, and the third is the man and the grass.

- #3 The battle of Chinese character forms: traditional, simplified or pinyin? (汉字之争); #10 Change (化); #60 Laws (法); #78 Blessing and the unfortunate Song dynasty (宋朝年号与'祐'); #115 Japanese era names feature common Chinese characters (日本年号中的汉字); #161 Antithetical couplets (对联); #179 Discrimination of women (女人干坏事); #184 Wives, housewives and brooms (妻子, 妇女与扫帚); #225 Chinese cooking methods (中国菜的做法); #238 Quality and rice (质量与大米); #272 Vegetables introduced to China (传入中国的蔬菜); #274 Brothers' names and radicals (兄弟人名的汉字与部首); #276 Southern Chinese names and 阿* (南方人名中的'阿'); #282 Chinese characters composed of 人 (比, 从, 北, 化)

3. The battle of Chinese character forms: traditional, simplified or pinyin? (汉字之争) 5

After China was defeated by Japan in the first Sino-Japanese War (1894–1895), Chinese intellectuals owed the defeat considerably to traditional characters since they were hard to learn and thus prevented Chinese ordinary people from being literate. From that time on, the call for the abolition of Chinese characters (废除汉字) and their replacement with romanized pinyin (拼音) has surged time to time until the turn of the 21st century when typing on computers made producing Chinese characters easier. Chinese characters have been preserved, but there is divergence between the simplified form (简体字) used in mainland China and the traditional form (繁体字 or 正体字) used mainly in Taiwan, Hong Kong and Singapore. There have been appeals made for the reintegration of some traditional characters back into mainland China.

- #2 Chinese characters and way of thinking (汉字与思维)

4. Auditory impression of the Chinese language (汉语的听觉印象) 10

Chinese sounds loud (if not noisy to many non-Chinese peoples); fluctuant (because of tones); and rhythmic (because of complex cultural, educational and ethnic reasons that will not be expounded here). Below are two lines of verse from Chapter 40 of 西游记 (*Journey to the West*). They will be annotated only with pinyin, tone patterns and syllable finals, ignoring the meaning for the moment.

一叶浮萍归大海,[1] yi ye fu ping gui da hai, | | − − − | |
人生何处不相逢. ren sheng he chu bu xiang feng. − − | | | | − −

---

1 一叶浮萍归大海, 人生何处不相逢 [-葉--歸--, ---處---] yí yè fú píng guī dà hǎi, rén sheng hé chù bù xiāng féng

First, the tone patterns (平仄) are regulated: alternating between level and oblique within one line and opposite between two lines. Second, all syllables except the middle syllable of the first line end with a vowel sound, and all syllables except the three middle syllables of the second line end with a nasal sound. If possible, ask a Cantonese speaker to read the verse aloud to get a sense of the Chinese language.

- #5 Sound and culture (语音与文化); #49 Nonverbal love (无言的爱); #77 Four magnificent characters and the declination of the Northern Song ('丰亨豫大'与北宋的衰败); #102 Long live (万岁); #264 Homophonic puns (谐音双关); #265 Fish and 'surplus' (鱼和余); #266 Prosperity and prostitution (繁荣'娼'盛); #271 Forget-me-not (勿忘我)

5. Sound and culture (语音与文化) 2

Besides onomatopoeia such as 嚎啕 (háotáo, as in 嚎啕大哭 'cry loudly') and 嘤嘤 (yīngyīng, as in 嘤嘤啜泣 sob), which imitate sounds, how the names of Chinese traditional musical instruments sound reflect the instruments' timbres, for example, 琴 (qín, zither with seven strings); 瑟 (sè, zither with more strings than 琴); 笙 (sheng, mouth-blown free reed instrument); 箫 (xiāo, vertical end-blown flute); 钟 (zhōng, bell); 鼓 (gǔ, drum); 笛 (dí, flute); 琵琶 (pípa, pipa) etc.

- #86 Naming taboo (避讳); #162 Music one gets to kneel down when listening (跪着听的音乐); #220 Bats (蝙蝠); #264 Homophonic puns (谐音双关); #265 Fish and 'surplus' (鱼和余); #266 Prosperity and prostitution (繁荣'娼'盛); #267 Dilution of vulgar words (傻*); #271 Forget-me-not (勿忘我)

6. Temporal sequence (时间顺序) 5

Researchers have found that Chinese sentence structure usually follows temporal sequence, for example, 星期日/早上/八点/我开车/去机场/接朋友/来我家/住三天 (literally 'Sunday morning 8 o'clock I drive a car to the airport to pick up a friend who comes to my home to live for three days.') with each event after another by strict temporal sequence.

- #252 Modal verb serial (能愿动词的连用); #258 Heavenly Stems and Earthly Branches to compute time (天干地支纪年); #274 Brothers' names and radicals (兄弟人名的汉字与部首); #285 Chinese ordinal numbers (汉语顺序号)

7. Idioms with markers of simile (带比喻词的成语) 3

Chinese idioms were coined roughly at the same pace that the Chinese language evolved in history. Main markers of simile in idioms include 犹 (yóu), 若 (ruò), 如 (rú) and 似 (sì). There is no idiom with 像, the most common marker of simile in modern Chinese. If there are two markers in one idiom, the structure is very likely to be '如X似X,' for example, 如花似玉 (like-flower-as-jade, very beautiful) and 如饥似渴 (rújī sikě, as-hungrily-as-thirstily, eagerly).

- #259 Idioms with 'heaven/earth' (带'天/地'的成语)

8. Electricity and Chinese idioms (成语中的电) 2

电 (電, diàn) can mean 'electricity' or 'lightning'; however, 'electricity' was introduced into the language a few thousand years later than 'lightning.' For this reason, all uses of 电 in Chinese idioms (a marker of traditional and formal language) mean 'lightning.'

4 *Overall (总论)*

9. Getting rich and building roads (致富与修路) 1

要想富, 先修路[2] (if [you] want to get rich, first build a road) is a slogan that emerged in the 1980s. This slogan is surprisingly popular among both ordinary people and government officials. New roads pave new ways for the local people to go outside and outsides to come in to do business. Therefore, the local people cheer for new roads from the bottom of their hearts. As for government officials, building news roads brings them power-for-money deals, so they are keen to build roads, parks, subways and airports, here and there, again and again. However, the idea of building a road is not at all new. The first emperor of China, Qin Shi Huang (259 BCE–210 BCE) built many broad highways that radiated out from Xianyang, the capital of the Qin dynasty. Why had not the slogan 要想富, 先修路, an easy but catchy slogan, emerged in Chinese feudal times? Rhyming is a problematic since 富 and 路 rhyme in Standard Chinese but not in ancient Chinese. However, the real reason might be a verse. . . 损人利己骑马骡, 正直公平挨饿. *修桥补路瞎眼*, 杀人放火儿多[3] (. . . those who are selfish ride horses, but those of integrity starve. Those *who repair bridges and roads will be blind*, but those who commit murder and arson have many sons.) in an extremely popular legendary novel 济公全传 (*Adventures of the Mad Monk Ji Gong*), published in the late Qing dynasty. In brief, building roads (修路 or 补路) is meritorious, but ordinary people dare not for fear of bad karma.

- #54 Men's three treasures (农民的三宝)

10. Change (化) 3

The oracle form of 化 depicts one man straight up and one man upside down, thus 化 got the meaning 'change.' For example, 化学 (chemistry) is a subject about change. Now 化 functions almost as a suffix with high productivity, for example, 绿化 (to green), 美化 (beautify, to glorify), 西方化 (to Westernize) and 机械化 (jīxièhuà, to mechanize) etc. 化 and its compound words or phrases can serve as an indicator of your proficiency of Chinese. If you understand all of the above-mentioned words with 化, you are at the intermediate level. More advanced words or phrases and their levels are as follows: 去中国化 (De-sinicization) and 大事化小, 小事化了 (to reduce a big problem into a small one, and a smaller one into nothing), advanced level, 化悲痛为力量[4] (to turn sorrow into strength), superior, 化干戈为玉帛[5] (to turn hostility into friendship, to bury the hatchet), near native, 化腐朽为神奇[6] (literally 'to turn decadent into miraculous,' a more free translation would be close to 'to wave a magic wand,') native.

- #2 Chinese characters and way of thinking (汉字与思维); #282 Chinese characters composed of 人 (比, 从, 北, 化)

11. The verse that changed China the most (影响中国最大的一句话) 5

British historian Joseph Needham, editor of the book series 'Science and civilization in China,' raised the interesting question of why modern science had developed in Europe but

---

2 要想富, 先修路 [-] yào xiǎng fù, xiān xiūlù (if-want-be rich, first-build-road)
3 修桥补路瞎眼, 杀人放火儿多 [-橋補---, 殺---兒-] xiūqiáo bǔlù xiāyǎn, shārén fànghuǒ ér duō (build-bridge-mend-road-blind-eye, kill-people-set-fire-son-many)
4 化悲痛为力量 [---為--] huà bēitòng wéi lìliàng (turn-sorrow-into-strength)
5 化干戈为玉帛 [---爲--] huà gāngē wéi yùbó (turn-weapons-into-gift)
6 化腐朽为神奇 [---為--] huà fǔxiǔ wéi shénqí (turn-decadent-into-miraculous)

Overall (总论)   5

not in China. This may have been closely related to one incident that happened in China in 1402. After the Prince of Yan (later Yongle Emperor of the Ming dynasty) overthrew the reign of his nephew, the Jianwen Emperor, he ordered an orthodox Confucian scholar-bureaucrat 方孝孺 (Fāng Xiàorú, 1357–1402) to write an inaugural address to glorify his usurpation of the throne. When Fang rejected firmly, the Yongle Emperor threatened to kill nine of Fang's agnates (kin through ancestral ties). The emperor's advisor had previously warned him not to kill Fang because Fang was 天下读书种子[7] (literally 'the seed of learning under the heaven,' the sole heir of Chinese culture). But Fang answered, 莫说九族, 十族何妨[8] (never mind nine agnates, go ahead with ten!) Consequently, of all Fang's blood relatives, students and peers – 873 people in total – were executed. When the news was made public, all intellectuals in China wept. From that time on, Chinese intellectuals have intentionally stayed away from politics and indulged themselves in ancient texts.

- #76 Prime ministers must be chosen from Confucian scholars (宰相须用读书人); #77 Four magnificent characters and the declination of the Northern Song ('丰亨豫大'与北宋的衰败)

---

7 天下读书种子 [--讀書種-] tiānxià dúshū zhǒngzi (under the heaven-school-seed)

8 莫说九族, 十族何妨 [-说--, -] mòshuō jiǔzú, shízú héfáng (not-mention-nine-agnate, ten-agnate-so what)

2 National character (民族性格)

12. Change (改变) 5

Greek philosopher Heraclitus said, 'The only thing that is constant is change' (唯一不变的是变化). However, all things remain essentially the same despite all apparent changes (万变不离其宗).[9] Chinese scholar Dong Zhongshu (179 BCE–104 BCE) said, '天不变, 道亦不变'[10] (Heaven does not change, nor does Tao/Dao/way), with which he justified the rule of 'three principles and five virtues.' One of the Thirteen Classics of Confucianism, *I Ching*, or *Book of Changes* contains a different concept: 穷则变, 变则通, 通则久[11] (When it is exhausted, it mutates; by mutation it achieves continuity; by continuity it endures). The ordinary people have a saying: 树挪死, 人挪活[12] (literally 'if trees are removed, they will die; if men move, they will survive.') Therefore, you cannot stick to 老皇历[13] (anachronistic practices), which claims that a woman loyal to her husband to death (从一而终)[14] is virtuous.

- #3 The battle of Chinese character forms: traditional, simplified or pinyin? (汉字之争); #37 Stress the past, not the present (厚古薄今); #39 Old or new (新与旧)

13. Change, in the wrong way (变坏) 3

变 (變, biàn) means 'transform, change.' Sun Wukong (孙悟空, the Monkey King) in the *Journey to the West* knows 72 transformations (七十二变) and is considered one of the mightiest warriors. There is a saying 女大十八变,[15] meaning 'there is no telling what a girl will look like when she grows up,' which is usually followed by 越变越好看 (the more changes, the more beautiful) in the positive and 越变越难看 (the more changes, the uglier) in the negative. Words with 变 usually carry a negative connotation, for example, 变心 (change loyalty), 变脸 (turn hostile suddenly), 变色 (change one's countenance), 变味 (go bad), 变相 (disguised), 变质 (deteriorate), 变卦 (go back on one's word), 变节 (betray), 变态 (abnormal, perverted) etc. If someone says '他/她/你变了' (S/he/you changed), the default meaning is 'S/he/you are not as good as before' unless there is a positive statement following.

- #154 Deterioration (变差); #267 Dilution of vulgar words (傻*)

---

9 万变不离其宗 [萬變-離--] wàn biàn bù lí qí zōng (10,000-change-not-away from-its-principle)

10 天不变, 道亦不变 [--變, ---變] tiān bú biàn, dào yì bú biàn (heaven-not-change, Dao-either-not-change)

11 穷则变, 变则通, 通则久 [窮則變, 變則-, -則-] qióng zé biàn, biàn zé tōng, tōng zé jiǔ (exhausted-then-mutate, mutate-then-continue, continue-then-endure)

12 树挪死, 人挪活 [樹--, -] shù nuó sǐ, rén nuó huó (tree-remove-die, people-move-survive)

13 老皇历 [--曆] lǎohuánglì (old-imperial-calendar)

14 从一而终 [從--終] cóng yī ér zhōng (stay with-one-and-die)

15 女大十八变 [----變] nǚ dà shíbā biàn (girl-grow up-18-changes)

National character (民族性格) 7

14. People, the (人民) 10

The word 'people' (人民) appears in the official name of China, the People's Republic of China (中国人民共和国),[16] and Article 2 of the Constitution of the People's Republic of China stipulates, 'All power in the People's Republic of China belongs to the people' (中华人民共和国的一切权力属于人民). However, when 'the people' (人民), 'the country' (国家) and 'the Party' (党, the Chinese Communist Party (CCP)) are mentioned together, the conventional sequence is the Party, the country and the people. For example, the Cultural Revolution (1966–1976) was 'responsible for the most severe setback and the heaviest losses suffered by the Party, the country and the people (党, 国家和人民[17]) since the founding of the People's Republic.' (Resolution on Certain Historical Issues of the Party Since the Founding of the People's Republic, the sixth plenary session of the 11th CPC Central Committee in June 1981.) Additionally, the top Chinese leader usually holds three titles: the General Secretary of the Communist *Party* of China, the President of the People's Republic of *China*, and the Chairman of the Central *Military Commission* (中共中央总书记, 国家主席, 中央军委主席).[18] The full name of the armed forces of China is the Chinese *People*'s Liberation Army (PLA, 中国人民解放军).[19] In contrast, the first three words of the Constitution of the United States of America are 'We the people.' President Lincoln has a famous quotation, 'Government of the people, by the people, for the people, shall not perish from the Earth.'

- #80 The pride of a great empire and the reluctance to lose power (帝国不愿舍弃的荣光); #96 Model of all Chinese (中国人的楷模)

15. Standpoint (立场) 5

The Chinese people are usually reluctant to take a firm stand and are inclined to sit on the fence (骑墙).[20] Fence-sitters (墙头草[21]) will swing to the side that is stronger (哪边风硬哪边倒).[22] It is beneficial to stand with the stronger side since 大树底下好乘凉[23] (an influential person provides protection for his associates). However, the winning side may only be in power temporarily, so it is better not to take a side too early. Many people would like to be a 老好人[24] (a man who tries never to offend anyone) or a 和事佬[25] (peacemaker) in order to 和稀泥[26] (patch things up, smooth things over). Lu Xun depicted this situation in a 1925 essay '立论' (make a point): when a person is approached to be introduced to a newborn boy, he should neither speak the truth such as 'The baby will die someday,' nor use flattering words such as 'The baby will be rich or influential,' but instead should say, '啊呀! 这孩子呵! 您瞧! 多么.... 阿唷! 哈哈! Hehe! He, hehehehe!' (Aha! This boy! You see! How . . . Wow! Ha! Ha! Ha-ha ha-ha!)

- #23 Who do you think you are? (你算老几啊?); #26 Not standing out (不出头); #116 North Korea and South Korea (北韩与南朝鲜)

---

16 中国人民共和国 [-華----國] Zhōnghuá Rénmín Gònghéguó (China-people-republic)

17 党, 国家和人民 [黨, 國----] dǎng, guójiā hé rénmín (Party, state and people)

18 中共中央总书记, 国家主席, 中央军委主席 [----總書記, 國---, --軍---] Zhōnggòng zhōngyāng zǒngshūjì, guójiā zhǔxí, zhōngyāng jūnwěi zhǔxí (CCP-central-general-secretary, state-chairman, central-military committee-chairman)

19 中国人民解放军 [-國----軍] Zhōngguó rénmín jiěfàngjūn (China-people-liberation army)

20 骑墙 [騎墻] qí qiáng (sit-fence/wall)

21 墙头草 [墻頭-] qiángtóu cǎo (wall-top-grass)

22 哪边风硬哪边倒 [-邊風--邊-] nǎbiān fēng yìng nǎ biān dǎo (which-side-wind-strong-which-side-swing)

23 大树底下好乘凉 [-樹----涼] dà shù dǐxià hǎo chéngliáng (big-tree-under-easy-get-shade)

24 老好人 [-] lǎohǎorén (always-good-man)

25 和事佬 [-] héshìlǎo (meddle-thing-guy)

26 和稀泥 [-] huò xīní (stir-thin-mud)

8 *National character (民族性格)*

16. Courage (勇气) 5

The best words to describe 'courage' might be 虽千万人, 吾往矣[27] ((if I found that I am right), I will go forward against thousands and tens of thousands people) in a positive way, and 竟无一人是男儿[28] ((among the 140,000 surrendered soldiers), none is a real man) in a negative way. Ironically, the later words were from the mouth of a woman in 965. If one has a great deal of courage, he can say 余勇可贾[29] (have plenty of fight left in me).

- #97 Three Immortal Deeds (三不朽); #268 The most heartbreaking vows (最让人心碎的誓言)

17. Times and heroes (时势与英雄) 3

Popular opinion is that 时势造英雄[30] (circumstances create heroes), not the opposite 英雄造时势 (heroes create times). Circumstances triumph any person (形势比人强).[31] However, Mao Zedong downgraded ancient heroes while endorsing modern ones, including himself. For example, in his poem 'Snow,' Mao wrote, '数风流人物, 还看今朝' (for truly great men, look to this age alone).

- #59 Mandate of Heaven, or God's will (天命, 天意); #139 Louis Cha Leung-yung (金庸, Jin Yong); #186 Heroines (女英雄); #187 The true. . . (真 . . .)

18. Tolerant (宽容) 5

Chinese morals advocate tolerance. When Chinese people fished, one side of the net would be left open (网开一面).[32] Intellectuals are strict with themselves and lenient to others (严以律己, 宽以待人).[33] Proverbs exhort that one should 得饶人处且饶人[34] (be easy on other people), 留有余地[35] (leave some leeway for oneself) and not 赶尽杀绝[36] (spare none). If one is not tolerant, he will 睚眦必报[37] (seek revenge for the smallest grievance). Lu Xun (1881–1936) was a writer and fighter highly praised by Mao Zedong. In his will, Lu Xun wrote of his foes, 让他们怨恨去, 我也一个都不宽恕[38] (Let them hate. I will forgive none of them).

- #244 Warning, mild (温和的警告)

19. Oneself and others (人与己) 2

人 (others) and 己 (oneself) are often used in Chinese idioms for contrast, for example, 损人利己[39] (benefit oneself at the expenses of others), 先人后己[40] (put the interest of

---

27 虽千万人, 吾往矣 [雖-萬-, -] suī qiān wàn rén, wǔ wǎng yǐ (although-thousand-ten thousand-people, I-go-*marker of affirmation*)

28 竟无一人是男儿 [-無----兒] jìng wú yì rén shì nánér (unexpectedly-no-one-man-is-man)

29 余勇可贾 [餘--賈] yú yǒng kě gǔ (my-courage-can-purchase)

30 时势造英雄 [時勢---] shíshì zào yīngxióng (time-create-hero)

31 形势比人强 [-勢---] xíngshì bǐ rén qiáng (situation-compared with-people-triumph)

32 网开一面 [網開--] wǎng kāi yī miàn (net-open-one-side)

33 严以律己, 宽以待人 [嚴---, 寬---] yán yǐ lǜ jǐ, kuān yǐ dài rén (strict-to-discipline-oneself, tolerant-to-treat-others)

34 得饶人处且饶人 [-饒-處-饒-] déráorénchùqiěráorén(should-forgive-others-occasion-then-forgive-others)

35 留有余地 [--餘-] liú yǒu yúdì (leave-aside-leeway)

36 赶尽杀绝 [趕盡殺絕] gǎn jìn shā jué (chase-to the end-kill-all)

37 睚眦必报 [-眥-報] yáozì bì bào (small grievance-must-avenge)

38 我一个都不宽恕 [--個--寬-] wǒ yígè dōu bù kuānshù (I-one-*measure word*-all-not-forgive)

39 损人利己 [損---] sǔnrén lìjǐ (harm-others-benefit-oneself)

40 先人后己 [--後-] xiānrén hòujǐ (first-others-later-oneself)

National character (民族性格) **9**

others above one's own), 舍己为人[41] (sacrifice one's own interests for the sake of others) and 人不为己，天诛地灭[42] (Every man for himself and the Devil take the last) etc.

- #21 Partial and impartial (公与私); #136 Individual vs. group (一人与一群); #200 Middlemen (中间人)

20. Utilitarianism (功利主义) 5

King Louis XV of France had an infamous quote, 'Après moi, le deluge' (After me, the flood, 我死之后，哪管洪水滔天). Chinese people usually judge heroes by success or failure (以成败论英雄[43]), and nothing succeeds like success (胜者王侯败者贼).[44] One will be mocked for being poor, but not for prostitution (笑贫不笑娼),[45] so some people will take whatever measures (不择手段[46]) as long as the end can justify the means.

- #23 Who do you think you are? (你算老几啊?); #25 No principles (无原则); #26 Not standing out (不出头); #31 Fame and fortune (名利); #134 Gain extra advantage and suffer losses (占便宜与吃亏)

21. Partial and impartial (公与私) 3

Both 私 (sī) and 公 (gōng) are related to '厶,' which probably means 'self-centered' as well representing a 'private part of the body.' 私 is a later form of 厶, and 公 means 'impartial, just, opposite of 厶' since the upper part of 公 (the 八) means 'opposite.' It is ideal to be impartial or just, i.e., 大公无私 (unselfish), to 公私兼顾 (take both public and private interests into account), and not to 假公济私 (exploit public office for private gain) or 公报私仇 (avenge a personal wrong in the name of public interests), which are unfortunately common.

- #19 Oneself and others (人与己); #108 Collectivism (集体主义); #136 Individual vs. group (一人与一群)

22. Speculative (投机) 5

Many Chinese people are keen to find out their superiors' likes and dislikes. If a superior likes something, their subordinates will go above and beyond to satisfy the supervisors' desires (上有所好，下必甚焉).[47] For example, King Ling of Chu (?–529 BCE) liked women with a small waist, so many concubines in his palace starved to death (楚王好细腰，宫中多饿死).[48] Emperor Xuanzong of Tang (685–762) doted on Imperial Consort Yang whose family was thus instantly promoted to very high level in the imperial court. This caused the concept of valuing sons and belittling daughters over the past thousand years to change temporarily. At that time, people instead valued girls over boys (不重生男重生女).[49] Opportunists (投机分子) do not have a firm standpoint because their knees are weak (膝盖软).[50]

---

41 舍己为人 [捨-爲-] shějǐwèirén (abandon-oneself-for-others)
42 人不为己，天诛地灭 [--爲-,-誅-滅] rénbúwèijǐ, tiānzhū dìmiè (one-not-for-oneself, heaven-execute-earth-destroy)
43 以成败论英雄 [--敗論--] yǐ chéngbài lùn yīngxióng (with-success or failure-judge-hero)
44 胜者王侯败者贼 [勝---敗-贼] shèngzhě wánghóu bàizhě zéi (succeeded-people-king-duke-failed-people-traitor)
45 笑贫不笑娼 [-貧---] xiào pín bú xiào chāng (mock-poor-not-mock-prostitute)
46 不择手段 [-擇--] bù zé shǒuduàn (not-choose-measure)
47 上有所好，下必甚焉 [-]shàngyǒusuǒhào, xiàbìshènyān (superior-have-what-like, subordinate-must-exceed-that)
48 楚王好细腰，宫中多饿死 [---細-, ---餓-] Chǔ Wáng hào xì yāo, gōng zhōng duō è sǐ (King-Chu-like-thin-waist, palace-inside-many-starve-dead)
49 不重生男重生女 [-] bú zhòng shēng nán zhòng shēng nǚ (not-value-bear-boy-value-bear-girl)
50 膝盖软 [-蓋軟] xīgài ruǎn (knee-soft)

10 *National character (民族性格)*

- #24 Snobbish (势利眼); #25 No principles (无原则); #41 Onlookers (看客); #125 Gamble (赌); #134 Gain extra advantage and suffer losses (占便宜与吃亏)

23. **Who do you think you are? (你算老几啊?) 1**

'你算老几啊?'[51] seems like a simple provoking sentence when two people argue. However, it reveals the Chinese mindset to only follow the boss (老大) or someone in a position of authority. If one is not the boss, they should shut up or go away.

- #20 Utilitarianism (功利主义); #22 Speculative (投机); #24 Snobbish (势利眼)

24. **Snobbish (势利眼) 1**

Snobbish people (势利小人) treat other people according to their social status (看人下菜碟),[52] or 狗眼看人低 (to be damned snobbish) colloquially. They usually fawn on those above and bully those below (谄上欺下).

- #22 Speculative (投机); #23 Who do you think you are? (你算老几啊?); #25 No principles (无原则)

25. **No principles (无原则) 5**

Most Chinese people submit to their superiors' orders (惟上是从[53]) and do not have principles of their own. When the Imperial Chancellor Zhao Gao (?–207 BCE), 'pointed at a deer and called it a horse' (指鹿为马[54]) in the presence of the emperor, other government officials either kept silent or agreed with him in order to butter him up. Sometimes, you have to do something without principle. For example, a child/son never considers his mother ugly, and a dog never shuns his owner's home however shabby it is (儿不嫌母丑, 狗不嫌家贫).[55] There is a modern catchphrase/couplet that vividly depicts this phenomenon: 说你行你就行, 不行也行; 说你不行你就不行, 行也不行[56] (If I say you can do it, you can do it; if I say you can't do it, you can't do it, can is can't). Many Chinese worship what the books teach.

- #22 Speculative (投机); #24 Snobbish (势利眼); #60 Laws (法)

26. **Not standing out (不出头) 5**

Well-educated Chinese say, '木秀于林, 风必摧之; . . . 行高于人, 众必非之,[57]' which means 'if a tree stands out of a woods, the wind will destroy it . . . if a man's behavior is nobler than other people, others will defame him' (tall trees catch the wind; good people attract envy). For ordinary people, similar sayings include 出头的椽子先烂[58] (the nail that sticks out gets

---

51 你算老几啊 [-] nǐ suàn lǎo-jǐ a (you-are-number-what-ah)
52 看人下菜碟 [-] kàn rén xià càidié (judge-people-place-dish)
53 惟上是从 [---從] wéi shàng shì cóng (only-superior-IS-follow)
54 指鹿为马 [--爲馬] zhǐ lù wéi mǎ (point at-deer-claim-horse)
55 儿不嫌母丑, 狗不嫌家贫 [兒---醜, ----貧] ér bù xián mǔ chǒu, gòu bù xián jiā pín (children-not-despise-mother-ugly, dog-not-despise-owner-poor)
56 说你行你就行, 不行也行; 说你不行你就不行, 行也不行 [說 . . ., 說 . . .] See in-text
57 木秀于林, 风必摧之 . . . 行高于人, 众必非之 [--於-, 風--- . . .--於-, 衆---] mù xiù yú lín, fēng bì cuī zhī . . . xíng gāo yú rén, zhòng bì fēi zhī (tree-outstanding-from-forest, wind-absolutely-destroy-it . . . behavior-better-than-people, masses-definitely-defame-him)
58 出头的椽子先烂 [-頭----爛] chūtóu de chuánzi xiān làn (stick-out-rafter-first-rot)

National character (民族性格) **11**

hammered down) and 人怕出名猪怕壮[59] (fame can be a double-edged sword). All of these concerns are out of worry about 枪打出头鸟[60] (the hunter will shoot the bird that sticks its head out). Deng Xiaoping knew this well and he set the tone for Chinese foreign policy in 1980s with 韬光养晦[61] (hide one's capacities and bide one's time) and 不当第一[62] (never to be the leader). In most cases Chinese politicians would rather 不作为[63] (not act) since if you 有作为 (do something), you are more likely to be criticized.

- #15 Standpoint (立场); #41 Onlookers (看客); #42 Silence (沉默); #43 Stay foolish (难得糊涂); #53 To survive by all possible means (活着); #110 Not flip flop (不折腾); #135 Find a happy medium (折中)

27. Sophistication (灵活) 1

Sophisticated people judge the hour and seize the situation (审时度势) and then play it by ear (见机行事).[64] They will change their tune when talking to different people (见什么人说什么话, 到什么山唱什么歌)[65] and are good at flattering others at the opportune moment (顺情说好话).[66] There is a vernacular saying, 不打勤, 不打懒, 专打不长眼[67] (do not punish those who work hard, do not punish those who are lazy, but do punish those who do not use their brain).

- #22 Speculative (投机); #25 No principles (无原则)

28. Kick someone to the curb (卸磨杀驴) 5

One of the Chinese rulers' innate weaknesses is to kick someone to the curb when he has outlived his usefulness (卸磨杀驴).[68] This bad habit can be traced back to the Spring and Autumn Period (771 BCE–476 BCE). The first richest person in Chinese history was named Fan Li (536 BCE–448 BCE), who was later revered as the God of Wealth. He helped King Goujian of Yue established a large kingdom but immediately left Goujian and concealed his identity in the masses. Later, he wrote to his good friend Wen Zhong (who was also an important minister of Goujian), 飞鸟尽, 良弓藏; 狡兔死, 走狗烹[69] (after all birds are shot, even good bows are to be put away; after cunning hares are killed, the hounds will be boiled). However, it was too late. Goujian ordered Wen Zhong to commit suicide. These phrases are too pretentious for ordinary people, who use the phrase 过河拆桥[70] (burn the bridge after crossing the river) more often.

- #20 Utilitarianism (功利主义); #98 Loyal and martial (忠武)

---

59 人怕出名猪怕壮 [-] rén pà chūmíng zhū pà zhuàng (people-fear-become-famous-pig-fear-fat)
60 枪打出头鸟 [槍--頭鳥] qiāng dǎ chūtóu niǎo (gun-shoot-stick out-head-bird)
61 韬光养晦 [韜-養-] tāo guāng yǎng huì (hide-limelight-stay-obscure)
62 不当第一 [-當--] bù dāng dì-yī (not-be-no.-1)
63 不作为 [--為] bú zuòwéi (no-act)
64 见机行事 [見機--] jiàn jī xíng shì (observe-opportunity-do-thing)
65 见什么人说什么话, 到什么山唱什么歌 [見-麼-說-麼話, --麼---麼-] jiàn shénme rén shuō shénme huà, dào shénme shān chàng shénme ge (seen-whatsoever-people-speak-whatsoever-words, arrived-whatsoever-mountain-sing-whatsoever-song)
66 顺情说好话 [順-說-話] shùnqíng shuō hǎohuà ()
67 不打勤, 不打懒, 专打不长眼 [-, --懶, 專--長-] bù dǎ qí, bù dǎ lǎn, zhuān dǎ bù zhǎng yǎn (not-punish-diligent, not-punish-lazy, only-punish-not-having-eye)
68 卸磨杀驴 [--殺驢] xiè mò shā lú (unload-millstone-kill-donkey)
69 飞鸟尽, 良弓藏; 狡兔死, 走狗烹 [飛鳥儘, -; -, -] fēi niǎo jìn, liáng gōng cáng; jiǎo tù sǐ, zǒu gǒu pēng (flying-bird-extinct, good-bow-store up; sly-hare-dead, running-dog-boiled)
70 过河拆桥 [過--橋] guò hé chāi qiáo (crossed-river-remove-bridge)

12 *National character (民族性格)*

29. **Mental balance (心理平衡) 2**

Chinese people achieve mental balance by thinking of these sayings in the following scenarios: when losing money, 破财免灾[71] (lose money to avert misfortune); when losing money in casinos, 赌场失意, 情场得意[72] (defeated at a casino, triumphant in love affairs); or when something is smashed, 碎碎平安[73] (safe and sound, all year round, 岁岁 (all year round) is homophonous with 碎碎 (smashed)).

30. **Success and failure (胜负, 成败) 5**

Chinese people can have difficulty maintaining inner peace (平常心[74]) and are very obsessive about results because those who win will become nobles while those who are defeated will be bandits (胜者王侯败者贼,[75] nothing succeeds like success). At the same time, they often say, 'a temporary setback means nothing (in war)' (胜败乃兵家常事[76]) and believe that one should not judge whether a person is a hero on the basis of whether he is successful or not (不以成败论英雄).[77] The game of Go has a term called a 胜负手[78] (all-or-nothing move). The Chinese doctrine on success or failure is 胜不骄, 败不馁[79] (neither be made dizzy by success, nor discouraged by failure). One should not find excuses for his failure, although it is human to find excuses. A tragic hero and prominent warlord in the late Qin dynasty, Xiang Yu (232 BCE–202 BCE), made excuses for his failures to the founding emperor of the Han dynasty, Liu Bang: (此)天之亡我, 非战之罪[80] (It is that the Heaven defeated me, not my failure in battles).

   • #17 Times and heroes (时势与英雄); #59 Mandate of Heaven, or God's will (天命, 天意)

31. **Fame and fortune (名利) 10**

名利 (fame and fortune/wealth) is 功名利禄[81] (功名, fame; 利禄, fortune). Some people are indifferent to fame and fortune (淡泊名利),[82] for example, one of the greatest national heroes of China, Yue Fei (1103–1142) said, '三十功名尘与土'[83] (30 years' fame and fortune is but dirt and dust) in his famous poem 'Man Jiang Hong.' However, most people are thirsty for both, i.e., 名利双收[84] (to gain both fame and wealth). Fame and fortune are like chains

---

71 破财免灾 [-财-灾] pò cái miǎn zāi (lose-money-avoid-disaster)
72 赌场失意, 情场得意 [賭場--, -場--] dǔchǎng shīyì, qíngchǎng déyì (gambling-place-be frustrated, love-arena-be content)
73 碎碎平安 [-] suìsuì píng'ān (smashed/year-smashed/year-safe and sound)
74 平常心 [-] píngcháng xīn (normal-mind)
75 胜者王侯败者贼 [勝---敗-賊] shèng zhě wánghóu bài zhě zéi (win-people-king-duke-defeated-people-traitor)
76 胜败乃兵家常事 [勝敗-----] shèng bài nǎi bīngjiā chángshì (win-defeated-is-military-personnel-normal-thing)
77 不以成败论英雄 [---敗論--] bù yǐ chéngbài lùn yīngxióng (not-by-success or failure-measure-hero)
78 胜负手 [勝負-] shèng fù shǒu (win-lose-move)
79 胜不骄, 败不馁 [勝-驕, 敗-餒] shèng bù jiāo, bài bù něi (win-not-proud, fail-not-dispirited)
80 天之亡我, 非战之罪 [-, -戰--] tiān zhī wáng wǒ, fēi zhàn zhī zuì (heaven-particle-extinguish-me, not-battle-'s-failure)
81 功名利禄 [-] gōngmíng lìlù (merit-fame-wealth-rank)
82 淡泊名利 [-] dànbó mínglì (indifferent-fame-fortune)
83 三十功名尘与土 [----塵與-] sānshí gōngmíng chén yǔ tǔ (30 years-fame-dust-and-dirt)
84 名利双收 [-] mínglì shuāng shōu (fame-fortune-both-achieve)

National character (民族性格) 13

(名缰利锁,[85] fetters of fame and fortune) preventing you from becoming a noble person, but people still cannot forget it. There is a song ('好了歌,'[86] 'Won-Done Song') in the greatest Chinese classic novel *Dream of the Red Chamber* and the first few lines are:

世人都晓神仙好, 惟有功名忘不了! 古今将相在何方? 荒冢一堆草没了. 世人都晓神仙好, 只有金银忘不了!

Men all know that salvation should be won. But with ambition won't have done, have done. Where are the famous ones of days gone by? In grassy graves they lie now, every one. Men all know that salvation should be won. But with their riches won't have done, have done!

(From Chapter 1 of *The Story of the Stone*, translated by David Hawkes, Penguin Books, 1973)

Life is like a vanity fair (名利场[87]), and as one Chinese proverb goes, 人为财死, 鸟为食亡[88] (people die for fortune and birds for food; the wages of avarice is death).

- #20 Utilitarianism (功利主义); #47 Legacy (功名); #83 Posthumous titles (谥号); #97 Three Immortal Deeds (三不朽)

32. Integrity vs. ability (德与才) 3

德 (dé) means 'integrity' and 才 'ability.' If a person owns both, 德才兼备[89] (have both integrity and ability), that is perfect, but some people 有才无德 (have talent without virtue). How about a person without talent? For women this is nevertheless not a bad thing according to the 'notorious' saying 女子无才便是德[90] (a woman is virtuous if she lacks talent, ignorance is a woman's virtue) popular during the Ming and Qing dynasties.

- #83 Posthumous titles (谥号); #94 Sages and men of virtue (圣贤); #138 Flunky vs. talent (奴才 vs. 人才)

33. Benevolence and justice (仁与义) 3

仁 means 'benevolence' and 义 'justice.' 仁 is Confucius's teaching and 义 Mencius's. 仁义礼智信 (rén, yì, lǐ, zhì, xìn) are the five Confucian virtues, meaning 'benevolence, justice, courtesy, wisdom, sincerity' respectively. There is also a folk saying, 你不仁, 我不义, which means 'since you are not sincere with me, don't blame me (for any improper behavior).' Ironically, the people who spoke '仁义' often were prone to do dirty things (满口仁义道德, 一肚子男盗女娼,[91] speak abundantly of justice and morality, but act like out-and-out scoundrels).

- #94 Sages and men of virtue (圣贤); #99 Ministry of Rites and its importance (礼部的地位); #110 Not flip flop (不折腾); #111 Warning inscription on a stone (戒石铭); #168 Filial (孝)

---

85 名缰利锁 [-繮-鎖] mīng jiāng lì suǒ (fame-rein-fortune-lock)
86 好了歌 [-] hǎoliǎogē (good-end-song)
87 名利场 [--場] mīnglìchǎng (fame-fortune-fair)
88 人为财死, 鸟为食亡 [-為财-, -為--] rén wèi cái sǐ, niǎo wèi shí wáng (people-for-wealth-die, bird-for-food-die)
89 德才兼备 [---備] décái jiānbèi (integrity-ability-both-have)
90 女子无才便是德 [--無----] nǚzǐ wúcái biànshì dé (woman-have no-talent-then-is-virtue)
91 满口仁义道德, 一肚子男盗女娼 [滿-義--, ----盗--] mǎnkǒu rényì dàodé, yí dùzi nándào nǚchāng (full-mouth-justice-morality, whole-belly-man-thief-woman-prostitute)

14 *National character (民族性格)*

34. **Refined and popular** (雅俗) 2

People can be elegant or vulgar and have good or poor taste. Some things do not appeal to refined tastes (不登大雅之堂) and are unbearably vulgar (俗不可耐).[92] It is ideal to suit to both refined and popular tastes (雅俗共赏),[93] but if one pretends to be elegant, he 附庸风雅.[94] One can say that oneself is a 俗人 (not pretending to be lofty or elegant), but the phrase is very negative if used to describe others.

- #37 Stress the past, not the present (厚古薄今); #213 Four Noblemen (四君子); #275 Forms of address: respectful, honorific and modest (尊称, 敬称, 谦称)

35. **Humorous** (幽默) 2

A good sense of humor is greatly appreciated in the Western world; however, it was condemned in ancient China based on Confucius's teaching '巧言令色鲜矣仁'[95] (fine words and an insinuating appearance are seldom associated with true virtue). Humorists were rare, but some were recorded in the *Records of the Grand Historian* (史记). The most humorous person in Chinese history might be a Han scholar-official 东方朔 (Dongfang Shuo, 154 BCE–93 BCE). He spoke in an absurd way his entire life, but when he was dying, he admonished the emperor 远巧佞, 退谗言 (to stay away from sycophants, and ignore calumnies.) The emperor wondered, 'Why had Dongfang Shuo spoken so many nice words today?' Soon Dongfang Shuo died. The mindset to speak seriously, not humorously, leads many Chinese people's speak in a very boring manner. But the situation is changing rapidly.

- #70 Sharp-witted remarks (机锋); #261 Language play on internet (网络上的语言游戏)

36. **Good or bad** (优劣) 5

Economic law states that 'bad money drives out good.' There is one aspect of Chinese culture that is similar to this concept. In the famous novel 水浒传 (*All Men Are Brothers*), every hero had to kill someone, guilty or innocent, to join the Liangshan rebels, so that in this way they would all be birds of a feather (物以类聚, 人以群分).[96] Now a popular (bad) joke goes like this: 一起同过窗不如一起扛过枪, 一起扛过枪不如一起分过赃, 一起分过赃不如一起嫖过娼,[97] which means 'Who are the most trustworthy? Classmates are less trustworthy than comrades-in-arms; comrades-in-arms are less than the people who share dirty money; the people who share dirty money are less than the people who visit brothels together.'

- #135 Find a happy medium (折中)

37. **Stress the past, not the present** (厚古薄今) 3

Chinese people have a strong tendency to stress the past, not the present (厚古薄今).[98] This tradition can be traced back to Confucius who admired the political systems and morals of

---

92 俗不可耐 [-] sú bù kě nài (vulgar-not-able to-endure)
93 雅俗共赏 [---赏] yǎ sú gòng shǎng (elegant-vulgar-both-appreciate)
94 附庸风雅 [--風-] fùyōng fēngyǎ (follow-elegance)
95 巧言令色鲜矣仁 [----鲜--] qiǎoyán lìngsè xiǎnyǐ rén (fine-word-flattering-appearance-seldom-indeed-benevelent)
96 物以类聚, 人以群分 [--類-, -] wù yǐ lèi jù, rén yǐ qún fēn (thing-by-kind-gather, people-by-group-split)
97 一起同过窗不如一起扛过枪/分过赃/嫖过娼 [. . . 過槍/-過赃/-過-] yìqǐ tóng guò chuāng bùrú yìqǐ káng guò qiāng/fēn guò zāng/piáo guò chāng (together-share-*experience marker*-school window-not-as good as-shoulder-*experience marker*-rifle/divide- *experience marker*-dirty money/visit- *experience marker* -brothel)
98 厚古薄今 [-] hòugǔ bójīn (value-ancient-devalue-contemporary)

National character (民族性格) **15**

the Zhou dynasty (吾从周,[99] I follow the Zhou). For most well-educated Chinese people, the ideal society was at the era of 三皇五帝 (Three Sovereigns and Five Emperors, a period before recorded history). They often complain that 人心不古 (public morality is not as good as it used to be) and 世风日下 (public morals are declining day by day). As for language, this tendency is still strong. In essence, ancient Chinese words are inclined to have positive connotations, for example, 面 and 脸 (☞ #148 Face and dignity). For another example, 口 is relatively more ancient than 嘴, so 口若悬河 (speak with a flow of eloquence) is much more positive than 满嘴跑火车 (blow smoke, be full of it).

- #12 Change (改变); #34 Refined and popular (雅俗); #39 Old or new (新与旧)

38. Vast land and abundant natural resources (地大物博) 3

Before 1990s, the Chinese government used the following phrases to maintain people's patriotism: 中国历史悠久, 地大物博,[100] 人口众多, China has a long history, a vast territory and a large population. Now the phrase has changed to 世界第二大经济体, the second largest economy (and going to surpass the U.S. in some years).

- #80 The pride of a great empire and the reluctance to lose power (帝国不愿舍弃的荣光); #114 One Belt One Road Initiative (一带一路); #203 Foreign and rustic (洋与土)

39. Old or new (新与旧) 10

Chinese people have the mentality of 喜新厌旧[101] (be fond of the new and tired of the old). There is a famous verse in a poem by the Tang dynasty poet Du Fu (712–770): 但见新人笑, 哪闻旧人哭[102] (he only sees his new bride's smile, and cannot hear his deserted wife cry). One slang saying goes: 旧的不去, 新的不来[103] (the new should replace the old). This mentality prompted Mao Zedong's young red guards to chant the slogan, 破四旧[104] (cast away the four olds – old ideas, old culture, old customs and old habits, 旧思想, 旧文化, 旧风俗, 旧习惯) in the mid-1960s during the Cultural Revolution and to destroy whatever was considered to be old. This included thousands of Confucian temples across the country, innumberable ancient paintings and books, to name only a few. Additionally, this mentality prevented second-hand/used/thrift stores from developing quickly in China. For many ordinary Chinese people, not collectors, a tea cup used by Queen Elizabeth II is not as good as a new cup bought from a dollar store. Women who are widows or have had sex before marriage were once commonly called 破鞋[105] (a worn-out shoe, a loose woman) or 二手货[106] (second-hand goods, a widow). This could partially explain why innovation is so scarce in China.

- #12 Change (改变); #189 Innovation and Chinese college mottos (大学校训与创新)

40. Lu Xun (鲁迅) 5

Some say that of the 20th century Chinese writers, only Lu Xun (鲁迅, 1881–1936) and Jin Yong (金庸, Louis Cha Leung-yung, 1924–2018) will be frequently mentioned in the 21st

---

99 吾从周 [-從-] wú cóng Zhōu (I-follow-Zhou dynasty)
100 历史悠久, 地大物博 [歷---, -] lìshǐ yōujiǔ, dìdàwùbó (history-long, land-vast-product-rich)
101 喜新厌旧 [--厭舊] xǐ xīn yàn jiù (like-new-dislike-old)
102 但见新人笑, 哪闻旧人哭 [-見---, -聞舊--] dàn jiàn xīnrén xiào, nǎ wén jiùrén kū (only-saw-person/wife-smile, not at all-heard-ex-person/wife-cry)
103 旧的不去, 新的不来 [舊---, ---來] jiùde bú qù, xīnde bù lái (old-thing-not-gone, new-thing-not-come)
104 破四旧 [--舊] pò sì jiù (cast awy-4-old)
105 破鞋 [-] pòxié (worn out-shoe)
106 二手货 [--貨] èrshǒu huò (second-hand-goods)

16 *National character (民族性格)*

century. Lu Xun is known for profoundly exposing the dark side of Chinese society through his essays and works of short fictions. Mao Zedong's eulogy of Lu Xun helped make him the greatest writer in the history of modern Chinese literature. Lu Xun had more works selected into Chinese national textbooks than any other writers. For many decades after Lu Xun's death, it remained fashionable to quote his words in writings. This book quotes Lu Xun's famous sayings in Entries #7, 9, 23, 24, 27, 57, 64, 81, 84, 105, for a total of ten times. His most famous works include *A Madman's Diary* (1918), *Kong Yiji* (孔乙己, 1918) and *the True Story of Ah Q* (阿Q正传, 1921).

- #41 Onlookers (看客); #112 Thoughtcrimes (思想罪); #113 Discuss in an open manner (妄议); #139 Louis Cha Leung-yung (金庸, Jin Yong)

41. Onlookers (看客) 5

Life is a journey and too many Chinese are onlookers (看客) who were constantly criticized as national inferiority (民族劣根性) by Lu Xun. As long as their own interests are not affected, onlookers will not act even if justice is violated as long as their own interests are not affected. Some stand by (袖手旁观[107]) and let things happen if they are not personally affected (事不关己, 高高挂起).[108] Some make irresponsible and sarcastic remarks (说风凉话[109]) since talk is cheap (站着说话不腰疼).[110] Some will want to sit this one out (坐山观虎斗[111]) and reap the spoils later (鹬蚌相争, 渔翁得利).[112] Either way, the more bustling the scene becomes, the happier the onlookers are (看热闹的不嫌事大).[113] More than a few onlookers are eager to see the world in disorder (唯恐天下不乱).[114]

- #22 Speculative (投机); #26 Not standing out (不出头); #40 Lu Xun (鲁迅)

42. Silence (沉默) 2

There is a proverb, 'silence is golden' (沉默是金[115]) in the West, and Chinese people understood its essence although there was not a similar proverb in Chinese. Many Chinese people kept silence when they should have spoken out in circumstances such as when justice was being trampled, and so Lu Xun said, '不在沉默中爆发, 就在沉默中灭亡'[116] (break out in the silence, or die in it). An influential modern writer Wang Xiaobo (1952–1997) had a collection of essays 沉默的大多数 (the silent majority), which analyzed the Chinese national character. Despite the calls from Lu Xun, Wang Xiaobo and others,

---

107 袖手旁观 [---觀] xiù shǒu páng guān (sleeved-hand-bystand-watch)

108 事不关己, 高高挂起 [--關-, -] shì bù guān jǐ, gāogāo guà qǐ (thing-not-concerning-oneself, high-*reduplication*-hang-up)

109 说风凉话 [說風涼話] shuō fēngliánghuà (speak-cool-wind-remark)

110 站着说话不腰疼 [-著說話---] zhànzhe shuōhuà bù yāoténg (stand–ing-speak-not-waist-painful)

111 坐山观虎斗 [--觀-鬥] zuò shān guān hǔ dòu (sit-mountain-watch-tiger-fight)

112 鹬蚌相争, 渔翁得利 [鷸--爭, 漁--] yù bàng xiāng zhēng, yúwēng délì (snipe-clam-each other-fight, fishing-man-reap-profit)

113 看热闹的不嫌事大 [-熱鬧-----] kàn rènao de bù xián shì dà (watch-thrilling sight-person-not-mind-thing-big)

114 唯恐天下不乱 [-----亂] wéikǒng tiānxià bú luàn (only-fear-world-not-chaotic)

115 沉默是金 [-] chénmò shì jīn (silence-is-gold)

116 不在沉默中爆发, 就在沉默中灭亡 [------發, -----滅-] bú zài chénmò zhōng bàofā, jiù zài chénmò zhōng mièwáng (not-in-silence-break out, then-in-silence-die)

most ordinary Chinese people are still, in their own words, 三脚踢不出一个屁来[117] (literally 'kick him three times and he dare not let out a fart.') Buddhism has a saying '一默如雷[118]' (silence is like thunder). There are so many Buddhists in China but the thunders are so few, so far.

- #26 Not standing out (不出头); #49 Nonverbal love (无言的爱)

43. Stay foolish (难得糊涂) 3

糊涂 means 'mud-headed,' which is not desirable, however, a motto of Zheng Banqiao (1693–1765), '难得糊涂[119]' has since been vastly cherished by the Chinese people. It means 'Where ignorance is bliss, 'tis folly to be wise.' The calligraphy of this phrase is usually written in traditional characters and can be found almost on every stand selling Chinese calligraphy works. The best way to be 难得糊涂 is to turn a blind eye (睁一只眼, 闭一只眼) to the things that may cause you trouble.

- #15 Standpoint (立场); #25 No principles (无原则)

44. Shortcuts (捷径) 2

Most Chinese people are diligent, but some do embrace shortcuts to achieve their goals, especially for wealth and fame. A common phenomenon is that most casino guests are Chinese. But there were certain shortcuts in certain times. For example, 'secluding' oneself in the Zhongnan Mountains in the Tang dynasty was a shortcut to achieve fame faster. This is called 终南捷径.[120] Great skill is acquired through hours upon hours of practice. Ouyang Xiu, a chancellor and scholar in the Song dynasty, wrote a fable that tells the story of an old street peddler who sells oil and can drip oil through the hole of a coin. A great archer admired the old man, but the old man said 我亦无他, 唯手熟耳,[121] which means 'I have nothing special, it is only that I got too used to this.' Even though this is true, many people still wait for windfalls, i.e., 仰天掉馅饼.[122]

- #232 Importance of tools (工具的重要性)

45. Greedy (贪婪) 3

Some people are never satisfied with what they have got (贪得无厌[123]) because avarice knows no boundaries (欲壑难填).[124] Give someone an inch and he will take a mile (得寸进尺,[125] or 得陇望蜀[126]). A man who rests content with nothing is like a snake trying to swallow an elephant (人心不足蛇吞象),[127] and for him the grass is always greener on the other side of

---

117 三脚踢不出一个屁来 [------個-來] sán jiǎo tī bù chū yīge pì lái (3-kick-kick-not-out-one-fart)
118 一默如雷 [-] yī mò rú léi (long-silence-like-thunder)
119 难得糊涂 [難--塗] nándé hútu (rare-be mud-headed)
120 终南捷径 [終--徑] Zhōngnán jiéjìng (Zhongnan mountain-short-path)
121 我亦无他, 唯手熟耳 [--無-, -] wǒ yì wú tā, wéi shǒushú ěr (I-too-have not-others, only-hand-skillful-that is all)
122 仰天掉馅饼 [---餡餅] yǎngtiān diào xiànbǐng (look up-sky-fall-stuffing-cake)
123 贪得无厌 [貪-無厭] tān dé wú yàn (greedy-gain-never-satisfied)
124 欲壑难填 [--難-] yù hè nán tián (greed-valley-hard-fill)
125 得寸进尺 [--進-] dé cùn jìn chǐ (get-inch-further ask-foot)
126 得陇望蜀 [-隴--] dé Lǒng wàng Shǔ (get- area of Long-hope-area of Shu)
127 人心不足蛇吞象 [-] rénxīn bùzú shé tūn xiàng (man-heart-not-content-snake-swallow-elephant)

18 *National character (民族性格)*

the fence (这山望着那山高).[128] When eating, this kind of person will keep one eye on the bowl and the other on the pan (吃着碗里的, 看着锅里的).[129]

- #31 Fame and fortune (名利); #54 Men's three treasures (农民的三宝)

46. Repent (回头) 2

Buddhism tells all living creatures that the sea of bitterness has no bounds, so repent, and the shore is at hand (苦海无边, 回头是岸).[130] One false step brings about external regret (一失足成千古恨),[131] so a prodigal son returned home is worth more than gold (浪子回头金不换).[132] But some people are headstrong. They believe that there is no turning back of an arrow once it is shot (开弓没有回头箭)[133], and those people would never come back until there is a dead end (不撞南墙不回头).[134] The egos of young people in China are bigger and bigger. According to a survey of about a thousand college students by the author of this book in 2012, their most favorite proverb is 好马不吃回头草[135] (a good man doesn't backtrack).

- #66 Retribution, karma (报应); #90 Penitential decrees and letters of self-criticism (罪己诏与检讨书)

47. Legacy (功名) 5

Westerners wish to leave a legacy for their families and society. On the other hand, the legacy Chinese people wish to leave is 名垂青史[136] (leave a name in history) because 人过留名, 雁过留声[137] (a man leaves behind a name, a wild goose leaves behind a voice). Wen Tianxiang (1236–1283), a famous scholar-general of the Southern Song dynasty, left a famous verse before he died, 人生自古谁无死, 留取丹青照汗青[138] (All men are mortal, but my loyalty will illuminate the annals of history forever). 功名 (achievements and fame, scholarly honor and official rank) was the ideal for most if not all Chinese intellectuals and officials in ancient times. Yue Fei (1103–1142), a military general of the Southern Song dynasty, mentioned the word 功名 twice in only three poems recorded, i.e., 三十功名尘与土, 八千里路云和月[139] (30 years: rank and honor, just so much dust; 800 leagues: traveling with the moon and clouds) and 白首为功名[140] (spend one's entire life striving for rank and honor). Another

---

128 这山望着那山高 [這--著---] zhè shān wàngzhe nà shān gāo (this-mountain-look into distance–*ing*-that-mountain-high)

129 吃着碗里, 看着锅里 [-著-裏, -著鍋裏] chīzhe wǎn lǐ, kànzhe guō lǐ (eat–*ing*-bowl-inside, look–*ing*-wok-inside)

130 苦海无边, 回头是岸 [--無邊, -頭--] kǔhǎi wú biān, huítóu shì àn (bitter-sea-no-boundary, turn around-head-is-shore)

131 一失足成千古恨 [-] yì shīzú chéng qiāngǔ hèn (once-lose-footstep-become-1,000-ages-regret)

132 浪子回头金不换 [---頭---] làngzǐ huítóu jīn bú huàn (prodigal-boy-turn around-head-gold-not-exchangeable)

133 开弓没有回头箭 [-----頭] kāigōng méiyǒu huítóu jiàn (draw-bow-not-have-turn around-head-arrow)

134 不撞南墙不回头 [---墙--頭] bú zhuàng nán qiáng bù huítóu (not-hit-south-wall-not-turn around-head)

135 好马不吃回头草 [-馬---頭-] hǎo mǎ bù chī huítóu cǎo (good-horse-not-eat-turn around-head-grass)

136 名垂青史 [-] míng chuí qīngshǐ (name-leave-history)

137 人过留名, 雁过留声 [-過--, -過-聲] rén guò liú míng, yàn guò liú shēng (man-pass-leave-fame, wild goose-pass-leave-voice)

138 人生自古谁无死, 留取丹心照汗青 [----誰無-, -] rénshēng zìgǔ shéi wú sǐ, liúqǔ dānxīn zhào hànqīng (life-from-ancient-who-no-die, reserve-loyal heart-shine-history)

139 三十功名尘与土, 八千里路云和月 [----塵與-, ----雲-] sānshí gōngmíng chén yǔ tǔ, bā qiān lǐ lù yún hé yuè (30 years-rank and honor-dust-and-dirt, 8,000-*li*-road-cloud-and-moon)

140 白首为功名 [--為--] báishǒu wèi gōngmíng (white-head hair-for-rank and honor)

National character (民族性格) 19

scholar-general of the Southern Song dynasty, Xin Qiji (1140–1207), had a similar verse, 了却君王天下事, 赢得生前身后名[141] (We will finish the monarch's mission to unify the realm, and be immortalized both in this life and the next). A modern poem, '有的人' (some people), which was written for the 13th anniversary of Lu Xun's death, begins like this: 有的人活着, 他已经死了; 有的人死了, 他还活着[142] (literally 'some people are alive, but they already died, but they are still alive.') The inscription on the Monument of the People's Heroes is 人民英雄永垂不朽[143] (people's heroes never die). Maybe we should not take the idea of 'legacy' too seriously and behave like chivalrous men described in Li Bai's poem: 事了拂衣去, 深藏身与名[144] (Leave the things done with nothing left behind).

- #30 Success and failure (胜负, 成败); #31 Fame and fortune (名利); #73 Outstanding statecraft and brilliant military exploits (文治武功); #94 Sages and men of virtue (圣贤); #97 Three Immortal Deeds (三不朽)

48. Integrity in one's later years (晚节) 1

Famous Chinese people who have great achievements want to leave a legacy or a name in history (名垂青史[145]) and they are afraid to lose integrity in their later years (晚节不保),[146] since no final verdict can be pronounced until after a man's death (盖棺定论[147] or 盖棺论定, only when the lid is laid on a person's coffin, can the final judgement be passed on him). How can one keep his integrity in his later years? For ordinary people, they can 含饴弄孙[148] (spend one's remaining years happily in the company of one's grandchildren) and for the famous people, especially politicians, they should 闭门谢客读书[149] (shut their door, deny visitors and read books, signifying no involvement with politics). For example, former Chinese Premier Zhu Rongji (in office 1998–2003) retired in 2003 and his main rules for social activities are 不谈工作[150] (no talking about work/politics) and 闭门谢客, 在家读书 (deny visitors and read books).

- #83 Posthumous titles (谥号)

49. Nonverbal love (无言的爱) 3

爱 (ài, love) is a lovely word, but it was almost never vocalized in Chinese. The character 爱 in proverbs and idioms typically means 'like, 喜欢.' For example, 爱屋及乌 (love me, love my dog; i.e., when you like someone, it is more likely that you will like the things related to him or her), 君子爱财, 取之有道 (while wealth is desirable for a gentleman, he takes it only as he can get it, in its natural course). 爱 appears only seven times in five poems from 诗经 (*Classic of Poetry, Book of Odes*). Among the seven 爱, only one truly means 'love.' It is 心乎爱矣, 遐不谓矣 (in my heart I love them, and why should I not say so?) in the poem of Xi Sang. It is what the modern poet Xi Murong said in her poem '信仰' (Belief): '我相

---

141 了却君王天下事, 赢得生前身后名 [-, 赢----後-] liǎoquè jūnwáng tiānxià shì, yíngdé shēngqián shēnhòu míng (finish-monarch-rule the world-ambition, win-this life-after life-fame)

142 有的人活着, 他已经死了; 有的人死了, 他还活着: See in-text.

143 人民英雄永垂不朽 [-] rénmín yīngxióng yǒngchuíbùxiǔ (people-hero-forever-live-never-perish)

144 事了拂衣去, 深藏功与名 [-, ---與-] shì liǎo fú yī qù, shēn cáng gōng yǔ míng (thing-done-flick-clothes-leave, deep-hide-rank and honor)

145 名垂青史 [-] míng chuí qīngshǐ (name-leave-history)

146 晚节不保 [-節--] wǎnjié bù bǎo (later-integrity-not-kept)

147 盖棺定论 [蓋--論] gài guān dìng lùn (cover-coffin-settle-verdict)

148 含饴弄孙 [-飴-孫] hán yí nòng sūn (keep in the mouth-candy-tease-grandchildren)

149 闭门谢客读书 [閉門謝-讀書] bìmén xièkè dúshū (shut-door-reject-visitor-read-book)

150 不谈工作 [-談--] bù tán gōngzuò (not-talk about-work)

20 *National character (民族性格)*

信/三百篇诗/反复述说著的/也就只是/年少时没能说出的/那一个字' (I believe, what the Classic of Poetry repeatedly tells, is the word that could not be uttered aloud when we were young). That word is 爱.

- #42 Silence (沉默)

50. **Share weal or woe? (同甘还是共苦) 3**

同甘共苦[151] (share weal and woe) should be a virtue, but many people think the Chinese can 共苦 (share woe) but cannot 同甘 (share joys) because they would support each other through hardships but will likely break up after they make their fortune. However, the Americans can 同甘 but not 共苦 since they are likely to break up during hardships.

- #173 Husband and wife: good (夫妻: 关系好); #174 Husband and wife: bad (夫妻: 关系差)

51. **Life and death (生死)5**

Birth, aging, illness and death (生老病死[152]) are all part of natural law. Life and death is often associated with the phrase 'survive or perish' (生死存亡).[153] Life or death, rich or poor, everything is already determined (生死有命, 富贵在天),[154] so optimistic people take life and death relatively lightly. Couples or sworn friends can 生死相依, 生死与共 or 同生死, 共患难, all meaning 'go through thick and thin,' and they can die for each other (生死之交).[155] The most painful parting is 生离死别.[156] The highest eulogy an ordinary Chinese person in this age can get is what was given to Liu Hulan (1932–1947), a female CCP member who received written inscription from the top leaders of three generations, with Mao's inscription being 生的伟大, 死的光荣[157] (a great life, a glorious death).

- #55 Die, death (死); #56 Chinese condolences (节哀顺变); #262 Euphemisms for 'to die' ('死'的委婉语)

52. **'Death penalty' and modesty (死罪死罪) 5**

From around the Western Han dynasty to the Tang dynasty, 死罪死罪[158] was widely used to mean 'pardon me (if this is not appropriate)' in memos to the emperor or higher rank officials or even between friends. In a short 1,274-character letter *劝进表* (quànjìnbiǎo) to the emperor on the lunar date March 18, 317, 刘琨 (Liú Kūn) used死罪 (death penalty) and unsurprisingly 顿首 (dùnshǒu, kowtow).

- #79 To take or decline the throne (劝进与固辞); #149 Civilities (客套); #275 Forms of address: respectful, honorific and modest (尊称, 敬称, 谦称)

---

151 同甘共苦 [-] tónggān gòngkǔ (same-sweet-together-hard)
152 生老病死 [-] shēng lǎo bìng sǐ (birth-aging-illness-death)
153 生死存亡 [-] shēngsǐ cúnwáng (live-die-survive-perish)
154 生死有命, 富贵在天 [-, -貴--] shēngsǐ yǒu mìng, fùguì zài tiān (life or death-have-destiny, rich and powerful-depend on-heaven)
155 生死之交 [-] shēng sǐ zhī jiāo (life-death-'s-friendship)
156 生离死别 [-離-别] shēng lí sǐ bié (life-separate-death-part)
157 生的伟大, 死的光荣 [--偉-, ---榮] shēng de wěidà, sǐ de guāngróng (born-great, died-glory)
158 死罪死罪 [-] sǐzuì (death penalty-death penalty)

National character (民族性格)   21

53. To survive by all possible means (活着) 3

Many Chinese people have a belief that 好死不如赖活着[159] (a living ass is better than a dead lion). They value too much, and that is why when the Hungarian poet Sándor Petőfi's 1847 poem 'Szabadság, szerelem!' first introduced to China in 1925. The Chinese translation and English equivalent are read as 生命诚可贵, 爱情价更高; 若为自由故, 两者皆可抛 (Freedom love! // I need these two. // For my love I sacrifice // Life, I // sacrifice // My Love for Freedom). In fact, Americans had similar sayings such as 'Give me liberty or give me death' (1775) and 'Live free or die' (1809, 1945), which can be translated into Chinese as 不自由, 毋宁死[160] (literally, 'if without freedom, I would rather die').

- #54 Men's three treasures (农民的三宝)

54. Men's three treasures (农民的三宝) 3

Northern Chinese peasants had a saying, 丑妻薄田破棉袄,[161] which were called 'three treasures' for men. 丑妻 means 'ugly wife,' 薄田 'infertile land' and 破棉袄 'worn cotton-padded jacket.' For those peasants, an ugly wife (丑妻) was safe since others had no interest in her and she could focus on housework. Infertile land (薄田) was safe since the rich had no interest in it, and if the peasant worked hard, the land could yield enough grains to support the family. A worn cotton-padded jacket (破棉袄) could keep one warm although it did not look magnificent. This saying reflects that the ambition of those peasants was extremely low. What they really wanted in life was safety, not prosperity.

- #31 Fame and fortune (名利); #132 Poor (穷)

55. Die, death (死) 5

Some people die for fortune, just like birds die for food (人为财死, 鸟为食亡[162]); some die for fame or legacy, as in 人生自古谁无死, 留取丹心照汗青[163] (All men are mortal, but my loyalty will illuminate the annals of history forever). Death pays all debts (一死百了)[164]; therefore, if a person's life is not so happy, he may hope to 早死早超生[165] (have an early death/early reincarnation). Chinese people respect the dead and will turn a blind eye to the dead's wrongdoings in his life (死者为大).[166] Many Chinese government officials have chosen to commit suicide to save their families. If one's wishes were not fulfilled, he would die with his eyes open (死不瞑目).[167]

- #51 Life and death (生死); #56 Chinese condolences (节哀顺变); #262 Euphemisms for 'to die' ('死'的委婉语)

---

159 好死不如赖活着 [----赖-著] hǎo sǐ bùrú lài huózhe (gracefully-die-not-as good as-disgracefully-live)

160 不自由, 毋宁死 [-, -宁-] bú zìyóu, wúnìng sǐ (not-free, rather-die)

161 丑妻薄田破棉袄 [醜-----襖] chǒuqībótiánpòmiánǎo (ugly-wife-infertile-land-worn-cotton-jacket)

162 人为财死, 鸟为食亡 [-為财-, -為--] rén wèi cái sǐ, niǎo wèi shí wáng (people-for-wealth-die, bird-for-food-die)

163 人生自古谁无死, 留取丹心照汗青 [----誰無-, -] rénshēng zìgǔ shéi wú sǐ, liúqǔ dānxīn zhào hànqīng (life-from-ancient-who-no-die, reserve-loyal heart-shine-history)

164 一死百了 [-] yì sǐ bǎi liǎo (once-die-100-end)

165 早死早超生 [-] zǎo sǐ zǎo chāoshēng (earlier-die-earlier-reincarnate)

166 死者为大 [--為-] sǐzhě wéi dà (dead-person-is-unsurpassable)

167 死不瞑目 [-] sǐ bù míng mù (die-not-close-eye)

22   *National character (民族性格)*

56. **Chinese condolences** (节哀顺变) **2**

In the English-speaking world, when one hears of someone's passing, he would usually say, 'My condolences' or 'I am sorry for your loss,' etc. For Chinese people, the traditional way is to ask the speaker to 节哀顺变[168] (restrain one's grief and accord with inevitable changes). 变 means 'change,' which is caused by Heaven. 顺便 means 'accept this change.' The phrase 节哀顺变 shows the Confucian concept of 天人合一[169] (oneness of heaven and man).

- #55 Die, death (死); #262 Euphemisms for 'to die' ('死'的委婉语)

57. **Same and different** (同与异) **5**

In ancient China, 'being different' (异) was bad and even dangerous. If someone 有异志 (has different ambitions), it meant he would rebel. Words with 异 often have a negative connotation, for example, 异心 (disloyalty), 异族 (different race or nation) and 异端 (heterodoxy). On the other hand, words with 同 (same) usually have a positive connotation, for example, 同志 (comrade), 同学 (classmate) and 同窗 (classmate). Two Chinese people 同庚 (of the same age) can make their bond closer, and 'being different' or 'individualism' (个人主义) was not welcome in China.

- #109 Boldest proclamation of reform (三不足); #113 Discuss in an open manner (妄议)

---

168 节哀顺变 [節-順變] jié'āi shùnbiàn (restrain-grief-at ease-change)
169 天人合一 [-] tiānrén héyī (heaven-human-integrate-one)

3 Religion, philosophy, politics, history (宗教, 哲学, 政治, 历史)

58. Heavenly principles (天理) 10

This term can mean 'natural law,' but it usually means 'heavenly principle.' Prominent Neo-Confucian philosopher, Zhu Xi (1130–1200) advocated these Confucian ethics, as reflected in his infamous slogan 存天理, 去人欲[170] (maintain the heavenly principles and eradicate human desires). What were heavenly principles? A perfect example is embodied in a sentence by a Neo-Confucian philosopher Cheng Yi (1033–1107), 饿死事(极)小, 失节事(极)大[171] (Death by starvation is preferable to loss of chastity). However, 300 years later, another influential Neo-Confucian philosopher Wang Yangming (1472–1529) promoted the opposite idea 人欲即天理[172] (human desires are the heavenly principles). 天理 was sometimes regarded as the highest justice by the common people. They would say, '还有没有天理?' (is there any justice?) or 天理难容[173] (heaven forbid) when they did not feel that there was any justice. Some inhuman acts are said to 伤天害理[174] (be against reason and nature). Who guarantees that the heavenly principles are followed? Heaven itself, because 人在做, 天在看[175] (God is watching you) or 举头三尺有神灵[176] (God is watching over you).

- #63 Fairness (公道); #109 Boldest proclamation of reform (三不足); #183 Earthquakes and women (地震与女人); #268 The most heartbreaking vows (最让人心碎的誓言)

59. Mandate of Heaven, or God's will (天命, 天意) 5

The concept of the Mandate of Heaven is related to rulers and God's will to the common people. All Chinese emperors called themselves 天子[177] (son of Heaven) since they all received the mandate from Heaven (受命于天).[178] The mandate was carved on a precious jade (He Shi Bi) seal, the Heirloom Seal of the Realm or the Imperial Seal of China, along with the phrase '既寿永昌' (may the emperor lead a long and prosperous life). The mandate of Heaven could not be violated (天命不可违),[179] and one had to submit to the will of Heaven

---

170 存天理, 去人欲 [-] cún tiānlǐ, qù rényù (preserve-heaven-principle, eradicate-human-desire)
171 饿死事极小, 失节事极大 [餓--極-, -節-極-] è sǐ shì jí xiǎo, shījié shì jí dà (starve-dead-thing-extremely-small, lose-chastity-thing-extremely-big)
172 天理即人欲 [-] tiānlǐ jí rényù (heaven-principle-i.e.-human-desire)
173 天理难容 [--難-] tiānlǐ nán róng (heaven-principle-hardly-tolerate)
174 伤天害理 [傷---] shāng tiān hài lǐ (hurt-heaven-harm-norm)
175 人在做, 天在看 [-] rén zài zuò, tiān zài kàn (people-is-doing, heaven-is-watching)
176 举头三尺有神灵 [舉頭----靈] jǔ tóu sān chǐ yǒu shénlíng (raise-head-three-inch-have-god-spirit)
177 天子 [-] tiānzǐ (heaven-son)
178 受命于天 [--於-] shòu mìng yú tiān (receive-mandate-from-heaven)
179 天命不可违 [----違] tiānmìng bùkě wéi (heaven-mandate-not-allowed-violate)

24   *Religion, philosophy, politics, history*

(听天由命).[180] Some things are destined to happen (命中注定).[181] Man can propose, but God disposes (谋事在人, 成事在天).[182] When Chinese are hopeless or feel incredulous, they often say, '这是天意[183]' (this is Heaven's will).

- #12 Change (改变); #17 Times and heroes (时势与英雄); #30 Success and failure (胜负, 成败); #66 Retribution, karma (报应); #78 Blessing and the unfortunate Song dynasty (宋朝年号与'祐'); #88 Feudal (封建)

60. Laws (法) 5

法 (fǎ, law) was originally written as 灋, which is related to 氵 (水, water), 廌 (zhì, a mythic celestial animal) and 去 (to go, away). 氵 (water) is naturally inclined to be level, thus indicating 'fair, just.' 廌 was said to be able to identify the person who was wrong in court and use his horns to strike the offender and make him leave (去). It is interesting that, if the myth had some ground, it indicates that the legitimacy of Chinese laws comes from heaven (天, tian), and is not based on a common contract. It is natural for a country to have national laws (国法). However, many ancient Chinese families had their own regulations that were called 家法 (literally 'family law'). Interestingly, if someone violated 家法, he would be punished. And the rod for punishing children or servants was also called 家法.

- #25 No principles (无原则); #58 Heavenly principles (天理)

61. Auspicious signs and the color white (祥瑞与白色) 3

In ancient China, many things and signs could be considered auspicious (祥瑞, xiángruì), for example, chilin (麒麟, qílín, a mythical creature), phoenix (凤凰, fènghuáng), turtle (龟, guī), dragon (龙) and clouds (祥云/庆云), etc. White animals and birds were usually considered auspicious, for example, a white elephant (白象), white fox (白狐), white deer (白鹿), white tiger (白虎), white wolf (白狼), 白兔 (white rabbit), 白燕 (white swallow), 白雀 (white tit), and白雉 (white pheasant), etc.

- #77 Four magnificent characters and the declination of the Northern Song ('丰亨豫大' 与北宋的衰败); #155 Colors and culture (颜色与文化)

62. Locations of the four temples in Beijing (北京四坛的方位) 2

The four temples 天坛 (Temple of Heaven), 地坛 (Temple of Earth), 日坛 (Temple of the Sun) and 月坛 (Temple of the Moon) in Beijing are located in the south, the north, the east and the west, respectively. Why? Ancient Chinese believed 天 is *yang* and 地 is *yin*, so the two temples are in the south and north. The sun rises in the east, and the moon sets in the west, so 日坛 and 月坛 are in the east and west. Ancient Chinese also believed 天圆地方[184] (the heaven is round and the earth square), so the main buildings in the Temple of Heaven are round and those in the Temple of Earth are square.

---

180 听天由命 [聽---] tīng tiān yóu mìng (submit to-heaven-arranged-fate)
181 命中注定 [-] mìng zhōng zhùdìng (fate-course-destined)
182 谋事在人, 成事在天 [謀---, -] móu shì zài rén, chéng shì zài tiān (plan-things-at-people, accomplish-thing-by-heaven)
183 这是天意 [這---] zhè shì tiānyì (this-is-heaven-will)
184 天圆地方 [-圓--] tiānyuán dìfāng (heaven-round-earth-square)

Religion, philosophy, politics, history 25

63. Fairness (公道) 2

Fairness or justice (公道) is what we have been pursuing but have not yet fully achieved. We hope that others are fair/impartial (说句公道话[185]) or uphold justice (主持公道, redress the scales). But where is justice and who knows it? It is in the people's hearts (公道自在人心,[186] the masses know clearly about the merits of the matter), and probably only god knows (你说你公道, 我说我公道, 公道不公道, 只有天知道,[187] words recited in the most popular Beijing opera *Susan Qijie*.) For ordinary people, fairness is the fact that everyone, rich or poor, will have gray hair (公道世间唯白发, 贵人头上不曾饶).[188]

- #21 Partial and impartial (公与私); #66 Retribution, karma (报应)

64. Men vs. ghosts (人与鬼) 5

Ghosts are ugly. If a person is ugly, a Chinese person might say of him, '三分像人, 七分像鬼[189]' (30% is like a man and 70% a ghost). After the Western troops invaded China in the mid-19th century, they were given a derogatory name 鬼子[190] (ghost) such as 洋鬼子 (Westerners) and 日本鬼子 (Japanese ghosts). There is also a taboo term for black people. A person may have an ulterior objective (心里有鬼).[191] Ghosts are also scary. Ancient Chinese people liked to say 我死了以后变成鬼也要找你算账 (I will settle with you even after I die and become a ghost) when they were threatened in desperation. However, ghosts are invisible, and no one has really seen them. Therefore, it is easiest to draw a ghost and hardest to draw a dog or a horse (画鬼最易,[192] in *Han Feizi*). The Chinese word 鬼 is not always derogatory. There are two Western movies that were popular in China: *Ghost* (1990, 人鬼情未了) and *Home Alone* (1990, 小鬼当家). Cantonese people will call a smart and naughty child 人小鬼大[193] (a kid is wise beyond his years).

- #268 The most heartbreaking vows (最让人心碎的誓言)

65. Yin and yang (阴阳) 5

The original meaning of 阴 is the north side of a mountain/hill or the south side of a river, and 阳 is the opposite of 阴. This sentiment exists widely in Chinese place names, for example, there are 117 county-level-city names containing 阳 (i.e., 沈阳, 贵阳, 淮阳) and 9 containing 阴 (i.e., 江阴, 山阴, 淮阴). Feng shui masters can judge if houses or tombs (阴阳宅) are blessed. In reference to Chinese place names, the common phrase is 阳盛阴衰[194] ('yang 阳' prevails over 'yin 阴.') However, in many other social areas, it is a prevailing belief that

---

185 说句公道话 [說---話] shuō jù gōngdào huà (speak-measure word-fair-words)
186 公道自在人心 [-] gōngdào zì zài rénxīn (fair-)
187 你说你公道, 我说我公道, 公道不公道, 只有天知道 [-說---, -說---, -, -] nǐ shuō nǐ gōngdào, wǒ shuō wǒ gōngdào, gōngdào bù gōngdào, zhǐ yǒu tiān zhīdào (you-say-yourself-fair, I-say-myself-fair, fair-not-fair, only-heaven-know)
188 公道世间惟白发, 贵人头上不曾饶 [---間--髮, 貴-頭---饒] gōngdào shìjiān wéi báifà, guìrén tóushang bùcéng ráo (fairness-in the world-only-grey-hair, noble-people-head-on-not-once-spared)
189 三分像人, 七分像鬼 [-] sān fēn xiàng rén, qī fēn xiàng guǐ (3–1/10-like-man, 7–1/10-like-ghost)
190 鬼子 [-] guǐzi (ghost-people)
191 心里有鬼 [-裏--] xīnlǐ yǒu guǐ (heart-inside-have-ghost)
192 画鬼最易 [畫---] huà guǐ zuì yì (draw-ghost-most-easy)
193 人小鬼大 [-] rén xiǎo guǐ dà (person-young-trick-wild)
194 阳盛阴衰 [陽-陰-] yáng shèng yīn shuāi (masculine/yang-flourishing-feminine/yin-decline)

26 *Religion, philosophy, politics, history*

阴盛阳衰[195] (women do better than men). A typical field where this phrase is used is sports, and this will not be wrong until the Chinese national football team wins the second place at the FIFA World Cup. Yin and yang are also applied to human bodies and genders. Yin indicates 'weak,' 'dead' or 'feminine,' whereas yang is 'strong,' 'alive' or 'masculine.' If a person behaves or speaks weirdly, he or she is considered eccentric (阴阳怪气).[196]

- #64 Men vs. ghosts (人与鬼); #183 Earthquakes and women (地震与女人); #250 Juxtaposition of male and female (连绵词: 雌雄)

66. Retribution, karma (报应) 10

Chinese people believe in karma, often saying 人在做天在看[197] (God is watching you) and 举头三尺有神灵[198] (God is watching over you). The idea is expressed in the following sayings: 善有善报, 恶有恶报[199] (good is rewarded with good, and evil with evil; what goes around comes around), 善恶到头终有报, 只争来早与来迟[200] (what goes around will come around, sooner or later), 好人有好报[201] (good people will eventually be rewarded), 恶人自有恶人磨[202] (the wicked have their own evildoers), and 多行不义必自毙[203] (what is unjust is doomed to be destroyed). However, this understanding is not always satisfying, and the outcome may be just the opposite. Good intentions do not pay off (好心没好报[204]) or even evil outlives good for a long time (好人不长寿, 祸害一千年).[205] When Chinese people are begging Heaven, they hope 'the Heaven is attentively watching' (老天有眼[206]); when complaining, they hope that 'Heaven's eyes are not open' (老天不睁眼[207]); when satisfied, 'the Heaven is acting' (老天显灵[208]); when unsatisfied, 'Heaven is blind' (老天瞎了眼).[209]

- #46 Repent (回头); #63 Fairness (公道); #268 The most heartbreaking vows (最让人心碎的誓言)

67. Buddhism and emperors with a posthumous title of 武 (佛教与'*武帝') 1

Buddhism condemns violence and killing. However, there were three emperors who caused the greatest harm to Chinese Buddhism, and they all had a posthumous title of 武. This is

---

195 阴盛阳衰 [陰-陽-] yīn shèng yáng shuāi (female/yin-flourishing-male/yang-decline)
196 阴阳怪气 [陰陽-氣] yīnyáng guàiqì (feminine/yin-masculine/yang-queer-manner)
197 人在做, 天在看 [-] rén zài zuò, tiān zài kàn (people-is-doing, heaven-is-watching)
198 举头三尺有神灵 [舉頭----靈] jǔ tóu sān chǐ yǒu shénlíng (raise-head-three-inch-have-god-spirit)
199 善有善报, 恶有恶报 [---報, 惡-惡報] shàn yǒu shàn bào, è yǒu è bào (good-have-good-beget, evil-have-evil-beget)
200 善恶到头终有报, 只争来早与来迟 [-惡-頭終-報, -爭來-與來遲] shàn è dàotóu zhōng yǒu bào, zhǐ zhēng lái zǎo yǔ lái chí (good-evil-arrive at-end-eventually-have-retribution, only-different-come-early-or-come-late)
201 好人有好报 [----報] hǎorén yǒu hǎo bào (kind-man-have-kind-reward)
202 恶人自有恶人磨 [惡---惡--] èrén zì yǒu èrén mó (evil-people-definitely-have-evil-people-trouble)
203 多行不义必自毙 [---義--斃] duō xíng búyì bì zì bì (much-do-not-justice-must-self-die)
204 好心没好报 [----報] hǎo xīn méi hǎo bào (kind-heart-no-good-reward)
205 好人不长寿, 祸害一千年 [---長壽, 禍----] hǎorén bù chángshòu, huòhài yīqiān nián (kind-people-not-long-live, wrongdoer-1000-year)
206 老天有眼 [-] lǎotiān yǒu yǎn (heaven-have-eye)
207 老天不睁眼 [---睜-] lǎotiān bù zhēngyǎn (heaven-not-open-eye)
208 老天显灵 [--顯靈] lǎotiān xiǎnlíng (heaven-reveal-itself)
209 老天瞎了眼 [-] lǎotiān xiāle yǎn (heaven-blind–*ed*-eye)

called 三武灭佛 (sān wǔ miè fó, Three Disasters of Wu). The emperors were 北魏太武帝 (Emperor Taiwu of Northern Wei), 北周武帝 (Emperor Wu Di of the Northern Zhou dynasty), and 唐武宗 (Emperor Wuzong of the Tang dynasty), starting approximately in the mid-5th, 6th, and 9th centuries, respectively, and each lasted approximately five years.

- #69 Buddhist texts and knife (佛经与刀)

68. Buddha and monks (佛与和尚/僧) 3

Chinese people generally respect Buddha but mock monks. Buddha (佛) is referred to positively in the following sayings: 借花献佛 (offer presents provided by someone else), 送佛送到西 (do not stop half way in doing a good deed), 放下屠刀, 立地成佛 (to achieve salvation after giving up evil), 平时不烧香, 临时抱佛脚 (to do nothing until one is driven to desperation) etc. Meanwhile, monks (和尚) are the subject of mocking, for example, 僧多粥少 (not enough to go round), 当一天和尚撞一天钟 (to go through the motions), 经是好的, 可是让歪嘴的和尚念歪了 (scriptures are good, but they are twisted by monks with a wry mouth). The most representative example is 不看僧面看佛面[210] (if not for the monk's sake, then for the Buddha' sake, i.e., do something out of respect for a higher authority) in which Buddha is held superior to monks.

- #67 Buddhism and emperors with a posthumous title of 武 (佛教与'*武帝')

69. Buddhist texts and knife (佛经与刀) 1

放下屠刀, 立地成佛[211] means 'a butcher becomes a Buddha the moment he drops his cleaver,' which is meant to convince that people can change if he believes in Buddhism. Interestingly, 鲁迅 (Lǔ Xùn, 1881–1936), a great writer once wrote after this famous quotation '放下佛经, 立地杀人' (literally 'one puts down Buddhist scripture, right at that place he will kill others.')

- #67 Buddhism and emperors with a posthumous title of 武 (佛教与'*武帝')

70. Sharp-witted remarks (机锋) 2

While 机锋 (jīfēng) originally refers to short, sharp-witted Buddhist remarks, it now can be used to refer to any sharp-witted remarks. There are more than a thousand recorded Buddhist 机锋 throughout history. For example, one asked Monk Tungshan 'What is Buddha?' He replied, 'Three pounds of hemp (麻三斤).'[212] In fact, answer could have been almost anything, such as 'five pounds of hemp,' 'three pounds of salt,' 'a wisp of breeze' or anything else. Simply put, Buddha is anything and anywhere. As another example, when the Sixth Ancestor of Chan Buddhism Dajian Huineng (惠能, 638–713) was preaching, the wind was blowing a pennant. One monk said it was the wind that was blowing. Another said that it was the pennant that was moving. They argued endlessly. Huineng argued that the wind was not blowing, and the pennant was not moving, but a benevolent person's heart moved (仁者心动).[213] Simply put, if one's mind was focused on Buddha, he could not observe external things.

- #35 Humorous (幽默); #71 'Go drink tea' (吃茶去)

---

210 不看僧面看佛面 [-] búkàn sēngmiàn kàn fómiàn (not-for-monk-sake-for-Buddha-sake)

211 放下屠刀, 立地成佛 [-] fàngxià túdāo, lìdì chéng fó (put-down-butcher-knife, right-that place-become-Buddha)

212 麻三斤 [-] má sān jīn (hemp-3-catty)

213 仁者心动 [---動] rénzhě xīndòng (benevolent-people-heart-move)

28   *Religion, philosophy, politics, history*

71. 'Go drink tea' (吃茶去) 2

This is a famous Chinese Zen saying and story. In the Tang dynasty, two monks visited a Zen master in a temple in modern Hebei Province. The master asked a monk, 'Have you been here recently?' The answer was 'Yes.' Then, the master said, '吃茶去'[214] (go drink tea). He then asked the other monk the same question. The answer was 'No.' Then, the master said, '吃茶去' (go drink tea) again. A follower of the master was curious and asked the master why he treated the two monks the same even though their answers were the opposite. The master told his follower the same thing, i.e., 吃茶去 (go drink tea). This story derived a famous thought '茶禅一味' (literally 'tea and Zen are the same sense'), which indicates that practicing Zen can happen anywhere and anytime, just like drinking tea.

- #70 Sharp-witted remarks (机锋)

72. Dusts and the human world (尘与世) 2

The celestial heaven is spotless whereas the human world is not (尘世/塵世, literally 'dust-world,' this mortal world; 凡尘/凡塵, literally 'ordinary-dust,' this mortal life). One's bonds with the world is called 尘缘 (塵緣). 一尘不染[215] originally came from Buddhism, meaning 'clear of six dusts that might pollute the ordinary people's six external sense bases, namely eye, ear, nose, tongue, body and mind.' Now it is used mainly as 'spotlessly clean (of rooms or other objects)' and 'maintain pure-hearted (in the bureaucratic environment etc.' The most famous saying on 尘 is '本来无一物, 何处惹尘埃[216]' (Originally there is not one thing, what place could there be for dust?) by the Sixth Ancestor of Chan, Dajian Huineng (638–713).

- #34 Refined and popular (雅俗)

73. Outstanding statecraft and brilliant military exploits (文治武功) 5

This term is not related to the common people but refers to the highest rulers of China. They wanted to have their names perpetuated throughout history (名垂青史[217]), and their egos craved for greatness and success (好大喜功).[218] Due to their extreme power and ambition, they would mobilize too many people (兴师动众[219]) and therefore exhaust the people and drain the treasury (劳民伤财).[220] At the very least they caused such utter confusion by making everybody nervous (鸡犬不宁,[221] even fowls and dogs are not left in peace). The only people who benefited from their ambition were brown-nosers who would heap praises and eulogies (歌功颂德).[222] There were many such rulers in Chinese history: Qin Shi Huang (259 BCE–210 BCE), Emperor Wu of Han (157 BCE–87 BCE), Emperor Yang of Sui (569–618), Emperor Qianlong of Qing (1711–1799), etc.

- #47 Legacy (功名); #77 Four magnificent characters and the declination of the Northern Song ('丰亨豫大'与北宋的衰败); #84 Temple names of emperors (庙号); #85 Temple names and achievements of emperors (庙号与成就); #97 Three Immortal Deeds (三不朽)

---

214 吃茶去 [-] chīcháqù (drink-tea-go)
215 一尘不染 [-塵--] yìchén bùrǎn (one-dust-not-polluted)
216 本来无一物, 何处惹尘埃 [--無--, -處-塵-] běnlái wú yīwù, héchù rě chén'āi (originally-no-one-thing, what-place-fall-dust)
217 名垂青史 [-] míng chuí qīngshǐ (name-leave-history)
218 好大喜功 [-] hào dà xǐ gong (fond-great-like-merit)
219 兴师动众 [興師動衆] xīng shī dòng zhòng (send-army-mobilize-masses)
220 劳民伤财 [勞-傷財] láo mín shāng cái (exhaust-people-harm-treasury)
221 鸡犬不宁 [鷄--寧] jī quǎn bù níng (chicken-dog-not-peaceful)
222 歌功颂德 [--頌-] gē gōng sòng dé (laud-merit-eulogize-virtue)

Religion, philosophy, politics, history　29

74. The first thing to do after a new emperor ascended the throne in ancient China (新皇继位后做的第一件事) 1

The first thing to do was 尊皇后为皇太后[223] (to honor the empress, the widow of the late emperor, as empress dowager). This was to display filial piety to his mother.

- #167 Ancestors (祖宗); #168 Filial (孝); #169 Parents (父母)

75. What was needed to rule China? (如何治理中国?) 5

Chinese philosopher Laozi said 治大国若烹小鲜[224] (govern a great nation as you would cook a small fish). A high-level official of the Sui dynasty, 苏威 (Su Wei, 542–623) once said in 581 CE that '唯读《孝经》一卷，足以立身治国，何用多为?' which means 'one only needs to read the *Classic of Filial Piety*, and it is enough to be a man of integrity and rule the country. What else is needed!' Su Wei's courtesy name is 无畏 (fearless). No wonder he proclaimed this so fearlessly! A Grand Chancellor of the Song dynasty 赵普 (Zhao Pu, 922–992) said 半部论语治天下,[225] which means 'one can rule the whole country with half of the *Analects*.'

- #91 Emperors, kings, generals, ministers (帝王将相)

76. Prime ministers must be chosen from Confucian scholars (宰相须用读书人) 3

This was a rule set by the founding emperor of the Song dynasty Zhao Kuangyin (927–976), that was obeyed by all of the following emperors. In 1249, 赵葵 (Zhao Kui, 1186–1266) was appointed as vice prime minister because of his great military achievements. However, he had to resign the next year because he was accused of not being a Confucian scholar, so even the emperor could not save him. For the Song dynasty, placing Confucian scholars in important positions had maybe only one great advantage, which was 不杀士大夫 (not to kill scholar-officials).

- #77 Four magnificent characters and the declination of the Northern Song ('丰亨豫大'与北宋的衰败); #91 Emperors, kings, generals, ministers (帝王将相); #109 Boldest proclamation of reform (三不足)

77. Four magnificent characters and the declination of the Northern Song ('丰亨豫大'与北宋的衰败) 3

In a time such as the Song dynasty when scholars were overvalued, cleverly quoting from ancient books such as 尚书 (*Book of Documents*), 易经 (*I Ching*) and 诗经 (*Classic of Poetry*) would justify a person's points greatly. 蔡京 (Cai Jing, 1047–1126) was chancellor of the Northern Song dynasty. He wanted to flatter the emperor Huizong who believed in Taoism. In 1106, Cai Jing advocated a concept and policy called 丰亨豫大,[226] in which all the four characters are from *I Ching*. Simply put, 丰亨豫大 means 'greatly prosperous and extremely comfortable.' This concept led to a proactive fiscal policy, the abuse of expenditures on works of art, and the overthrow of the Northern Song dynasty by the Great Jin only 20 years later. That is not to say that 丰亨豫大 was the only thing to blame for the overthrow

---

223 尊皇后为皇太后 [---為---] zūn huánghòu wéi huángtàihòu (honor-empress-be-royal-grand empress)
224 治大国若烹小鲜 [--國---鮮] zhì dàguó ruò pēng xiǎoxiān (govern-large-country-like-to cook-small-fish)
225 半部论语治天下 [--論語---] bàn bù Lúnyǔ zhì tiānxià (half-volume-Analects-govern-world)
226 丰亨豫大 [豐---] fēng hēng yù dà (prosperous-greatly-comfortable-extremely)

30   *Religion, philosophy, politics, history*

of the Northern Song, but even if many people wanted to object, how could they argue against these four magnificent characters?

- #76 Prime ministers must be chosen from Confucian scholars (宰相须用读书人)

78. **Blessing and the unfortunate Song dynasty** (宋朝年号与'祐') 3

The Song dynasty (960–1279) suffered endless intrusion and invasion from the 西夏 (Western Xia), 辽 (the Great Liao, or Khitan), 金 (the Great Jin, or Jurchen), and 蒙古 (Mongol Empire) almost entirely throughout her history. Among all the characters of era names, 祐 (yòu, to bless) is the most common one and appeared seven times, namely 景祐, 皇祐, 嘉祐, 元祐, 淳祐, 宝祐 and 德祐. However, the Song dynasty was not blessed and even considered 崖山之后无中华[227] (China no longer existed after the naval battle of Mount Ya in 1279) by some Japanese scholars.

- #59 Mandate of Heaven, or God's will (天命, 天意); #115 Japanese era names feature common Chinese characters (日本年号中的汉字)

79. **To take or decline the throne** (劝进与固辞) 2

Imagine this drama: a leader overthrew the previous emperor and his subordinates urged him to take the throne (劝进, quànjìn, urge a leader to take the throne), but the leader resolutely declines (固辞, gùcí, resolutely decline), again and again, until he finally accepts it. This happened time and again in the Chinese history. For example, after Zhu Di (朱棣), Prince of Yan, overthrew the reign of his nephew Emperor Jianwen, the second emperor of the Ming dynasty, in 1402, this drama happened and Zhu Di said, '今辞弗获, 勉循众志 . . . ' (since my declination is not approved by you, I am obliged to follow your will. . .) before taking the throne.

- #101 The last bit of an emperor's dignity (皇帝最后的尊严)

80. **The pride of a great empire and the reluctance to lose power** (帝国不愿舍弃的荣光) 3

Chinese feudal society was at her peak during the reign of the Qianlong Emperor (1735–1796) of the Qing dynasty, which was around the same time as the rise of the Second British Empire (1783–1825). The two empires had first official contact at the Macartney Embassy (1792–1794). During the British King George III's envoy to China, Lord George Macartney met the Qianlong Emperor in 1793. The Chinese insisted that Macartney was a 'conveyor of tribute' (贡使, gòngshǐ), not a 'legate of the sovereign' (钦差, qīnchāi), and that he should kowtow (三跪九叩, sānguì jiǔkòu) to the Qianlong Emperor. Since then, China went downhill rapidly, losing almost all wars with foreign countries, such as the First Opium War (1840–1842), the Second Opium War (1856–1860), the First Sino-Japanese War (1894–1895), the Siege of the International Legations (Western intervention during the Boxer Rebellion, 1900), etc. Under great external and internal pressure, the Qing dynasty attempted to establish a constitutional monarchy and in 1908 issued 钦定宪法大纲 (*Qīndìng Xiànfǎ Dàgāng*, Outline of the Constitution by Imperial Order), in which the people were still called 臣民 (chénmín, subject of the kingdom), not 人民 (the people) or 公民 (citizen). The dream to preserve a great empire lingered.

- #14 People, the (人民); #38 Vast land and abundant natural resources (地大物博)

---

227 崖山之后无中华 [---後無-華] Yáshān zhīhòu wú Zhōnghuá

Religion, philosophy, politics, history 31

81. Open and aboveboard (光明正大) 2

光明正大 means 'open and aboveboard.' An alternative form is 正大光明,[228] which you can find above the throne at the Palace of Heavenly Purity (Qiánqīng Gōng) in the Forbidden City in Beijing. The script is written from right to left like most ancient Chinese scripts. Both 正大 (fair and square) and 光明 (bright) are highly positive words, and they are understandably registered as trademarks. 正大 is often associated with the Thai Charoen Pokphand Group (C.P. Group, 正大集团), which was established by two Chinese brothers in 1921. The four second-generation leaders of that group are named 谢正民, 谢大民, 谢中民 and 谢国民. Their given names are 正大中国 in combination. 光明 is often associated with a major Chinese newspaper 光明日报 (*Guangming Daily*, established in 1949) and a major dairy and food company 光明乳业 (Bright Dairy and Food Co., Ltd) whose name '光明' was proposed in 1952 by the factory's Vice Director Jiang Zemin who would later become President of China from 1993 to 2003.

- #33 Benevolence and justice (仁与义)

82. Correctness of names (名正言顺) 5

Confucius said 名不正则言不顺, 言不顺则事不行[229] (If names are incorrect, language is not in accordance with the truth of things. If language is not in accordance with the truth of things, affairs cannot be carried on to success. (From Book XIII Tsze-loo of Confucian Analects, translated by James Legge, The Chinese Classics, Volume 1, London: Trübner & Co., 1861, pp. 127–128.), and Chinese people, prominent or ordinary, pay great attention to names. Chinese girls in ancient times demanded a ceremony of 吹喇叭 (blowing trumpets) and 走正门 (entering the husband's home through the main gate), which was to show the 'name/status' of the woman as a 'wife,' not a 'concubine' who was not qualified for the ceremony. The recent top leaders of China are always granted three titles, namely General Secretary of the Party (党的总书记), Head of the State (国家主席), and Chairman of the Military (军委主席), to justify through name the legality of his leadership. Usually rankings of Chinese leaders are General Secretary of the Party (总书记), Premier (总理), Chairman of the People's Congress (人大委员长) and so on. However, when former Chinese leader Li Peng stepped down from the position of Premier and took the post of Chairman of the People's Congress in 1998, his ranking in politics did not change from the second place to the third place. This reflects the correctness of names.

- #23 Who do you think you are? (你算老几啊?); #59 Mandate of Heaven, or God's will (天命, 天意); #77 Four magnificent characters and the declination of the Northern Song ('丰亨豫大' 与北宋的衰败); #101 The last bit of an emperor's dignity (皇帝最后的尊严)

83. Posthumous titles (谥号) 5

Queen Elizabeth II has an official title in the United Kingdom after May 29, 1953: Elizabeth the Second, by the Grace of God of the United Kingdom of Great Britain and Northern Ireland and of Her other Realms and Territories Queen, Head of the Commonwealth, Defender of the Faith. If you omit the place names, the title is actually not as complicated as the Chinese posthumous titles. It was likely starting from the mid-Zhou dynasty that kings, royal family members and prominent figures had posthumous titles (谥号), which would later become longer

---

228 正大光明 [-] zhèngdà guāngmíng (square-open)

229 名不正则言不顺, 言不顺则事不行 [---则--顺, --顺则---] míng bú zhèng zé yán bú shun (name-not-correct-then-language-not-coordinated, language-not-coordinated-then-thing-not-succeed)

32 *Religion, philosophy, politics, history*

and nicer than ever. Confucius was revered as 大成至圣先师文宣王[230] (literally the 'most accomplished, greatest sage, the Master, exalted king of culture'). The last Chinese emperor who had a posthumous title was Emperor Guang Xu (1871–1908) of the Qing dynasty, his title being 同天崇运大中至正经文纬武仁孝睿智端俭宽勤景皇帝, which is very hard, if not impossible to translate into English. The very last characters are 皇帝 (emperor) and all other 21 words are tributes to his nature, virtue and achievements. For all feudal officials of the last few Chinese dynasties, the posthumous title 文正 was the highest honor to be awarded. 文 and 正 are two simple characters, but they could refer to almost anything that is brilliant. It is beyond the scope of this book to explain all of the meanings in detail, and only the first meanings are annotated. 文 could mean 经纬天地 (administer the universe) 曰文; 道德博闻曰文; 慈惠爱民曰文; 愍民惠礼曰文; 赐民爵位曰文; 勤学好问曰文; 博闻多见曰文; 忠信接礼曰文; 能定典礼曰文; 经邦定誉曰文; 敏而好学曰文; 施而中礼曰文; 修德来远曰文; 刚柔相济曰文; 修治班制曰文; 德美才秀曰文; 万邦为宪, 帝德运广曰文; 坚强不暴曰文; 徽柔懿恭曰文; 圣谟丕显曰文; 化成天下曰文; 纯穆不已曰文; 克嗣徽音曰文; 敬直慈惠曰文; 与贤同升曰文; 绍修圣绪曰文; 声教四讫曰文. 正 could mean 内外宾服 (all people, domestic and foreign, are convinced and showing due respect to) 曰正; 大虑克就曰正; 内外用情曰正; 清白守洁曰正; 图国忘死曰正; 内外无怀曰正; 直道不挠曰正; 靖恭其位曰正; 其仪不忒曰正; 精爽齐肃曰正; 诚心格非曰正; 庄以率下曰正; 息邪讵诐曰正; 主极克端曰正; 万几就理曰正; 淑慎持躬曰正; 端型式化曰正; 心无偏曲曰正; 守道不移曰正.

- #32 Integrity vs. ability (德与才); #59 Mandate of Heaven, or God's will (天命, 天意); #84 Temple names of emperors (庙号)

84. Temple names of emperors (庙号) 3

A 庙号 (miàohào, temple name of an emperor) was bestowed upon only the emperors who achieved a great deal in early Chinese history. However, after the Sui dynasty, almost all emperors received temple names. The temple name convention followed many rules, one of which was a distinction between 祖, 宗 and 帝. 祖 means 'ancestor' and was used on only founding emperors such as 唐高祖 (Emperor Gaozu of Tang), 宋太祖 (Emperor Taizu of Song), and 清太祖 (Nurhaci). The only two exceptions were 明成祖 (Yongle Emperor of Ming, 1360–1424), the third emperor of the Ming dynasty and 清世祖 (康熙, Kangxi Emperor of Qing, 1654–1722), the second emperor of the Qing dynasty. After Kangxi died, although Kangxi was the second emperor of the Qing dynasty, the ministers thought his achievements were as significant as the founding emperor's, so they revered Kangxi as a 祖, not a 宗. 宗 means 'ancestor, forefather,' and it was used for all emperors except the last ones of each dynasty who were usually given names of 帝 by later dynasties.

- #59 Mandate of Heaven, or God's will (天命, 天意); #73 Outstanding statecraft and brilliant military exploits (文治武功); #85 Temple names and achievements of emperors (庙号与成就)

85. Temple names and achievements of emperors (庙号与成就) 3

Throughout the history of imperial China, ministers would thoughtfully discuss temple names after an emperor died. There were a large set of rules dictating temple names, and we can guess what an emperor achieved from his temple name. For example, 文 indicates

---

230 大成至圣先师文宣王 [---聖-師---] dàchéng zhìshèng xiānshī wénxuānwáng: See in-text.

Religion, philosophy, politics, history 33

the emperor had achievements such as '经天纬地' (plan the world affairs) or '学勤好问' (studious and inquisitive), among others. 武 indicates the emperor might be 刚强直理 (firm, strong and uphold integrity) or 克定祸乱 (put down rebellions) etc. 成 indicates the emperor will 安民立政 (stabilize the lives of the people and set up effective administration), etc. The aforementioned temple names are complimentary. A few temple names were derogatory, such as 灵, 炀, 厉 etc. A few were sympathetic, such as 哀, 愍 and 怀 etc.

- #73 Outstanding statecraft and brilliant military exploits (文治武功); #84 Temple names of emperors (庙号)

86. Naming taboo (避讳) 5

In ancient China, names of monarchs, royal family members, sages, and one's ancestors were holy and should be avoided. For example, the founding emperor of the Western Han dynasty was named (刘)邦 (Liu Bang, 256 BCE–195 BCE, with 邦 meaning 'country'), which was replaced by 国 (meaning 'country'). Liu Bang's wife was named 吕雉 and 雉 (pheasant), which was replaced by 野鸡 (literally 'wild-chicken,' pheasant). Confucius was revered as a sage, and his given name 丘 (hill) happened to also be the surname of many people. Due to the naming taboo, 丘 was replaced by 邱 (hill). Many people were killed as the result of not avoiding rulers' names. One had to respect his ancestors by avoiding using any character of their given names. Even when one wrote those characters, he should avoid them in one way or another. For example, Lin Daiyu is a character in the greatest Chinese classic novel *Dream of the Red Chamber*. When she came across the character 敏 (mǐn), which happened to be her mother's first name, she would pronounce it as 密 (mì) or write it with one or two strokes missing.

- #83 Posthumous titles (谥号); #84 Temple names of emperors (庙号); #85 Temple names and achievements of emperors (庙号与成就); #87 Given names: taboo and honor (改名); #105 Little * (*小*)

87. Given names: taboo and honor (改名) 3

Emperors' given names were taboo, and all people, both noble and ordinary, had to observe the taboo. For example, Prince 赵匡美 (Zhao Kuangmei, 947–984) was the youngest brother of the Song dynasty's founding emperor, Emperor Taizu of Song, whose name was 赵匡胤 (Zhao Kuangyin). Since Zhao Kuangyin was the emperor, Zhuang Kuangmei changed his given name to '*Guang*mei' (光美) in 960 CE, to observe the taboo of his brother's given name '*Kuang*yin.' Emperor Taizu's other brother observed this taboo as well and changed his name from Kuangyi to Guangyi. After Zhao Kuangyin died in 976 CE, Zhao Guangyi ascended the throne, and Zhao Guangmei had to change his given name once again, from Guangmei to *Ting*mei (廷美), to respect the taboo around his brother's name 'Guangyi.' Observing the taboo of emperors' given names was respectful to the emperors. On the other hand, not addressing feudal officials' given names was the emperor's respecting their subordinates. For example, one of the four greatest honors for an official was 赞拜不名,[231] which means a protocol official did not address an official's name but announced his official title when he was to meet the emperor in court. Emperor Zhenzong of Song respected 吕端 (Lü Duan, 935–1000) and did call his name, so too did Emperor Taizu of Ming to 刘基 (Liu Ji, 1311–1375).

- #86 Naming taboo (避讳); #105 Little * (*小*)

---

231 赞拜不名 [讚---] zànbài bùmíng (announce-greet-not-call names)

34   *Religion, philosophy, politics, history*

88. Feudal (封建) 2

封 means 'to subinfeudate' and 建 'to establish a state.' The compound word 封建 (fēngjiàn) means 'feudal.' Since the feudal society had such a long history in China, its influence will understandably last for a long time although the final feudal dynasty, the Qing dynasty, ended in 1911 officially. There is a saying that reflects the feudal mindset. It is 强龙压不住地头蛇,[232] which means 'the mighty dragon is no match for the native serpent.' The 地头蛇 (native serpent), in other words, is the 土皇帝 (local emperor). Chinese society is not a feudal society (封建社会) any more, but 封建思想[233] (feudal thought/mindset) is far from being eliminated.

- #59 Mandate of Heaven, or God's will (天命, 天意); #91 Emperors, kings, generals, ministers (帝王将相); #98 Loyal and martial (忠武); #102 Long live (万岁)

89. Peaceful and chaotic (治与乱) 2

乱 (luàn) means 'chaos,' and 治 (zhì) means 'peaceful and prosperous.' 天下大乱 (the whole country is great disorder) is what we would to avoid, and 天下大治[234] (the whole country is in great order and prosperity) is our ultimate goal. However, Chairman Mao started the Cultural Revolution (1966–1976) hoping that the country would progress from 天下大乱 to 天下大治, though he actually barely made it.

- #110 Not flip flop (不折腾); #119 Ordinary Chinese people's dream, now and then (河清海晏与岁月静好)

90. Penitential decrees and letters of self-criticism (罪己诏与检讨书) 2

In ancient China, when an emperor felt that he had done something wrong and had made his people suffer bitterly, he could issue a penitential decree. According to statistics, there were 79 emperors who issued 罪己诏. While the majority of them had few repercussions, the decrees at least demonstrated that the emperors had a basic guilty conscience. In contemporary China, many students wrote a 检讨书 (a letter of self-criticism) for this reason or that. Some letters could be archived in the person's official dossier. Mao Zedong liked to order high-level officials to write 检讨书, which, once written, would be tied to the officials forever.

- #33 Benevolence and justice (仁与义); #46 Repent (回头); #111 Warning inscription on a stone (戒石铭)

91. Emperors, kings, generals, ministers (帝王将相) 5

The Chinese history, at least the Orthodox Histories, 二十四史 (*Twenty-Four Histories*) are almost all about emperors, kings, generals, ministers (帝王将相). Those histories are recorded in biographies (纪传体) set forth by the *Records of the Grand Historian* (史记), which was finished around 94 BCE. 史记 contains 12 Basic Annuals (本纪), 30 Hereditary Houses (世家) and 70 Ranked Biographies (列传).

---

232 强龙压不住地头蛇 [-龍壓---頭-] qiánglóng yābúzhù dìtóushé (strong-dragon-oppress-not-able to-local-serpent)

233 封建思想 [-] fēngjiàn sīxiǎng (feudal-thought)

234 天下大治 [-] tiānxià dàzhì (the world-great order and prosperity)

Religion, philosophy, politics, history 35

- #76 Prime ministers must be chosen from Confucian scholars (宰相须用读书人); #94 Sages and men of virtue (圣贤); #97 Three Immortal Deeds (三不朽); #111 Warning inscription on a stone (戒石铭); #159 Gifted scholars and beautiful women (才子佳人)

92. Keeping the emperor company (与大人物相处) 2

In China, especially in the past, keeping the emperor company is like living with a tiger (伴君如伴虎[235]) because the emperor would probably not feel at ease if one's merits are great (功高震主,[236] so great is one's achievements as to make one's boss feel uneasy or insecure), so the founding emperor of the Song dynasty deprived his generals' military power with a cup of wine (杯酒释兵权[237]) in 962. The most skillful person in dealing with this situation was the first Premier of the People's Republic of China, Zhou Enlai (1898–1976) who survived and thrived in Mao Zedong's company.

- #141 Fawn (吹捧)

93. Not even recognize cows and goats (见牛羊亦不识) 3

Ancient Chinese emperors cared about, and feared most, being overthrown. After Emperor Jianwen of the Ming dynasty was overthrown in 1402, his youngest son was incarcerated for the next 56 years. When he was finally released in 1458, he could not even recognize cows and goats (见牛羊亦不识),[238] let alone the human world. He died soon afterward. We can infer that, in his 56-year confinement, the poor dethroned prince had no opportunity to meet anyone other than a few servants, if that. He was so unlucky to have been born in a royal family (生在帝王家).[239]

- #91 Emperors, kings, generals, ministers (帝王将相)

94. Sages and men of virtue (圣贤) 3

Sages are perfect, and we are human and imperfect (人非圣贤, 孰能无过).[240] Famous sages that Confucians endorsed include Emperor Yao (尧), Emperor Shun (舜), Yu the Great (禹), Tang of Shang (商汤), King Wen of Zhou (周文王), King Wu of Zhou (周武王), Duke of Zhou (周公), Confucius (孔子) and Mencius (孟子). Mencius advocated that 人皆可以为尧舜[241] (everyone can be as good as Yao and Shun). For young people, if you want to be Yao or Shun, you need to 两耳不闻窗外事, 一心只读圣贤书[242] (pay no attention to what is going on beyond one's study and bury oneself in the classics). However, Taoism despises sages. Laozi advocated that one should 绝圣弃智[243] (renounce sageness and discard wisdom), and Zhuangzi mocked Confucian sages with the idea 圣人不死, 大盗不止[244] (if sages do not die, great robbers will not cease to appear). The great poet Li Bai was unconcerned with fame and

---

235 伴君如伴虎 [-] bàn jūn rú bàn hǔ (accompany-monarch-like-accompany-tiger)
236 功高震主 [-] gōng gāo zhèn zhǔ (merit-high-surpress-master)
237 杯酒释兵权 [--释-權] bēi jiǔ shì bīngquán (cup-wine-deprive-military-power)
238 见牛羊亦不识 [見----識] jiàn niúyáng yì bùshí (saw-ox-goat-either-not-know)
239 生在帝王家 [-] shēngzàidìwángjiā (born-in-royal-family)
240 人非圣贤, 孰能无过 [--聖賢, --無過] rén fēi shèngxián, shú néng wú guò (people-not-sage, who-can-no-fault)
241 人皆可以为尧舜 [----為堯-] rēn jiē kěyǐ wéi Yáo Shùn (people-all-can-become-Yao-Shun)
242 两耳不闻窗外事, 一心只读圣贤书 [---聞---, ---讀聖賢書] liǎng ěr bù wén chuāngwài shì, yìxīn zhǐ dú shèngxián shū (2-ear-not-hear-window-outside-thing, whole-heart-only-read-sage-book)
243 绝圣弃智 [絕聖棄-] jué shèng qì zhì (renounce-sage-discard-wisdom)
244 圣人不死, 大盗不止 [聖---, -盜--] shèngrén bù sǐ, dàdào bù zhǐ (sage-not-die, great-robber-not-cease)

36 *Religion, philosophy, politics, history*

virtues, and he wrote 古来圣贤皆寂寞, 惟有饮者留其名[245] (since ancient times, sages have all been solitary, only drinkers can leave their names behind).

- #32 Integrity vs. ability (德与才); #33 Benevolence and justice (仁与义); #47 Legacy (功名); #83 Posthumous titles (谥号); #91 Emperors, kings, generals, ministers (帝王将相); #95 Master (*子); #96 Model of all Chinese (中国人的楷模); #97 Three Immortal Deeds (三不朽); #137 Mean person (小人)

95. Master (*子) 2

If a person in Chinese history was called 'surname + 子,' he must be outstanding in philosophy or a closely related field. The well-known '子' include 孔子 (Confucius), 孟子 (Mencius), 荀子 (Xúnzǐ), 老子 (Lǎozǐ), 庄子 (Zhuāngzǐ), 墨子 (Mòzǐ), 韩非子 (Hánfēizǐ), 孙子 (Sūnzǐ) and so on. The last one might be 朱子 (朱熹, Zhū Xī, 1130–1200).

- #94 Sages and men of virtue (圣贤)

96. Model of all Chinese (中国人的楷模) 2

Confucius said the model (楷模, kǎimó) of all Chinese people was 周公 (Zhōu Gōng, the Duke of Zhou, 11th century BCE), but the people after Confucius said Confucius should be the model and thus revered him as 大成至圣先师 (dàchéng zhìshèng xiānshī, most accomplished, greatest sage, first teacher). The Duke of Zhou and Confucius were too obscure to be modeled, but there was a man who lived in the late Qing dynasty. He is 曾国藩 (Zēng Guófān, 1811–1872), a statesman, military general and Confucian scholar who was revered as 千古完人 (a flawless/perfect man through the ages).

- #97 Three Immortal Deeds (三不朽)

97. Three Immortal Deeds (三不朽) 10

This phrase is a short form of '大上有立德,[246] 其次有立功, 其次有立言' (set moral examples, perform great deeds and achieve glory by writing), which is from *Zuo's Commentary on The Spring and Autumn Annals* (左传) and was revered by Chinese rulers and literati in ancient times. To 立德, they would glorify their ancestors and pretend to do something of high morals. For example, some emperors would 耕籍田, which means 'to plow the emperor's registered land.' The protocol required that the emperor give three pushes; however, many emperors gave one push only. To 立功, emperors were keen on doing gigantic projects. To 立言, they would quote magnificent words from ancient books with help from their aides. But history is merciless: 粪土当年万户侯[247] (literally 'the remains of previous princes are only dirt').

- #31 Fame and fortune (名利); #47 Legacy (功名); #83 Posthumous titles (谥号)

98. Loyal and martial (忠武) 2

It was the highest posthumous honor for generals in ancient China. Among the famous generals who received this title are 诸葛亮 (Zhuge Liang, 181–234) and 岳飞 (Yue Fei,

---

245 古来圣贤皆寂寞, 唯有饮者留其名 [-來聖賢---, --飲----] gǔ lái shèngxián jiē jìmò, wéi yǒu yǐn zhě liú qí míng (ancient-since-sage-all-lonely, only-is-drinker-leave-his-name)

246 大上有立德 [-] dàshàng yǒu lìdé (superior-is-set-morals)

247 粪土当年万户侯 [糞-當-萬--] fèntǔ dāngnián wànhùhóu (dirt-then-year-10,000-household-duke)

Religion, philosophy, politics, history   37

1103–1142). Chinese emperors considered generals a real threat to the throne, so 'loyalty' (忠) was the foremost virtue for them. As for civil officials, they could not constitute real threat, for as a saying goes '秀才造反, 三年不成[248]' (scholars cannot even start a rebellion in three years). Therefore, 'upright' (正), especially '文正,' was the highest posthumous honor for them.

- #47 Legacy (功名); #91 Emperors, kings, generals, ministers (帝王将相)

99. Ministry of rites and its importance (礼部的地位) 1

From the 7th century to early 20th century, the main central government structure in China was a system called Three Departments and Six Ministries (三省六部), among which the Ministry of Rites (礼部) ranked third in the Six Ministries, which also included the 吏部 (Ministry of Personnel), 户部 (Ministry of Revenue), 礼部, 兵部 (Ministry of War), 刑部 (Ministry of Justice) and 工部 (Ministry of Works). The Ministry of Rites oversaw religious rituals, court ceremonials, imperial examinations and foreign relations and was even more important than the Ministries of War and Justice. This indicated that 礼 (rites) played an important role in the religious, political and civil lives of the Chinese people.

- #33 Benevolence and justice (仁与义); #118 Purpose of life (生活的目的)

100. Chinese emperors should thank historians. (中国皇帝应该感谢史官) 5

Historians are supposed to be objective, and most Chinese historians were indeed objective and had recorded a great deal of absurd, immoral or inhuman things done by Chinese emperors. However, Chinese emperors should heartfeltly thank Chinese historians who tried their best to maintain the dignity of emperors. Here are some examples. (1) 为尊者讳 (為尊者諱, wèi zūnzhě huì) means 'to cover up for respectable people.' Confucius put forward and practiced this principle when he edited 春秋 (*The Spring and Autumn Annals*). For example, Duke Zhuang of Zheng killed his younger brother Duan, but Confucius avoided the word 'killed' (杀) and used 'conquered' (克, as in 郑伯克段于鄢, Zhèngbó kè Duàn yú yān). (2) 帝在房州 means 'The Emperor lives in Fangzhou.' 帝 refers to Emperor Ruizong of Tang (662–716), and 房州 was a city considerably far from Chang'an and Luo Yang, the two capitals of the Tang dynasty. This line appeared in Chinese history book 12 times from 686 to 697. The fact is that, during that period, the only empress in all of Chinese history, Empress Wu (624–705), was the actual ruler of China, but historians regarded the Li (李) family, not Empress Wu as the orthodox rulers. So they wrote this line again and again to restate the orthodoxy of the ruling of the Li family.

- #82 Correctness of names (名正言顺); #86 Naming taboo (避讳); #101 The last bit of an emperor's dignity (皇帝最后的尊严)

101. The last bit of an emperor's dignity (皇帝最后的尊严) 1

This phrase refers to the emperor maintaining a term of self-address '朕' (zhèn). In 5 CE Wang Mang usurped the throne of the Han dynasty, but he did not call himself 朕, in order to show the least respect to the previous dynasty and emperors.

---

248 秀才造反, 三年不成 [-] xiùcái zàofǎn, sān nián bùchéng (scholar-rebell, 3-year-not-successful)

38 *Religion, philosophy, politics, history*

- #84 Temple names of emperors (庙号); #85 Temple names and achievements of emperors (庙号与成就); #102 Long live (万岁)

102. Long live (万岁) 3

It was likely starting from the Late Han dynasty that the emperors were called and worshipped 万岁 (long live, Your Majesty, His Majesty). This address continued all the way down to the last emperor of China, Puyi (1906–1967, abdicated on February 12, 1912) and to Mao Zedong and to Mao's successor Hua Guofeng until about 1978. The intensified form of 万岁 is 万岁, 万岁, 万万岁.[249] Mao Zedong was often chanted 毛主席万岁, 万岁, 万万岁 by thousands of people's representatives and as many as 2 million ordinary people. The Chinese people had shouted 万岁 for 2,000 years, and it was not easy for them to change this form of address. When the last emperor Puyi returned to Beijing in 1959 after almost 40 years of exile and penal labor, his former eunuchs visited him and called him 万岁爷[250] (Your Majesty) upon seeing him. Now the word 万岁 is still visible in places such as Tiananmen Square. You can find the slogans 中华人民共和国万岁, 世界人民大团结万岁[251] (Long live the People's Republic of China. Long live the great unity of the peoples of the world.), along with a giant portrait of Mao Zedong on the wall of Tiananmen. The word 万岁 is sometimes used in fields other than politics. Students may shout 60分万岁! (Hooray! 60 points!) when they passed an exam.

- #84 Temple names of emperors (庙号); #85 Temple names and achievements of emperors (庙号与成就); #88 Feudal (封建)

103. One man (一人) 2

There is an antithetical couplet written by the Yongzheng Emperor (1678–1735) on two pillars of 故宫养心殿西暖阁 (the Xi'nuan Pavilion, Yangxin Temple, the Imperial Palace): 惟以一人治天下, 岂为天下奉一人,[252] which can be rendered roughly as 'although the lasting tradition is *one man* rules the country, does it justify that the whole country should submit/attend to *that man*'s will?' This couplet reveals the essence of Chinese rule – only one man matters. Therefore, the goal of billions of Chinese was to be the 'one man' (一人[253]) or 'that man.' After the Chinese politician Deng Xiaoping (1904–1997) died, another prominent politician Bo Yibo (1908–2007) presented a couplet: 一人千古, 千古一人,[254] which means 'one man died, and he is the only one person standing out through one thousand ages.' If there would indeed be such a man, he must be lonely (高处不胜寒,[255] it's lonely at the top). Additionally, Mencius held the opinion that 独乐乐不如众乐乐[256] (enjoying happiness alone is not as happy as sharing it).

- #102 Long live (万岁)

---

249 万岁, 万岁, 万万岁 [萬歲, 萬歲, 萬萬歲] wànsuì, wànsuì, wànwànsuì (10,000-years old, 10,000-years old, 10,000–10,000-years old)

250 万岁爷 [萬歲爺] wànsuìyé (10,000-years old-lord)

251 中华人民共和国万岁, 世界人民大团结万岁 [-華----國萬歲, -----團結萬歲] Zhōnghuá Rénmín Gònghéguó wànsuì, shìjiè rénmín dàtuánjié wànsuì (PRC-long live, world-people-great-unity-long live)

252 惟以一人治天下, 岂为天下奉一人 [-, -為-----] wéi yǐ yī rén zhì tiānxià, qǐ wéi tiānxià fèng yī rén (only-because-one-man-rule-world, how could-justify-world-attend to-one-man)

253 一人 [-] yī rén (one-man)

254 一人千古, 千古一人 [-] yī rén qiāngǔ, qiāngǔ yī rén (one-man-pass away, 1,000-ages-one-man)

255 高处不胜寒 [-處-勝-] gāochù bú shèng hán (high-place-not-endure-cold)

256 独乐乐不如众乐乐 [獨樂樂--衆樂樂] dú lè bùrú zhòng lè (oneself-enjoy-happiness-not as good as-masses-enjoy-happiness)

Religion, philosophy, politics, history   39

104. Savior (救星) 1

God or Jesus Christ is the Savior (救世主) of Christians. For Chinese people, one could say that the Savior is Confucius (孔子) because 天不生仲尼, 万古如长夜[257] (without Confucius, all ages would have been like an endless night), living Buddha (活菩萨) for the common folks, and starting from the 1940s, Mao Zedong, who is called the People's Great Savior (人民的大救星[258]) in a song 'The East Is Red' (东方红).

- #90 Penitential decrees and letters of self-criticism (罪己诏与检讨书); #103 One man (一人)

105. Little * (*小*) 2

The fourth Premier of the People's Republic of China was Li Peng (李鹏, 1928–2019), and he had two sons and one daughter. His eldest son is named Li Xiaopeng (李小鹏, with 小 meaning 'little' or 'Jr.') and his daughter is named Li Xiaolin (李小琳). On the surface, this seems just like Donald Trump naming his son Donald Trump, Jr. However, there is a huge difference between these two circumstances. Donald Trump followed the Western practice, but Li Peng broke from traditional Chinese culture. All Chinese people in the past, and most people in the present, have strictly abided by the naming taboo. People cannot use the characters that were previously in the names of their ancestors. Li Peng, as the son of a Chinese Communist Party revolutionist and raised by the first Premier of China, Zhou Enlai, had the courage to oppose the old culture, and his way of naming his children reflected his ideology. It seems only Li Xiaopeng's name is relevant and Li Xiaolin's name is not. But in fact, Li Peng's wife is named Zhu Lin (朱琳), and Li Xiaolin (李小琳) and Zhu Lin (朱琳) share a common character (琳) in their names.

- #86 Naming taboo (避讳)

106. Party, the (党) 5

The word 党 had a negative connotation in history, meaning 'clique, faction, gang,' such as 奸党 (cabal), 朋党 (clique), 死党 (sworn followers), 余党 (remaining confederates), 黑手党[259] (mafia), etc. However, after the Chinese Communist Party (CCP, 中国共产党[260]) came into power, the meaning of 党 became specialized to refer to the CCP. Therefore, the negative connotations of 党 have been artificially eliminated or limited. For example, the Gang of Four is called 四人帮,[261] not 四人党. Now the CCP propagandizes herself as 'the mother' of the masses in songs such as '党啊, 亲爱的妈妈'[262] ('Party Ah, Dear Mother!'), so Chinese dissidents call the CCP 党妈[263] (Party Mom) in a sarcastic tone.

- #107 Ignorant young ladies (无知少女); #110 Not flip flop (不折腾); #113 Discuss in an open manner (妄议); #114 One Belt One Road Initiative (一带一路)

---

257 天不生仲尼, 万古如长夜 [-, 萬--長-] tiān bù shēng Zhòngní, wàngǔ rú chángyè (heaven-not-having borne-Confucius, 10,000-ages-like-long-night)

258 人民的大救星 [-] rénmín de dà jiùxīng (people-'s-great-savior)

259 黑手党 [--黨] hēi shǒu dǎng (merciless-hand-clique)

260 中国共产党 [-國-產黨] Zhōngguó Gòngchǎndǎng (Chinese-communist-party)

261 四人帮 [--幫] sì rén bāng (4-people-fraction)

262 党啊, 亲爱的妈妈 [黨-, 親愛-媽媽] dǎng a, qīnài de māma (Party-oh, dear-mom)

263 党妈 [黨媽] dǎng mā (Party-mom)

40 *Religion, philosophy, politics, history*

107. Ignorant young ladies (无知少女) 2

无知少女 literally means 'ignorant young lady' or 'knowledge shallow,' but now this term is also political slang for four kinds of people: 无党派人士 (non-partisan), 知识分子 (known intellectuals), 少数民族 (national minorities) and 女性 (female) who have greater chances of being promoted in the government.

- #106 Party, the (党); #117 The history and a young girl (历史与小姑娘); #277 White Bone Spirit (白骨精)

108. Collectivism (集体主义) 3

Chinese collectivism was based on the common people's naive materialism, which is reflected in proverbs such as 众人拾柴火焰高[264] (everyone collects and adds twigs to a fire, and the flames rise high, the more people, the more strength), 人多力量大[265] (the more people, the more strength, there is strength in numbers, a common saying popularized by Mao Zedong), 单丝不成线, 独木不成林[266] (one thread does not make a yarn, one tree does not make a forest, one person alone cannot accomplish much), 聚沙成塔, 集腋成裘[267] (many a little makes a mickle, many small amounts make a large amount), 众志成城[268] (unity is strength) etc.

- #21 Partial and impartial (公与私); #136 Individual vs. group (一人与一群)

109. Boldest proclamation of reform (三不足) 2

Northern Song chancellor Wang Anshi (王安石, 1021–1086) put forward his famous 三不足 (Three No-Fears) to justify his socioeconomic reforms, the New Policies. 三不足[269] refers to 天变不足畏, 祖宗不足法, 人言不足恤,[270] which means 'One should not fear changes under heaven and one should not blindly follow old conventions and one should not be deterred by complaints of others.' This was extremely bold because, according to Chinese philosophy and morals, 天 (the heaven) and 祖宗 (ancestors) were to be followed and revered.

- #12 Change (改变); #57 Same and different (同与异); #58 Heavenly principles (天理)

110. Not flip flop (不折腾) 5

折腾 means 'much ado about nothing.' Chinese rulers like to 折腾 in order to realize their outstanding statecraft and brilliant military exploits (文治武功).[271] Mao Zedong liked to stir up class struggle. He once said, '与天斗, 其乐无穷, 与地斗, 其乐无穷, 与人斗, 其乐无穷,'[272] which literally means 'struggle with the Heaven, the joy is boundless, struggle

---

264 众人拾柴火焰高 [衆------] zhòngrén shíchái huǒyàn gāo (massive-people-collect-charcoal-fire-flame-high)

265 人多力量大 [-] rén duō lìliàng dà (people-many-strength-much)

266 单丝不成线, 独木不成林 [單絲--綫, 獨----] dān sī bù chéng xiàn, dú mù bù chéng lín (single-thread-not-make-yarn, single-tree-not-make-forest)

267 聚沙成塔, 集腋成裘 [-] jù shā chéng tǎ, jí yè chéng qiú (gather-sand-become-tower, collect-armpit hair-become-fur coat)

268 众志成城 [衆---] zhòng zhì chéng (massive-will-make-fortress)

269 三不足 [-] sān bù zú (three-no-fear)

270 天变不足畏, 祖宗不足法, 人言不足恤 [-變---, -, ----卹] tiānbiàn bùzú wèi, zǔzōng bùzú fǎ, rényán bùzú xù (heaven-change-not-adequate-fear, ancestor-not-adequate-follow, people's-rumor-not-adequate-worry)

271 文治武功 [-] wén zhì wǔ gōng (civil-administration-military-merit)

272 与天斗, 其乐无穷, 与地斗, 其乐无穷, 与人斗, 其乐无穷 [與-鬥, -樂無窮, 與-鬥, -樂無窮, 與-鬥, -樂無窮] yǔ tiān dòu, qílèwúqióng, yǔ dì dòu, qílèwúqióng, yǔ rén dòu, qílèwúqióng: See in-text

Religion, philosophy, politics, history 41

with the Earth, the joy is boundless, struggle with somebody, the joy is boundless.' Chinese leader Hu Jintao advanced a theory called 不折腾[273] (to not flip flop) on the 30th anniversary of China's decision to open itself up to the outside world in 2008. Philosophically, the essence of 'not flip flop' is close to a major concept of Taoism, 无为[274] (non-action).

- #33 Benevolence and justice (仁与义); #47 Legacy (功名)

111. Warning inscription on a stone (戒石铭) 2

In 1132, Emperor Gaozong of Song ordered stone tablets with inscriptions (戒石铭, jièshímíng) to be erected in all government courts to remind government officials to be compassionate to the ordinary people. The inscriptions were 尔俸尔禄, 民膏民脂, 下民易虐, 上天难欺,[275] which means 'your salary as well as your pension, are flesh and blood of the people. The common people are prone to be abused, but the heavens cannot be cheated.' These warning words were adopted by later dynasties, including the Ming and Qing dynasties.

- #33 Benevolence and justice (仁与义); #90 Penitential decrees and letters of self-criticism (罪己诏与检讨书); #110 Not flip flop (不折腾)

112. Thoughtcrimes (思想罪) 3

The term 'thoughtcrime' first appeared in George Orwell's novel *Nineteen Eighty-Four*. However, the practice of it occurred in China long before. For example, 腹诽[276] (criticize inwardly) appeared as early as the Han dynasty. Emperor Gaozong of the Southern Song ordered to execute the greatest national hero in Chinese history, Yue Fei (岳飞, 1103–1142) for his crime 莫须有[277] ('perhaps there is' or 'no reason needed'). In 1457, Emperor Yingzong of the Ming dynasty ordered the execution of the famous general Yu Qian (于谦, 1398–1457) because of 'intended' (意欲) treason.

- #40 Lu Xun (鲁迅); #103 One man (一人); #106 Party, the (党); #113 Discuss in an open manner (妄议)

113. Discuss in an open manner (妄议) 3

Currently, for members of Chinese Communist Party, 'discussing party policy in an open manner' (妄议中央[278]) is violation of the Party's regulations. '妄议' is not a new term because in 1256 the powerful Southern Song Prime Minister Ding Daquan (丁大全) erected stone tablets, with the inscription '不得妄议国政'[279] (not allowed to discuss the nation's administration recklessly or in an open manner) in the highest educational institutions of the country.

- #40 Lu Xun (鲁迅); #57 Same and different (同与异); #112 Thoughtcrimes (思想罪)

---

273 不折腾 [--騰] bù zhēteng (not-flip-flop)
274 无为 [無爲] wú wéi (no-action)
275 尔俸尔禄, 民膏民脂, 下民易虐, 上天难欺 [爾-爾-,-,-,--難-] ěr fèng ěr lù, mín gāo mín zhī, xià mín yì nüè, shàng tiān nán qī (your-salary-your-pension, people's-fat-people's-grease, lowly-people-apt to-be abused, holy-heaven-hard-be cheated)
276 腹诽 [-誹] fùfěi (belly-criticize)
277 莫须有 [-須-] mòxūyǒu (perhaps-must-have)
278 妄议中央 [-議--] wàngyì zhōngyāng (recklessly-discuss-central government)
279 不得妄议国政 [---議國-] bùdé wàngyì guózhèng (not-allowed-recklessly-discuss-state-politics)

114. One Belt One Road Initiative (一带一路) 2

Officially, this program is called 一带一路 (Belt and Road Initiative) in Chinese. The 'Belt' (带, dài) refers to '21st-century Maritime Silk Road,' and the 'Road' (路, lù) refers to 'the Silk Road,' which is much more famous than the former. Linguistically, it should be called 一路一带, however, leaving aside the 一, '路带' makes no sense, but '带路' (to lead) makes a lot of sense, for a country striving for worldly glory.

- #38 Vast land and abundant natural resources (地大物博); #106 Party, the (党); #126 Dream (梦)

115. Japanese era names feature common Chinese characters (日本年号中的汉字) 3

Japanese era names started from 645, and as of early 2019, there have been 247 Japanese era names so far. Among all the Chinese characters used in Japanese era names, 永, 天, 元, and 治 are the most common ones, occurring 29, 27, 27 and 21 times, respectively. It is easy to understand since 永 means 'forever, eternal,' 天 'heaven,' 元 'first, prime, origin' and 治 'peace and prosperity.' These words denote traditional Asian values, i.e., the divine right of kings.

- #78 Blessing and the unfortunate Song dynasty (宋朝年号与'祐'); #84 Temple names of emperors (庙号); #85 Temple names and achievements of emperors (庙号与成就)

116. North Korea and South Korea (北韩与南朝鲜) 5

This is a question of political correctness. Before the establishment of diplomatic relations between China and South Korea in 1992, South Korea was called 南朝鲜[280] (literally 'South-North Korea'), a name with an obvious standpoint on North Korea. The same thing happened with many Chinese people or media in the U.S., they call North Korea 北韩[281] (literally 'North-South Korea'), which is also wrong in terms of standpoint. To be fair, North Korea should be called 朝鲜 (Cháoxiǎn) and South Korea 韩国 (Hánguó), unless they unify one day.

- #15 Standpoint (立场)

117. The history and a young girl (历史与小姑娘) 3

While history should be objective, it was extremely hard to be objective in Chinese history because, as the Chinese proverb goes, 胜者王侯败者贼[282] (nothing succeeds like success; history is written by the victors). The official history of any Chinese dynasty was written by its succeeding dynasty, so readers should always pay extra attention to the facts of the end of the history of a Chinese dynasty since there was an overlap with the succeeding dynasty. It was common practice to defame the previous dynasty in China. It was said that the famous Chinese scholar 胡适 (Hu Shih, 1891–1962) said, '历史是个任人打扮的小姑娘' (literally, 'history is a little girl who can be dressed in whatever way you want (if you are in power)'). Whether or not this verse was really spoken by Hu Shih is unimportant. The verse itself stands when it comes to Chinese history.

- #91 Emperors, kings, generals, ministers (帝王将相)

---

280 南朝鲜 [--鲜] nán Cháoxiǎn (south-North Korea)
281 北韩 [-韩] běi Hán (north-South Korea)
282 胜者王侯败者贼 [勝---敗-贼] shèngzhě wánghóu bàizhě zéi (won-people-crowned-defeated-people-hanged)

4   Life, society, arts, literature (生活, 社会, 艺术, 文学)

118. Purpose of life (生活的目的) 10

享受生活[283] (enjoy life) became a mindset for many Chinese people only after the economic reform starting in 1978. Before that, they could not separate work and life (工作和生活). Their purpose in life was as simple as 吃得苦中苦, 方为人上人[284] (if you wish to be the best man, you should be able to withstand the bitterest of the bitter). Simply put, their purpose in life compromised two things: to 吃苦[285] (endure hardships) and to be considered 人上人[286] (upper class). When the Westerners say, 'this is life (这就是生活),' you can feel their willingness to accept what life has bestowed them. For many ancient Chinese, life (生活) was to live (活着).[287] The 1994 Chinese movie *To Live* (活着) presents a good depiction of the purposes of Chinese lives.

- #47 Legacy (功名); #83 Posthumous titles (谥号); #124 Bad habits (恶习)

119. Ordinary Chinese people's dream, now and then (河清海晏与岁月静好) 1

In 河清海晏,[288] 河 means Yellow River (黄河), which was said to be clear once in a thousand years, 清 'clear,' 海 'sea,' and 晏 'calm or peaceful.' This idiom refers to a harbinger of peace, an equivalent of 天下太平 (all is at peace) for emperors. For modern Chinese people, 山河 and 天下 are not their major concern, but their individual lives are more important. Therefore, 岁月静好[289] (a tranquil and comfortable life) is their dream. 岁月 means 'life'; 静, 'tranquil'; and 好, 'good.'

- #73 Outstanding statecraft and brilliant military exploits (文治武功); #89 Peaceful and chaotic (治与乱); #110 Not flip flop (不折腾)

120. Attitude to life (生活态度) 2

There are essentially two attitudes toward life. One is 入世[290] (literally 'enter the world') as advocated by Confucianism, and the other is 出世[291] (literally 'exit the world') as advocated

---

283 享受生活 [-] xiǎngshòu shēnghuó (enjoy-life)
284 吃得苦中苦, 方为人上人 [-] chī de kǔ zhōng kǔ, fāng wéi rénshàngrén (withstand-able to-bitter-of-bitter, only then-be-people-above-person)
285 吃苦 [-] chīkǔ (endure-harship)
286 人上人 [-] rénshàngrén (people-above-person)
287 活着 [-著] huózhe (be living)
288 河清海晏 [-] héqīng hǎiyàn (Yellow River-clear-sea-calm)
289 岁月静好 [歲-靜-] suìyuè jìnghǎo (life-tranquil-comfortable)
290 入世 [-] rùshì (enter-world)
291 出世 [-] chūshì (exit-world)

44 *Life, society, arts, literature*

by Taoism. Confucius advocated that 学而优则仕[292] (a good scholar will make an official), and a late Ming thinker Gu Yanwu (1613–1682) said, '天下兴亡, 匹夫有责[293]' (Everybody is responsible for the fate of the world). Laozi advocated for 小国寡民[294] (a small country with a small population), and his ideal was 邻国相望, 鸡狗之音闻, 民至老死不相往来[295] (The people of neighbouring states might be able to descry one another; the voices of their cocks and dogs might be heard all the way from one to the other; they might not die till they were old; and yet all their life they would have no communication together.) (From Book X Cutting Open Satchels of The Writings of Kwang Tse, translated by James Legge, in The Sacred Books of China: The Texts of Taoism, Oxford: At the Clarendon Press, 1891, P.288.) For some ordinary people, life should be enjoyed, i.e., 今朝有酒今朝醉[296] (drink today while drink you may – enjoy things while one can). Some even believe 人生苦短, 何不秉烛夜游[297]? (Life is too short, why not hold a candle and stroll in the night?) Lazy people drift along (得过且过),[298] just like a 寒号鸟[299] (Chinese fictional bird, similar to a flying squirrel) does.

- #31 Fame and fortune (名利); #50 Share weal or woe? (同甘还是共苦)

121. Custom (风俗) 5

风俗 (fēngsú) means 'custom.' Different places within China have remarkably different customs due to their long and complex histories. There is a Chinese saying that shows these remarkable differences, 十里不同风, 百里不同俗,[300] which means 'two different places have different customs even though they are just ten miles or a hundred miles apart.' Therefore it is important to 入境而问禁, 入国而问俗,[301] 入门而问讳, which means 'after entering a territory, one needs to inquire about prohibition; after entering a country, inquire about customs; after entering a home, inquire about taboos.'

- #122 Food and drink (饮食); #146 Gifts to avoid giving (不能送的礼物)

122. Food and drink (饮食) 5

Food, drink and sex are humanity's primary needs (食色性也,[302] by Mencius). The masses regard food as their Heaven (民以食为天,[303] food is the first necessity of the people), and they even conclude that food and drink is the sole purpose/meaning of life (人生在世, 吃喝二字).[304] However, Confucius considered food and drink less important than faith

---

292 学而优则仕 [學-優則-] xué ér yōu zé shì (study-and-excel-then-become an official)

293 天下兴亡, 匹夫有责 [--興-, ---責] tiānxià xīngwáng, pǐfū yǒu zé (world-rise and fall, ordinary man-have-responsibility)

294 小国寡民 [-國--] xiǎo guó guǎ mín (small-country-less-population)

295 鸡犬之声相闻, 民至老死不相往来 [雞--聲-聞, -------來] jīquǎn zhī shēng xiāng wén, mín zhì lǎo sǐ bù xiāng wǎnglái (chicken-dog-'s-sound-mutual-heard, people-until-naturally-die-not-each other-interact)

296 今朝有酒今朝醉 [-] jīnzhāo yǒu jiǔ jīnzhāo zuì (this-day-have-wine-this-day-drunk)

297 人生苦短, 何不秉烛夜游 [-, ---燭--] rénshēng kǔ duǎn, hébù bǐngzhú yèyóu (life-suffer-short, why-not-hold-candle-night-stroll)

298 得过且过 [-過-過] dé guò qiě guò (able to-pass-let-pass)

299 寒号鸟 [-號鳥] hánhàoniǎo (cold-cry-bird)

300 十里不同风, 百里不同俗 [----風, -] shílǐ bùtóng fēng, bǎilǐ bùtóng sú (10-mile-not-same-folkways, 100-mile-not-same-customs)

301 入国而问俗 [-國-問-] rù guó ér wèn sú (enter-country-then-ask-customs)

302 食色性也 [-] shí sè xìng yě (food-sex-nature-*marker of affirmation*)

303 民以食为天 [---為-] mín yǐ shí wéi tiān (masses-take-dining-as-heaven)

304 人生在世, 吃喝二字 [-] rén shēng zài shì, chīhē èr zì (people-live-in-world, eat-drink-two-words)

(去食, . . . 民无信不立,[305] when someone asked Confucius to disperse one from either food or faith, he said, 'part with the food, . . . if the people have no faith in their rulers, there is no standing for the state'). This idea was developed by a Neo-Confucian philosopher Cheng Yi (1033–1107) who said, '饿死事(极)小, 失节事(极)大'[306] (Death by starvation is a small thing, but loss of chastity is of the utmost importance).

- #123 Liquor and drinking (酒, 喝酒); #225 Chinese cooking methods (中国菜的做法); #226 Buns or dumplings (包子); #272 Vegetables introduced to China (传入中国的蔬菜)

123. Liquor and drinking (酒, 喝酒) 5

Drinking was a major part of Chinese people's entertainment in ancient times. There will be no banquet if there is not liquor (无酒不成席).[307] If you are successful, you need to drink, because 人生得意须尽欢, 莫使金樽空对月[308] (literally 'if your life is successful, you need to enjoy yourself to the fullest extent and not to make the golden goblets unfilled in a bright moon night'). If you met your soul mate, you also need to drink to him/her, since 酒逢知己千杯少, 话不投机半句多[309] (for a bosom friend a thousand toasts are too few, and in a disagreeable conversation, one word more is too many). You need to drink and sing while expressing your feeling of life (对酒当歌, 人生几何).[310] People may have hidden motives other than the wine itself (醉翁之意不在酒[311] though drunker, one's real interest is not in wine). Sometimes, it is not the wine that makes you drunk, but you yourself (酒不醉人人自醉).[312] Once drunk, one is prone to speak the truth (酒后吐真言[313]) and be loose with sex (酒后乱性).[314] Friends that only wine and dine together (酒肉朋友[315]) are superficial. People who indulge in sensual pleasures live a life of 花天酒地.[316] The God of wine in China may refer to several people one of whom is Li Bai (Li Po, 701–762), the greatest poet in China. It is said that Li Bai could write a hundred poems after drinking a big vessel of wine (李白斗酒诗百篇).[317] Another anecdote states that the poet Liu Ling (221–300) was drunk for three consecutive years.

- #122 Food and drink (饮食); #255 I'll think about it (研究研究)

124. Bad habits (恶习) 3

Buddhism says that people have three innate flaws, or the Three Poisons (三毒), i. e., 贪嗔痴[318] (greed, delusion, aversion). Traditional Chinese laws stipulated Ten Abominations

---

305 去食, . . . 民无信不立 [-, -無---] qù shí, . . . mín wú xìn bú lì (give up-food, . . . masses-without-faith-not-hold)

306 饿死事极小, 失节事极大 [餓--極-, -節-極-] è sǐ shì jí xiǎo, shījié shì jí dà (starve-dead-thing-extremely-small, lose-chastity-thing-extremely-big)

307 无酒不成席 [無----] wú jiǔ bù chéng xí (no-wine-not-complete-feast)

308 人生得意须尽欢, 莫使金樽空对月 [-----盡歡,-----對-] rénshēng déyì xūjìnhuān, mò shǐ jīnzūnkōng duì yuè (life-successful-should-maximize-enjoyment, not-make-gold-goblet-empty-face-moon)

309 酒逢知己千杯少, 话不投机半句多 [-, 話--機---] jiǔ féng zhījǐ qiān bēi shǎo, huà bù tóujī bàn jù duō (drinking-meet-soul mate-1,000-cup-less, conversation-not-congenial-half-sentence-too much)

310 对酒当歌, 人生几何 [對-當-, --幾-] duì jiǔ dāng gē, rénshēng jǐhé (facing-wine-accompany-singing, life-how short)

311 醉翁之意不在酒 [-] zuìwēng zhī yì bú zài jiǔ (drunk-man-'s-interest-not-at-wine)

312 酒不醉人人自醉 [-] jiǔ bú zuì rén rén zì zuì (wine-not-intoxicate-people-people-oneself-drunk)

313 酒后吐真言 [-後---] jiǔ hòu tǔ zhēn yán (after-drinking-speak out-true-words)

314 酒后乱性 [-後亂-] jiǔ hòu luàn xìng (drinking-after-loose-sex)

315 酒肉朋友 [-] jiǔròu péngyǒu (drinking-dining-friend)

316 花天酒地 [-] huā tiān jiǔ dì (woman-heaven-wine-earth)

317 李白斗酒诗百篇 [----詩--] Lǐ Bái dǒu jiǔ shī bǎi piān (Li Bai-vessel-wine-poem-100- *measure word*)

318 贪嗔痴 [貪-癡] tān chēn chī (greed-delusion-aversion)

46 *Life, society, arts, literature*

(十恶) that could not be pardoned (十恶不赦).[319] These abominations are plotting rebellion (谋反), plotting great sedition (谋大逆), plotting treason (谋叛), parricide (恶逆), depravity (不道), great irreverence (大不敬), lack of filial piety (不孝), discord (不睦), unrighteousness (不义) and incest (内乱). Ordinary people could have five bad habits, i. e., 吃喝嫖赌抽[320] (to dine, wine, whore, gamble, smoke), and if they have all of them, it is said that they 五毒俱全[321] (engage in all kinds of unlawful acts). Bad habits of nowadays include 黄赌毒[322] (pornography, gambling and drug abuse and trafficking).

- #123 Liquor and drinking (酒, 喝酒); #125 Gamble (赌); #150 Rumor (流言); #266 Prosperity and prostitution (繁荣'娼'盛)

125. Gambling (赌) 5

More than a few Chinese people are addicted to gambling. You can find about half of the gamblers in all casinos worldwide are Chinese, and Cantonese or Mandarin is the second most common language heard in casinos. Everyone knows if one gambles for a long time, he will definitely lose (久赌必输).[323] Some gamblers think that high-stakes gambling is harmful, but low-stakes gambling is entertaining (小赌怡情, 大赌伤身).[324] The rules in casinos include 'gamblers know neither fathers nor sons' (赌场无父子[325]) and 'admit defeat for a bet' (愿赌服输).[326] The result of gambling is probable theft (赌近盗).[327] It is strange that the Chinese people associate gambling with love affairs, and there is a saying 'lucky in cards, unlucky in love' (赌场得意, 情场失意),[328] and vice versa. The Chinese governments in almost all dynasties banned gambling, but this did not work. Nowadays the government juxtaposes gambling with prostitution and drugs (黄赌毒[329]) as major harms to society.

- #22 Speculative (投机); #124 Bad habits (恶习)

126. Dreams (梦) 10

We all dream dreams, good or bad. When a Chinese person is telling you about a dreadful dream (噩梦), it is appropriate for you to say '梦反'[330] or '梦是反的' (dreams are the opposite (of reality)) in return. If he is telling you a sweet dream or a fantasy, you can suitably say '祝你好' or '(美)梦成真'[331] (wish your dreams come true). Some people daydream (白日梦[332]), and some people speak in their dreams (说梦话,[333] also meaning 'put forward impractical ideas'). If some ideas

---

319 十恶不赦 [-恶--] shí è bú shè (10-obmination-not-pardon)
320 吃喝嫖赌抽 [---赌-] chī hé piáo dǔ chōu (dine-wine-whore-gamble-smoke)
321 五毒俱全 [-] wǔ dú jù quán (5-evil-all-complete)
322 黄赌毒 [-赌-] huáng dǔ dú (pornography-gamble-drug)
323 久赌必输 [-赌-輸] jiǔ dǔ bì shū (long-gamble-must-lose)
324 小赌怡情, 大赌伤身 [-赌--, -赌傷-] xiǎo dǔ yíqíng, dà dǔ shāngshēn (small-bet-cheer-mood, large-bet-hurt-body)
325 赌场无父子 [赌場無--] dǔchǎng wú fùzǐ (gamble place-no-father and son)
326 愿赌服输 [-赌-輸] yuàn dǔ fú shū (willing-gamble-accept-lose)
327 赌近盗 [赌-盜] dǔ jìn dào (gamble-close to-theft)
328 赌场得意, 情场失意 [赌場--, -場--] dǔchǎng déyì, qíngchǎng shīyì (gample place- be victorious, love affair- be defeated)
329 黄赌毒 [-赌-] huáng dǔ dú (pornography, gamble, drug)
330 梦反 [夢-] mèng fǎn (dream-opposite)
331 祝你好梦成真 [---夢--] zhù nǐ hǎomèng chéngzhēn (wish-you-sweet-dream-become-reality)
332 白日梦 [--夢] báiri mèng (day-dream)
333 说梦话 [説夢話] shuō mènghuà (speak-dream-words)

are truly nonsensical, the speaker is saying 痴人说梦[334] (idiotic nonsense). There are two legendary accounts of dreams in Chinese literature. One is 南柯一梦 and the other is 黄粱一梦[335] or 黄粱美梦, both having the extended meaning of 'pipe dream' (一场春梦[336] or 春梦一场). You can find books titled 周公解梦[337] in any non-academic bookstore. The book title originated from a sentence Confucius said, '甚矣, 吾衰也! 久矣, 吾不复梦见周公' (Extreme is my decay. For a long time, I have not dreamed of the Duke of Zhou). The Duke of Zhou (11th century BCE) was a great sage before Confucius. The most famous dream is a philosophical problem (庄周梦蝶[338]) raised by Zhuangzi (370 BCE–287 BCE): he dreamt he was a butterfly and awoke, saying, 'Now I do not know whether I was then a man dreaming I was a butterfly, or whether I am now a butterfly, dreaming I am a man.' Many Chinese emperors used dreams to glorify their ancestry. According to the Records of the Great Historian, the founding emperor of the Western Han, Liu Bang (256 BCE–195 BCE)'s birth story is this: Liu Bang's mother once slept by the side of a big lake and dreamt she met a god. At that time there was a severe thunderstorm. Liu Bang's father went to look for his wife and found that a dragon was on top of his wife's body. She then became pregnant and later gave birth to Liu Bang. Immigrants to the United States have the 'American dream' (美国梦),[339] and now China is pursuing her own 中国梦[340] (Chinese dream). If a dream is too ambitious to be realized, it will be 春秋大梦[341] (grand dream), vividly described by the character Murong Fu (慕容复) in the martial novel 天龙八部 (Demi-gods and semi-devils) by Jin Yong. The Chinese statesman Zhuge Liang (诸葛亮, 181–234) was revered as the smartest person in history by Chinese folks. In the historical novel *Romance of the Three Kingdoms*, Zhuge Liang was introduced with impressive chanting in a poem, and the first sentence is 大梦谁先觉[342] (who is the first to awake from a grand dream).

- #114 One Belt One Road Initiative (一带一路)

127. Beauty (美女) 10

Beauties were chased by men who possessed power and/or wealth. In ancient China, the standards of beauty were roughly the same as now. The first standard is to have smooth and white skin (肤如凝脂, skin is like smooth, soft and glossy cream) since 一白遮百丑[343] (A light complexion is powerful enough to hide seven faults). There were Four Beauties (四大美女[344]) in ancient China: Xi Shi (西施, 506 BCE–?), Wang Zhaojun (王昭君, 52 BCE–8 CE), Diao Chan (fictional character, active in 190s) and Yang Guifei (杨贵妃, 719–756). There is a saying to describe the Four Beauties, 沉鱼落雁, 闭月羞花.[345] Xi Shi 'sinks fish' (沉鱼). Wang Zhaojun 'entices wild geese into falling' (落雁). Diao Chan 'eclipses the moon' (闭月), and Yang Guifei 'shames flowers' (羞花).

- #185 Rosy cheeks (红颜)

---

334 痴人说梦 [癡-说夢] chīrén shuō mèng (idiot-man-tell-dream)

335 黄粱一梦 [---夢] huángliáng yí mèng (yellow-millet-one-dream)

336 一场春梦 [-場-夢] yì cháng chūnmèng (one-*measure word*-spring dream)

337 周公解梦 [---夢] Zhōugōng jiěmèng (Zhou-duke-interpret-dream)

338 庄周梦蝶 [莊-夢-] Zhuāng Zhōu mèng dié (Zhuang Zhou-dream-butterfly)

339 美国梦 [-國夢] Měiguó mèng (American-dream)

340 中国梦 [-國夢] Zhōngguó mèng (Chinese-dream)

341 春秋大梦 [---夢] chūnqiū dà mèng (ancient times-grand-dream)

342 大梦谁先觉 [-夢誰-覺] dà mèng shí xiān jué (grand-dream-who-first-awake)

343 一白遮百丑 [----醜] yì bái zhē bǎi chǒu (one-white-hide-hundred-ugly)

344 四大美女 [-] sì dà měinǚ (four-top-beautiful-woman)

345 沉鱼落雁, 闭月羞花 [-鱼--, 閉---] chén yú luò yàn, bì yuè xiū huā (sink-fish-fall-wild goose, eclipse-moon-shy-flower)

48　*Life, society, arts, literature*

128.　**Fondness for children (恋童) 5**

It seems that pedophilia is seldom associated with Chinese people; however, they do love children in other ways. Many people like to eat 童子鸡[346] (young chicken), and some even like to drink 童子尿[347] (boy urine). The worst is that some people like 雏妓[348] (child prostitutes). Aside from the above-mentioned behaviors, there is a very common scene in Chinese paintings called 童子烹茶[349] (children make tea) or 童子献茶[350] (children serve/present tea) when two old men are chatting or playing chess. In Chinese Buddhism, Avalokiteśvara has two followers, one of whom is called 善财童子[351] (*Sudhana Kumara*, literally 'child of wealth') or 散财童子 (child who disperses wealth). Children should spend more time in 童子军 (boy scouts, girl scouts), but Chinese children became attached to money and involuntary service too early. It is no wonder that, in 1918, the greatest Chinese modern writer, Lu Xun, wrote in his fame-making fiction *A Madman's Diary*:

> I read intently half the night, until I began to see words between the lines, the whole book being filled with the two words – 'Eat people' (吃人).[352] . . . Perhaps there are still children who have not eaten men? Save the children (救救孩子[353]). . . .

- #124 Bad habits (恶习); #175 Children (孩子)

129.　**Rich and powerful (富贵) 5**

Life or death, rich or poor, everything is already determined (生死有命, 富贵在天).[354] Therefore, some people are doomed to never become rich or powerful (没富贵命).[355] If you want to be rich and powerful, you must take risks (富贵险中求).[356] In the arts, fortune comes with blooming flowers (花开富贵),[357] usually peonies (牡丹). People who are rich and powerful usually consume a lot of sugar, and thus get diabetes, which is also called 富贵病[358] (literally 'rich-powerful-illness'). The rich and the powerful are bound to gather together, so members of their group are either rich or powerful (非富即贵).[359] In ancient China, if one became rich and powerful (大富大贵),[360] he should go to his hometown to show off; otherwise, it would be like wearing magnificent clothes and walking in the dark (富贵不还乡, 如锦衣夜行).[361] The first recorded Chinese peasants' uprising is called the Dazexiang Uprising (209 BCE) led by Chen Sheng who was once a peasant. One day he told a coworker, 'if I became rich and powerful one day, I will not forget you' (苟富贵, 无相忘).[362] The most profound words

---

346　童子鸡 [--鷄] tóngzǐjī (child-chicken)

347　童子尿 [-] tóngzǐ niào (child-urine)

348　雏妓 [雛-] chújì (chicken prostitute)

349　童子烹茶 [-] tóngzǐ pēngchá (child-boil-tea)

350　童子献茶 [--献-] tóngzǐ xiàn chá (child-present-tea)

351　善财童子 [-财--] shàn cái tóngzǐ (good at-fortune-child)

352　吃人 [-] chī rén (eat-people)

353　救救孩子 [-] jiùjiu háizi (save-children)

354　生死有命, 富贵在天 [-, -贵--] shēngsǐ yǒu mìng, fùguì zài tiān (life or death-have-destiny, rich and powerful-depend on-heaven)

355　没富贵命 [--贵-] méi fùguì mìng (no-rich and powerful-fate)

356　富贵险中求 [-贵险--] fùguì xiǎn zhōng qiú (rich and powerful-risk-among-seek)

357　花开富贵 [-开-贵] huā kāi fùguì (flower-blossom-rich and powerful)

358　富贵病 [-贵-] fùguìbìng (rich and powerful-illness)

359　非富即贵 [---贵] fēi fù jí guì (not-rich-then-powerful)

360　大富大贵 [---贵] dà fù dà guì (extremely-rich-extremely-powerful)

361　富贵不还乡, 如锦衣夜行 [-贵-還鄉, -锦---] fùguì bù huánxiāng, rú jǐnyī yè xíng (rich and powerful-not-return-home, like-splendid-clothes-night-travel)

362　苟富贵, 无相忘 [--贵, 勿--] gǒu fùguì, wù xiāngwàng (one day-rich and powerful, not-each other-forget)

on 富贵 were said by Confucius. He said, '邦有道, 贫且贱焉, 耻也; 邦无道, 富且贵焉, 耻也'[363] (When the Way prevails in your own state, to be poor and obscure is a disgrace. But when the Way does not prevail in your own state, to be rich and honored is a disgrace).

- #118 Purpose of life (生活的目的); #130 Noble temperament (贵族气质); #132 Poor (穷); #166 Rulers and the ruled, ancient and present (社会的两极); #212 Peonies and prosperous (牡丹和富贵)

130. Noble temperament (贵族气质) 1

Using the logic of two contradictory proverbs, no Chinese person has a noble temperament (贵族气质). One is 三代为官作宦, 方知穿衣吃饭,[364] which means that only after three generations of being government officials can one know how to dress and eat properly and gracefully. The other is 富不过三代,[365] which means 'wealth never survives three generations' or 'shirtsleeves to shirtsleeves in three generations.' In ancient China, wealth was roughly equal to being a government official.

- #34 Refined and popular (雅俗); #129 Rich and powerful (富贵)

131. Unrestrained (风流) 5

If a person, usually a woman, is unrestrained in sexual morals, she is a loose woman (风流女人 or 风流娘们). Young people need not conform to social conventions strictly, and they should be forgiven for doing something foolish (人不风流枉少年,[366] young, dumb, looking for fun). If a person is talented and unrestrained (and romantic), he is 风流潇洒/倜傥 or a 风流才子[367] (elegant and unrestrained). If one did something truly great in history, he is a 风流人物 (a truly great man), which was Mao Zedong's ideal as reflected in his poem 'Qinyuanchun Snow': 数风流人物, 还看今朝[368] (for truly great men, look to this age alone).

- #32 Integrity vs. ability (德与才); #159 Gifted scholars and beautiful women (才子佳人)

132. Poor (穷) 10

A pauper (穷光蛋[369]) does not have a penny to his name (穷得叮当响). He often does not know where his next meal will come from (吃了上顿没下顿)[370] and understandably has no or few visitors (贫居闹市无人问, 富在深山有远亲,[371] a poor man has no visitors even if he lives on a busy street, whereas a rich man who lives in a remote mountain will be called on by distant relatives).

---

363 邦有道, 贫且贱焉, 耻也; 邦无道, 富且贵焉, 耻也 [-, 貧-賤-, 恥-; -無-, --貴-, 恥-] bāng yǒu dào, pín qiě jiàn yān, chǐ yě; bāng wú dào, fù qiě guì yān, chǐ yě (state-have-Dao/way, poor-and-low-*emphatic marker*, shameful-*marker of affirmation*; state-no-Dao/way, rich-and-powerful-*emphatic marker*, shameful-*marker of affirmation*)

364 三代为官作宦, 方知穿衣吃饭 [--為---, -----飯] sān dài wéi guān zuò huàn, fāng zhī chuānyī chīfàn (3-generation-be-official-serve as-official, so that-know-wear-clothes-dine-food)

365 富不过三代 [--過--] fù búguò sān dài (rich-not-exceeding-3-generation)

366 人不风流枉少年 [--風----] rén bù fēngliú wǎng shàonián (people-not-fool around-vainly-young)

367 风流才子 [風---] fēngliú cáizǐ (unrestrained-talent-man)

368 数风流人物, 还看今朝 [數風---, 還---] shǔ fēngliú rénwù, hái kàn jīnzhāo (count-elegant and talent-people, still-look at-this day)

369 穷光蛋 [窮--] qióngguāngdàn (poor-penniless-guy)

370 吃了上顿没下顿 [---頓--頓] chīle shàng dùn méi xià dùn (eat-finished-last-meal-no-next-meal)

371 贫居闹市无人问, 富在深山有远亲 [貧-鬧-無-問, -----遠親] pín jū nàoshì wú rén wèn, fù zài shēnshān yǒu yuǎnqīn (poor-live-noisy-market-no-people-greet, rich-in-remote-mountain-have-distant-relative)

50 *Life, society, arts, literature*

Shoes are a superficial mark of wealth (脚上没鞋穷半截,[372] a person is half-judged by his shoes). Even if poor, you should not be stingy when traveling (穷家富路,[373] be frugal at home but well equipped for a journey). Intellectuals have an idiosyncratic look '穷酸相'[374] (poor and pedantic looking). Poverty chills ambition (人穷志短),[375] but the poor should not be helped (救急不救穷,[376] help those in emergency not those in poverty), according to a Chinese proverb. Children of the poor know the hardships of life sooner (穷人的孩子早当家).[377] Adversity leads to a desire for change (穷则思变).[378] Therefore, Deng Xiaoping asserted '贫穷不是社会主义，更不是共产主义'[379] (poverty is not a characteristic of socialism, not to mention communism) in 1987.

- #54 Men's three treasures (农民的三宝); #129 Rich and powerful (富贵); #166 Rulers and the ruled, ancient and present (社会的两极)

133. Debt (债) 2

Debt must be paid, either in blood (血债血偿,[380] debts of blood must be paid in blood) or by one's son (父债子还,[381] when a man dies, his debts must be repaid by his son). Either way, 躲得过初一，躲不过十五[382] (you cannot keep it up forever). Out of debts, out of worries (无债一身轻).[383] Therefore, Mao Zedong was very proud that China during his era 既无外债，也无内债[384] (had neither foreign nor domestic debts). However, nowadays, the debtors are cocky (欠债的是大爷[385]) because 虱子多了不咬，账多了不愁[386] (you need not worry if you have too much debt) since the creditors, usually state-owned banks, do not want to send the debtors to prison without getting anything back.

- #132 Poor (穷)

134. Gain extra advantage and suffer losses (占便宜与吃亏) 5

Fairly speaking, many Chinese people tend to gain extra advantage at expense of other people or the public. They say 有便宜不占王八蛋[387] or 不占白不占[388] (only a fool or a son of a bitch would not gain an extra advantage). But, you may gain a petty advantage at the cost

---

372 脚上没鞋穷半截 [----穷--] jiǎo shang méi xié qióng bànjié (foot-on-no-shoe-poor-half-way)

373 穷家富路 [穷---] qióng jiā fù lù (poor-home-rich-away)

374 穷酸相 [穷--] qióngsuān xiàng (poor-pedantic-looking)

375 人穷志短 [-穷--] rén qióng zhǐ duǎn (people-poor-ambition-short)

376 救急不救穷 [----穷] jiù jí bú jiù qióng (help-urgent-not-help-poor)

377 穷人的孩子早当家 [穷-----当-] qióngrén de háizi zǎo dāngjiā (poor-people-child-early-manage-house)

378 穷则思变 [穷则-變] qióng zé sī biàn (poor-then-think-change)

379 贫穷不是社会主义，更不是共产主义 [貧窮---會-义，----產-义] pínqióng búshì shèhuìzhǔyì, gèng búshì gòngchǎnzhǔyì (poverty-not-is-socialism, furthermore-not-is-communism)

380 血债血偿 [-债-償] xuèzhài xiě cháng (blood-debt-blood-return)

381 父债子还 [-债-還] fù zhài zǐ huán (father-debt-son-pay back)

382 躲得过初一，躲不过十五 [--過--, --過--] duǒ de guò chū-yī, duǒ bú guò shíwǔ (avoid-able-first of the month-avoid-not-able-the fifteenth)

383 无债一身轻 [無債--輕] wú zhài yìshēn qīng (no-debt-whole-body-light)

384 既无外债，也无内债 [-無-债, -無-債] jì wú wàizhài, yě wǔ nèizhài (either-no-external-debt, or-no-internal-debt)

385 欠债的是大爷 [-债---爺] qiànzhàide shì dàyé (owe-debt-person-is-idle and wayward man)

386 虱子多了不咬，账多了不愁 [-, 賬----] shīzi duō le bù yǎo, zhàng duō le bù chóu (lice-too many-not-bite, debt-too much-not-worry)

387 有便宜不占王八蛋 [-] yǒu piányi bú zhàn wángbādàn (have-advantage-not-take-bastard)

388 不占白不占 [-] bú zhàn bái bú zhàn (not-take-in vain-not-take)

Life, society, arts, literature   51

of suffering big losses (占小便宜吃大亏).[389] Therefore, some old men tell young people that 'suffering losses is a blessing' (吃亏是福).[390] If a male takes advantage of a female (占女人的便宜),[391] this usually means sexual harassment.

- #20 Utilitarianism (功利主义); #21 Partial and impartial (公与私); #45 Greedy (贪婪)

135. Find a happy medium (折中) 5

Most Chinese people like to find a happy medium and call it by the fine-sounding name of 不偏不倚[392] (impartial) or more philosophically, 中庸之道[393] (Doctrine of the Mean, the golden mean). Lu Xun pointed out why Written Vernacular Chinese was accepted in 1920s by conservative literati who preferred much elegant Classical Chinese, and the reason is unbelievably simple. There was an extremely radical scholar named Qian Xuantong who advocated the abolition of Chinese characters. Compared with abolishing characters, using Written Vernacular Chinese was not as bad, and thus acceptable. Lu Xun then gave an example,

> if you say you want to open a window in a dark room to let in some light, everyone will be against you. However, if you suggest the roof be removed, they would want to work with you and open a window.
>
> (from *Silent China*, 1927)

People who like to find a happy medium are peacemakers (和事佬[394]), and they always try to patch things up (和稀泥).[395]

- #36 Good or bad (优劣); #43 Stay foolish (难得糊涂)

136. Individual vs. group (一人与一群) 5

Collectivism (集体主义) is a major political and behavioral concept of East Asian peoples. Their true mindset is to follow the crowd (随大流/溜[396]) and not to stick one's neck out (不出头[397]) because the law fails where violators are legion (法不责众).[398] Individuals should follow this idea too. For example, it would be bad if you gave gifts to some or most of a group of people, but left someone out. You would rather neglect an entire group than neglect one person (宁落一群, 不落一人),[399] since the one left out would hate you because you looked down upon him.

- #19 Oneself and others (人与己); #21 Partial and impartial (公与私); #108 Collectivism (集体主义)

---

389 占小便宜吃大亏 [------虧] zhàn xiǎo piányi chī dà kuī (take-petty-advantage-suffer-huge-loss)
390 吃亏是福 [-虧--] chīkuī shì fú (suffer-loss-is-fortunate)
391 占女人的便宜 [-] zhàn nǚrén de piányi (take-woman-'s-advantage)
392 不偏不倚 [-] bù piān bù yǐ (not-favor-not-partial)
393 中庸之道 [-] Zhōngyōng zhī dào (unbiased-normal-'s-way)
394 和事佬 [-] héshìlǎo (mediate-thing-guy)
395 和稀泥 [-] huò xīní (meddle-thin-mud)
396 随大流/溜 [隨--] suí dàliú/liù (follow-main-stream)
397 不出头 [--頭] bù chūtóu (not-stick out-head)
398 法不责众 [--責衆] fǎ bù zé zhòng (law-not-punish-plenty)
399 宁落一群, 不落一人 [-] nìng là yì qún, bù là yì rén (would rather-leave out-one-group, not-leave out-one-person)

52 *Life, society, arts, literature*

137. **Mean person (**小人**) 5**

Everyone dislikes mean people, from as early as the year of Confucius who grouped mean persons and women together (唯女子与小人为难养也, 近之则不逊, 远之则怨.[400] Only women and mean persons are hard to get along with. If you become familiar with them, they lose their humility; if you are distant, they resent it). The smartest Chinese person in history, Zhuge Liang (181–234) warned the last emperor of Shu Han to 'be close to gentlemen and stay away from mean persons' (亲君子, 远小人).[401] Although you do not like whose who are mean, you cannot offend them. You need to respect but stay away from them (敬而远之).[402] Gentlemen are open and magnanimous, and mean persons are often sad (小人常戚戚)[403]; however, once they have won, they hold sway (小人得志).[404]

- #94 Sages and men of virtue (圣贤); #138 Flunky vs. talent (奴才vs. 人才); #141 Fawn (吹捧)

138. **Flunky vs. talent (**奴才 **vs.** 人才**) 3**

As an address by a master to his slaves or servants, the word 奴才 (minion, flunky) appeared as early as the Spring and Autumn period. However, it was extensively used as a form of self-address from the mid-Qing dynasty to the early 20th century. 奴才 must have had happy lives in the history, which is evident from the experiences of numerous well-known ones, including Deng Tong (邓通, in early Han dynasty), Li Linfu (李林甫, 683–753), Wei Zhongxian (魏忠贤, 1568–1627) and He Shen (和珅, 1750–1799). Notorious 奴才 were recorded in 佞幸列传[405] or 恩幸列传 (biographies of flatterers) in historical records such as the *Records of the Grand Historian*, the *History of Song* and the *History of Ming*, etc. The term 奴才 also encompasses 走狗[406] (lackey), 鹰犬 (hired thug) and 哈巴狗 (sycophant). 奴才 are easy to find, but talented people (人才) are hard to find, 千军易得, 一将难求[407] (capable people are hard to come by), not to mention whether they will actually be used. For many Chinese rulers, officials or leaders, their tactic when appointing people is 宁用奴才, 不用人才[408] (loyalty over talent). What happens if the talented people are not convinced? It does not matter, since there is a saying 说你行, 你就行, 不行也行; 说你不行, 你就不行, 行也不行[409] (if I say you are capable, you are capable, incapable is capable; if I say you are incapable, you are incapable, capable is incapable).

- #32 Integrity vs. ability (德与才); #137 Mean person (小人)

---

400 唯女子与小人为难养也, 近之则不逊, 远之则怨 [---與--為難養-, --則--, 遠-則-] wéi nǚzǐ yǔ xiǎorén wéi nán yǎng yě, jìn zhī zé bú xùn, yuǎn zhī zé yuan (only-women-and-mean person-is-hard-accommodate, close to-them-then-not-modest, stay away-from-them-then-resent)

401 亲君子, 远小人 [親--, 遠--] qīn jūnzǐ, yuǎn xiǎorén (close to-gentleman, stay away-from-mean person)

402 敬而远之 [--遠-] jìng ér yuǎn zhī (no offending-but-stay away from-him)

403 小人常戚戚 [-] xiǎorén cháng qīqī (mean person-often-anxious)

404 小人得志 [-] xiǎorén dézhì (mean person-realize-goal)

405 佞幸列传 [---傳] nìngxìng lièzhuàn (flatter-biography)

406 走狗 [-] zǒugǒu (walk-dog)

407 千军易得, 一将难求 [-軍--, -將難-] qiān jūn yì dé, yī jiàng nán qiú (1,000-soldier-easy-get, one-general-hard-seek)

408 宁用奴才, 不用人才 [寧---, -] nìng yòng núcái, bú yòng réncái (would rather-use-flunky, not-appoint-talent people)

409 See in-text.

Life, society, arts, literature   53

139. Louis Cha Leung-yung (金庸, Jin Yong, 1924–2018) 5

From the late 1950s to the late 2000s, when social media could be easily accessed, Jin Yong's martial arts novels and subsequently adapted movies and TV dramas were major sources of enjoyment for billions of Chinese people worldwide, mainly males. Deng Xiaoping (1904–1997) was a big fan of Jin Yong who maintained the traditional spirit of chivalry through the heroes and heroines he portrayed, including Guo Jing, Huang Rong, Xiao Feng, Wei Xiaobao, etc. Jin Yong wrote a total of 14 novels. Fans found that the first characters of the 14 novels form a couplet that also makes sense: 飞雪连天射白鹿, 笑书神侠倚碧鸳. A loose translation taken from Wikipedia is:

> Shooting a white deer, snow flutters around the skies;
> Smiling, [one] writes about the divine chivalrous one, leaning against bluish lovebirds (or lover).

In mainland China since the 1980s, if a male student had not read Jin Yong's novels, he would be mocked as a nerd. This book includes an entry 'Mystic Dragon Cult Leader' (神龙教主), which is from a character in Jin Yong's novel _The Deer and the Cauldron_ (鹿鼎记).

- #40 Lu Xun (鲁迅); #140 Mystic Dragon Cult Leader (神龙教主); #142 Kindness and hatred (恩仇)

140. Mystic dragon cult leader (神龙教主) 5

The Mystic Dragon Cult Leader, Hong Antong, is a fictional character in _The Deer and the Cauldron_ (鹿鼎记) written by Louis Cha Leung-yung (金庸) from 1969 to 1972. Hong Antong has the highest martial arts skills, but he enjoys watching how his accomplished colleagues are brought down by unsophisticated children he secretly trained. Some say that Hong Antong was based on Mao Zedong because Hong (here literally 'flood') is homophonous with the character 'hong' (red), which symbolizes communism. Additionally, An appears in the place name Yan'an, which was Mao Zedong's most important base for his revolution. Lastly, Tong sounds similar to 'dong.' In the book, there is a cult internal conflict that is similar to the Cultural Revolution started by Mao Zedong. It is of little importance to argue if Hong Antong was based on Mao Zedong, but this fictional character is a vivid depiction of many Chinese leaders who like to use young and meritless men to bring down those who are credited and capable.

- #139 Louis Cha Leung-yung (金庸, Jin Yong); #141 Fawn (吹捧)

141. Fawn (吹捧) 5

China, ancient or modern, has never lacked eulogists (吹鼓手[410]) whose main jobs are to 吹喇叭, 抬轿子[411] (blow the trumpet and carry somebody in a sedan chair, flatter) in order to gain benefits from wealthy people or superiors. Although this kind of behavior is disgusting, Chinese officials, in both ancient and modern times, like and have gotten used to it. As a result, eulogies that 捧臭脚[412] (bootlick) and 戴高帽[413] (flatter, lay it on thick) are enough to make people sick. For example, even when a subordinate Wei Xiaobao messed up the

---

410 吹鼓手 [-] chuī gǔ shǒu (blow a trumpet-beat a drum-person)
411 吹喇叭, 抬轿子 [-, 擡轎-] chuī lǎba, tái jiàozi (blow-trumpet, carry-sedan chair). 吹喇叭 has another meaning, oral sex.
412 捧臭脚 [-] pěng chòujiǎo (flatter-stinky-foot)
413 戴高帽 [-] dài gāomào (wear-high-hat)

54   *Life, society, arts, literature*

names of the first four greatest legendary emperors, 尧舜禹汤[414] (yao, shun, yu, tang) and said them as 鸟生鱼汤[415] (literally 'birds give birth to fish soup,'), the Qianlong Emperor (1711–1799) of the Qing dynasty was happy to accept this dumbfounding and stupid eulogy. (See the novel 鹿鼎记, *The Deer and the Cauldron* by Louis Cha Leung-yung). During the Cultural Revolution, all Chinese people were fawning Chairman Mao Zedong by saying 毛主席万岁[416] (Long live Chairman Mao!).

- #92 Keeping the emperor company (与大人物相处); #138 Flunky vs. talent (奴才vs. 人才)

142. **Kindness and hatred** (恩仇) 3

The Chinese doctrine is to be grateful in return for other's help (知恩图报),[417] not to return kindness with ingratitude (恩将仇报).[418] However, tremendous kindness is like great hatred (大恩如大仇),[419] since the beneficiary cannot pay it back. There was a story in the Tang dynasty in which a government official set free a prisoner facing the death penalty. Several years later, the official resigned and traveled north. He run across the prisoner, and the prisoner invited him to his home cordially. The prisoner asked his wife, 'This officer saved my life, how should we repay him?' His wife suggested loads of luxurious white silk. The man said it was not enough. Then his wife suggested to double the silk and he said, 'not enough' once again. Finally, his wife said, '大恩难报, 不如杀之'[420] (his tremendous kindness is impossible for us to repay, why don't we just kill him?). A servant heard this and thought it was too cruel, so he told the officer who immediately ran away (from *Tang Yu Lin* by Wang Dang). When people grew older, they might take hatred lightly and could resolve (the kindness and) hatred with a smile when he met his enemy ((相逢)一笑泯恩仇).[421] Kindness and hatred (恩仇) are a major theme of martial arts novels. The very first book of prolific novelist Jin Yong is called 书剑恩仇录 (*The Book and the Sword*, literally 'book-sword-kindness-hatred-legend.')

- #140 Mystic Dragon Cult Leader (神龙教主); #143 Kindness (恩); #144 Hatred (仇)

143. **Kindness** (恩) 3

Requiting a kindness (报恩) was a major theme in Chinese folklore. Who should be requited for their kindness? First of all, parents: 父母之恩[422] (kindness of parents for giving you a life) and 养育之恩[423] (gratitude for the love and care given by parents) were considered the greatest forms of kindness. Second, teachers or mentors: 恩师[424] (kind and respected teachers/mentors) should not be forgotten. Others include the people who helped you, and they were called 恩人or 恩公.[425] Prostitutes would call their guests 恩客.[426] Kindness should be repaid multiple times; a drop of water

---

414 尧舜禹汤 [堯--湯] Yáo, Shùn, Yǔ, Tāng

415 鸟生鱼汤 [鳥--湯] niǎo shēng yú tang (bird-bear-fish-soup)

416 毛主席万岁 [---萬歲] Máo Zhǔxí wànsuì (Mao-chairman-10,000-years old)

417 知恩图报 [--圖報] zhī ēn tú bào (recognize-kindness-wish-pay back)

418 恩将仇报 [-將-報] ēn jiāng chóu bào (kindness-with-hatred-return)

419 大恩如大仇 [-] dà ēn rú dà chóu (great-kindness-like-great-hatred)

420 大恩难报, 不如杀之 [--難報, --殺-] dà ēn nán bào, bùrú shā zhī (great-kindness-hard-pay back, had better-kill-him)

421 一笑泯恩仇 [-] yī xiào mǐn ēnchóu (one-smile-clear up-kindness and hatred)

422 父母之恩 [-] fùmǔ zhī ēn (parents-'s-kindness)

423 养育之恩 [養---] yǎngyù zhī ēn (bear-raise-'s-kindness)

424 恩师 [-師] ēnshī (kind-master)

425 恩公 [-] ēn'gōng (benefit-reverend)

426 恩客 [-] ēnkè (benefit-guest)

Life, society, arts, literature 55

shall be returned with gushing spring (滴水之恩当涌泉相报),[427] let alone 大恩大德[428] (great kindness), which is as heavy as a mountain (恩重如山). Not only humans but also animals, such as finches (stories of 结草衔环),[429] horses and dogs (stories of 马有垂缰之义, 狗有湿草之恩) know how to return others' kindness. A highly respected politician and the first Premier of the People's Republic of China, was named 周恩来,[430] in which the second character is 恩.

- #142 Kindness and hatred (恩仇); #144 Hatred (仇)

144. Hatred (仇) 5

To avenge something/someone (报仇 or 报仇雪恨[431]) was a major theme in Chinese literature. Vengefulness for murder of one's father is absolutely irreconcilable (杀父之仇, 不共戴天),[432] and both national and family hatred (国恨家仇[433]) should never be forgotten. Although profound hatred (深仇大恨[434]) is as deep as sea (仇深似海),[435] you need not take actions of vengeance until you are ready for it (君子报仇, 十年不晚).[436] Exhortations indicate 'it is better to resolve resentments than to settle them' (冤仇宜解不宜结).[437]

- #142 Kindness and hatred (恩仇); #143 Kindness (恩)

145. To one's face and in his back (当面与背后) 3

Many Chinese people are double-faced, acting one way to your face and another behind your back (当面一套, 背后一套).[438] They would 好话说尽[439] (say only good words) and be a 笑面虎[440] (smiling tiger – outwardly kind but inwardly cruel person) to your face, but would 坏事做绝[441] (commit every evil) and 背后捅刀子[442] (hurt you in your absence/behind your back). How a person acts to one's face and behind one's back are so different that a proverb goes 当面教子, 背后教妻[443] (admonish one's child in the presence of others, but admonish one's wife in privacy).

- #137 Mean person (小人)

---

427 点水之恩当涌泉相报 [點---當湧--報] diǎn shuǐ zhī ēn dāng yǒng yuán xiāng bào (drop-water-'s-benefit-should-gushing-spring-to-return)

428 大恩大德 [-] dà ēn dà dé (great-kindness-great-virtue)

429 结草衔环 [結-衔環] jié cǎo xián huán (knot-grass-hold in the mouth-ring jade)

430 周恩来 [--來] Zhōu Ēnlái

431 报仇雪恨 [報---] bàochóu xuěhèn (avenge-hatred-revenge-hatred)

432 杀父之仇, 不共戴天 [殺---, -] shā fù zhī chóu, bú gòng dài tiān (kill-father-'s-hatred, not-together-live under-heaven)

433 国恨家仇 [國---] guó hèn jiā chóu (national-hatred-family-hatred)

434 深仇大恨 [-] shēn chóu dà hèn (deep-hatred-great-hatred)

435 仇深似海 [-] chóu shēn sì hǎi (hatred-deep-as-sea)

436 君子报仇, 十年不晚 [--報-, -] jūnzǐ bàochóu, shí nián bù wǎn (gentleman-avenge-hatred, 10-year-not-late)

437 冤仇宜解不宜结 [------結] yuānchóu yí jiě bùyí jié (hatred-should-resolve-not-should-start)

438 当面一套, 背后一套 [當---, -後--] dāngmiàn yī tào, bèihòu yī tào (in one's presence-one-set, behind one's back-another-set)

439 好话说尽 [-話說盡] hǎo huà shuō jìn (good-words-speak-all out)

440 笑面虎 [-] xiàomiànhǔ (smiling-face-tiger)

441 坏事做绝 [壞--絕] huàishì zuò jué (bad-thing-do-to extreme)

442 背后捅刀子 [-後---] bèihòu tǒng dāozi (behind one's back-stab-knife)

443 当面教子, 背后教妻 [當---, -後--] dāngmiàn jiào zǐ, bèihòu jiāo qī (in one's presence-educate-child, behind one's back-teach-wife)

56　*Life, society, arts, literature*

146. Gifts to avoid giving (不能送的礼物) 3

Many items cannot be given as gifts for various reasons. For example, 钟 (clock) is homophonous with 终 (zhōng, end), thus 送钟 (to gift a clock) sounds like 送终 (to see a dying person). 梨 (pear) is homophonous with 离 (lí, to part, to leave). To gift pears could mean 'to part, to separate.' 伞 (sǎn, umbrella) sounds close to 散 (sàn, to break up) and could mean 'to part, to break up,' especially in the case of lovers. The worst gift is a green hat/cap (绿帽子) to a married gentleman because 绿帽子 is a symbol of being a cuckold. 戴绿帽(子)[444] means 'to be a cuckold.'

- #121 Custom (风俗); #147 Mirrors (镜子)

147. Mirrors (镜子) 1

Mirrors can reflect people's appearance and much beyond. Emperor Taizong of Tang (598–649) was one of the greatest emperors in Chinese history. He used 'mirrors' (镜子) as metaphors as follows: 以铜为镜，可以正衣冠；以古为镜，可以见兴替；以人为镜，可以知得失[445] (With bronze as a mirror one can correct his appearance; with history as a mirror, one can understand the rise and fall of a state; with good men as a mirror, one can distinguish right from wrong). But, you can never gift a mirror to other people in China because it implies the sentiment 'to look at yourself, do you know who you are?' that was expressed by an old proverb 撒泡尿照照自己[446] (pee and look at your reflection from it) or a colloquial saying 自己照镜子看看 (to look at yourself in the mirror).

- #146 Gifts to avoid giving (不能送的礼物)

148. Face and dignity (脸, 面子) 5

面子 (face, honor, dignity) is a major aspect of Chinese social life. All people want to 有面子[447] (have/enjoy the due/inflated honor). Some people 死要面子活受罪[448] (keep up appearances to cover up one's predicament). If one is not able to 有面子, one should at least not 丢脸[449] (lose face, be disgraced) since 人有脸, 树有皮[450] (a man has his face just like a tree has its bark, a man has a sense of shame). 丢人[451] is worse than 丢脸. Anyway, 面子是别人给的, 脸是自己丢的[452] (honor is conferred by others, but disgrace is done by yourself). Don't bring shame to your parents/family (别丢父母/你家的脸).[453]

- #101 The last bit of an emperor's dignity (皇帝最后的尊严)

149. Civilities (客套) 5

To be frank, it is hard for foreigners to understand Chinese civilities that are not even easily understood by many unsophisticated Chinese people themselves. Imagine this scenario:

444　戴绿帽 [-綠-] dàilǜmào (wear-green-hat)

445　以人为镜，可以知得失 [--為鏡, -] yǐ rén wéi jìng, kěyǐ zhī déshī (use-people-as-mirror, can-know-gain or loss)

446　撒泡尿照照自己 [-]sā pǎo niào zhàozhào zìjǐ (to urinate-mw-pee-reflect-oneself)

447　有面子 [-] yǒu miànzi (have-honor)

448　死要面子活受罪 [-] sǐ yào miànzi huó shòuzuì (obstinately-want-honor-simply-endure-torture)

449　丢脸 [-臉] diū liǎn (lose-face)

450　人有脸, 树有皮 [--臉, 樹--] rén yǒu liǎn, shù yǒu pí (man-have-face, tree-have-bark)

451　丢人 [-] diū rén (lose-dignity)

452　面子是别人给的, 脸是自己丢的 [-----給-, 臉-----] miànzi shì biérén gěi de, liǎn shì zìjǐ diū de (honor-is-others-give, face-is-oneself-lose)

453　别丢父母的脸 [-----臉] bié diū fùmǔ de liǎn (don't-lose-parents-'s-face)

Life, society, arts, literature 57

A person asks his friend for help and his friend answers: 没什么问题, 有一定难度, 应该差不多,[454] let me 研究研究[455] and 回头再说[456] (It won't be a problem, but there might be some difficulty. However, it should be alright. Let me think about it, and we will talk about it later). All of the five phrases actually mean 'no,' let alone what they would mean in most cases when combined. When a Chinese person says he wants to 随便聊聊[457] (just talk) with you, he might mean something else.

- #52 'Death penalty' and modesty (死罪死罪); #121 Custom (风俗); #255 I'll think about it (研究研究); #275 Forms of address: respectful, honorific and modest (尊称, 敬称, 谦称)

150. Rumor (流言) 3

Many Chinese people like to gossip (嚼舌头 or 八卦[458]) and spread rumors (串闲话). Supposedly, rumors stop with the wise (流言止于智者).[459] However, Chinese rumors are so powerful that the testimony of three men creates a tiger in the market (三人成虎,[460] repeated false reports will sound convincing), and even though the tongue is boneless, it breaks bones (众口铄金, 积毁销骨).[461] Even the mother of the Confucian sage Zengzi (505 BCE–435 BCE) was convinced that Zengzi killed a man (曾参杀人,[462] rumors are formidable). Nowadays, rumors (谣言) about Chinese politics are ridiculed as 遥遥领先的预言[463] (far ahead prophecies), and if the government wants to clarify, it would be 越描越黑[464] (the more one clarifies a rumor, the more likely it turns out to be).

- #124 Bad habits (恶习); #145 To one's face and in his back (当面与背后)

151. Find fault (找借口) 3

To nitpick is 鸡蛋里挑骨头[465] (to find bones in an egg, to find quarrel in a straw). If one wants to find fault in others, he will always have excuses (欲加之罪, 何患无辞,[466] give a dog a bad name and hang him). The most famous national hero in Chinese history is 岳飞 (Yue Fei, 1103–1142), who was accused of a fabricated crime and hanged. The crime was called 莫须有[467] ('maybe have') and could be used on anyone. In ancient China, emperors could fling accusations on officials for 腹诽[468] (criticizing inwardly) and then kill them.

- #59 Mandate of Heaven, or God's will (天命, 天意)

---

454 没什么问题, 有一定难度, 应该差不多: See in-text.

455 研究研究 [-] yánjiu (think about it-*reduplication*)

456 回头再说 [-頭-説] huítóu zàishuō (later-again-discuss)

457 随便聊聊 [隨---] suíbiàn liáoliao (casually-chat-*reduplication*)

458 八卦 [-] bā guà (8-trigram)

459 流言止于智者 [---於--] liúyán zhǐ yú zhìzhě (rumor-stop-at-wise-man)

460 三人成虎 [-] sān rén chéng hǔ (3-people-make-tiger)

461 众口铄金, 积毁销骨 [衆-鑠-, 積毀銷-] zhòng kǒu shuò jīn, jī huǐ xiāo gǔ (many-mouth-melt-metal, accumulated-defamation-melt-bone)

462 曾参杀人 [-參殺-] Zeng Shen shārén (Zeng Shen-kill-man)

463 遥遥领先的预言 [遙遙領--預-] yáoyáo lǐngxiān de yùyán (far-ahead-'s'-prophesy)

464 越描越黑 [-] yuè miáo yuè hēi (the more-describe-the more-black)

465 鸡蛋里挑骨头 [鷄-裏--頭] jīdàn lǐ tiāo gútou (chicken-egg-inside-nitpick-bone)

466 欲加之罪, 何患无辞 [-, --無辭] yù jiā zhī zuì, hé huàn wú cí (want-add-him-fault, why-worry-no-excuse)

467 莫须有 [-須-] mòxūyǒu (maybe-have)

468 腹诽 [-誹] fùfěi (abdomen-slander)

58 *Life, society, arts, literature*

152. Suspicious (怀疑) 2

Foxes (狐狸) are known for being suspicious (狐疑). Generally speaking, Chinese people are rather suspicious (疑神疑鬼,[469] terribly suspicious), and a suspicious heart will create imaginary ghosts (疑心生暗鬼).[470] However, when it comes to managing a man, you need to either trust him or skip him (疑人不用, 用人不疑).[471] In Chinese history, Cao (曹操, 155–220), a famous warlord was notorious for being too suspicious, said, '宁教我负天下人, 休教天下人负我'[472] (I would rather betray the whole world than leave them to betray me).

153. Seek others for help (求人) 2

Generally, Chinese people think others are not fully trustworthy or dependable, so the old doctrine was 求人不如求己[473] (God helps those who help themselves). Some people never ask for help (万事不求人).[474] Asking for help is not easy, but sometimes you need to 求爷爷, 告奶奶[475] (beg the grandpa and entreat the grandma, beg this one and that), but 求天天不应, 求地地不语[476] (beg whomever you can, but none responds). Therefore, if you are in trouble, you are on your own and 自求多福[477] (good luck).

154. Deterioration (变差) 1

Old men are often pessimistic and believe that society and young people are becoming progressively worse (世风日下).[478] One generation is worse than the previous one (一代不如一代,[479] also a key word that appeared repeatedly in Lu Xun's short fiction 风波, *Disturbance*), and each person is worse than the other (一蟹不如一蟹,[480] literally 'each crab is smaller than the one before.'

- #13 Change, in the wrong way (变坏); #267 Dilution of vulgar words (傻*)

155. Colors and culture (颜色与文化) 3

Colors were highly attached to culture in the Chinese language, and much of this cultural significance remains in contemporary society. For example, the color of red (红色) symbolizes many things: auspicious/lucky (吉祥, jíxiáng, auspicious as can be seen at a Chinese wedding), wealth/fortune (财富, as in 红包 red envelope, and 牛市, the bull market), and revolution (革命, as in 红卫兵, the Red Guards) etc. Pink (粉红) was dangerous during the Cultural Revolution because it was associated with the petty bourgeoisie (小资产阶级). On

---

469 疑神疑鬼 [-] yí shén yí guǐ (suspicious-god-suspicious-ghost)

470 疑心生暗鬼 [-] yíxīn shēng àn guǐ (suspicious-heart-create-imaginary-ghost)

471 疑人不用, 用人不疑 [-] yí rén bú yòng, yòng rén bù yí (suspect-people-not-use, use-people-not-suspect)

472 宁教我负天下人, 休教天下人负我 [宁--负---, -----负-] nìng jiào wǒ fù tiānxià rén, xiū jiào tiānxià rén fù wǒ (would rather-let-me-betray-world-people, not-let-world-people-betray-me)

473 求人不如求己 [-] qiú rén bùrú qiú jǐ (beg-others-not-as good as-beg-oneself)

474 万事不求人 [萬----] wàn shì bù qiú rén (10,000-thing-not-beg-others)

475 求爷爷, 告奶奶 [-爺爺, -] qiú yéye, gào nǎinai (beg-grandpa, tell-grandma)

476 求天天不应, 求地地不语 [----應, ----語] qiú tiān tiān bú yìng, qiú dì dì bù yǔ (beg-Heaven-Heaven-not-respond, beg-Earth-Earth-not-speak)

477 自求多福 [-] zì qiú duō fú (self-beg-more-luck)

478 世风日下 [-風--] shìfēng rì xià (social-practice-day by day-deteriorate)

479 一代不如一代 [-] yī dài bùrú yī dài (one-generation-not-as good as-one-generation)

480 一蟹不如一蟹 [-] yī xiè bùrú yī xiè (one-crab-not-as good/big as-one-crab)

Life, society, arts, literature   59

the internet, 小粉红 refers to those who glorify the Chinese communist administration. In ancient China, colors were bound with 五德 or 五行 (The Five Elements, 金木水火土, i.e. metal, wood, water, fire, earth). Once a dynasty revered a certain virtue, a corresponding color would be decided and a process called 易服色 (to change the state/official color). For example, the state color of the Qin dynasty was black (黑), the Tang dynasty yellow (黄) and the Song dynasty red (红), etc.

- #61 Auspicious signs and the color white (祥瑞与白色); #121 Custom (风俗)

156. Representatives of Chinese literature (中国文学的代表) 2

Chinese people are very proud of their literature, especially 唐诗, 宋词, 元曲[481] (Tang poetry, Song *ci*/poetry, Yuan *qu*/poetry/opera). Actually, *诗经* (*Classic of Poetry*), 先秦散文 (pre-Qin prose), 汉赋 (Han *fu*/poetry) and 明清小说 (Ming and Qing novels) are as excellent as the three forms of literature mentioned before.

- #157 Common lengths of forms in Chinese literature (几种中国文学体裁的长度); #160 Chinese literary works with the richest culture (富含中国文化的文艺作品)

157. Common lengths of forms in Chinese literature (几种中国文学体裁的长度) 2

Common lengths of forms in Chinese literature vary: quatrain (绝句), either 20 or 28 characters; regulated verse (律诗), either 40 or 56 characters; *ci* (词, a form of poetry), mostly 58 ± 12 characters; a volume of histories (一卷史书), approximately 8,000 characters, based on statistics of the History of Song and the History of Ming; a chapter of a novel, approximately 8,000 characters, based on statistics of the Four Classic Novels (四大名著). Chinese emperors read numerous memorials (表) from ministers. What length was recommended by the emperors? 156 characters, based on the two model memorials written by Liu Zongyuan (柳宗元) and Han Yu (韩愈).

- #156 Representatives of Chinese literature (中国文学的代表)

158. Confucius says (子曰) 1

子 here refers to Confucius (孔子), and 曰 means 'say.' 子曰 often appears at the beginning of many paragraphs in the Analects, therefore 子曰 became synonymous to old sayings, whether they were real or fabricated. A similar phrase is 太史公曰 (the Grand Historian says), which appears at the end of each biography in the *Records of the Grand Historian*. Both phrases are used to justify the authority of the following content, usually in a joking way.

- #95 Master (*子)

159. Gifted scholars and beautiful women (才子佳人) 3

才子佳人 (cáizǐ jiārén, gifted scholars and beautiful women) is a genre of ancient Chinese fiction typically about a romance between a gifted scholar and a beautiful woman. Stories about 才子佳人 were extremely popular because they reflected traditional Chinese values

---

481 唐诗宋词元曲 [-詩-詞--] Tángshī Sòngcí Yuánqǔ (Tang-poem-Song-*Ci*-Yuan-opera)

60 *Life, society, arts, literature*

on marriage, 郎才女貌 (lángcái nǚmào), which means the husband should be talented and the wife beautiful.

- #91 Emperors, kings, generals, ministers (帝王将相); #131 Unrestrained (风流)

160. Chinese literary works with the richest culture (富含中国文化的文艺作品) 3

The following is the personal view of the author. (1) 红楼梦 (Hónglóumèng, *Dream of the Red Chamber*, mid-18th century) is regarded almost undisputedly as the greatest work of Chinese literature. It is an encyclopedia of Chinese feudal society. (2) Jin Yong's martial/*wuxia* novels (金庸的武侠小说, 1955–1972) captured the fascination of almost all literate Chinese before the internet era. The novels depict a fascinating world of rivers and lakes (江湖, jiānghú). No. 3: The movie 霸王别姬 (Bàwáng Biéjī, *Farewell My Concubine*, 1993) explores individual experiences of living in political turmoil. Any non-Chinese who can understand half of any of the aforementioned works deserves a PhD in Chinese culture.

- #139 Louis Cha Leung-yung (金庸, Jin Yong); #156 Representatives of Chinese literature (中国文学的代表)

161. Antithetical couplets (对联) 5

对联 (duìlián) means 'antithetical couplet' and was the basic training for ancient Chinese literature. 对联 are commonly seen at important cultural sites such as palaces, temples, tombs, funerals and on many families' gates in the spring festival. A 对联 is composed of two parts that are usually opposite in tone patterns and meanings, for example, 黑发不知勤学早, 白首方悔读书迟, which means 'at a young age I did not know that I should have studied diligently, and when I became old, I just regretted/found that it was too late to read books.'

黑	发	不	知	勤	学	早
hēi	fà	bù	zhī	qín	xué	zǎo
black	hair	not	know	diligently	study	early
white	head	just	regret	read	book	late
bái	shǒu	fāng	huǐ	dú	shū	chí
白	首	方	悔	读	书	迟

Many well-educated Chinese love 对联, so does the author of this book. Here is the upper scroll or first line of a 对联 for readers of this book to complete: 林森入森林, 只见树木.[482] Here are notes for readers' attention. (1) It includes 木林森, all of which have the radical 木, (2) 林森 (Lín Sēn, 1868–1943) was Chairman of the National Government of the Republic of China from 1931 until his death. (3) It implies a proverb '只见树木, 不见森林,'[483] which means 'unable to see the forest for the trees.' This is supposedly hard for 99.99% of, if not all, native Chinese.

- #281 Difficulty levels of Chinese rhyme (韵脚的难易)

---

482 林森入森林, 只见树木 [-, -见树-] Lín Sēn rù sēnlín, zhǐ jiàn shùmù (Lin Sen-enter-forest, only-saw-trees)

483 只见树木, 不见森林 [-见树-, -见--] zhǐ jiàn shùmù, bú jiàn sēnlín (only-saw-trees, not-saw-forest)

Life, society, arts, literature 61

162. Music one gets to kneel down when listening (跪着听的音乐) 1

This *erhu* music is '二泉映月' ('Èrquán Yìngyuè,' the Moon's Reflection on the Second Spring) written and originally played by a blind Chinese musician ABing (registered name 华彦钧 Huà Yánjūn, 1893–1950). Èrquán Yìngyuè is treasure of Chinese music. After listening to this piece, Japanese conductor Seiji Ozawa made the comment '跪着听的音乐'[484] in 1978. In Chinese, this piece is 此曲只应天上有, 人间能得几回闻[485] (the song only belongs to the heaven, it is hardly heard on earth), two lines of a poem by the greatest Chinese poet Du Fu (712–770).

- #34 Refined and popular (雅俗)

163. Painting (画画) 2

It is easiest to paint ghosts (画鬼最容易).[486] According to a story in *Han Fei Zi* (韩非子), the hardest thing to paint is a dog or a horse and the easiest a ghost, since dogs and horses are known to all people, but nobody has ever seen a ghost so you can paint it as whatever you imagine. There is a rule for Chinese landscape painting: 丈山尺树, 寸马分人.[487] It means the scales between a mountain, a tree, a horse and a man are 10 feet, 1 foot, 1/10 foot, 1/100 foot. Dragons and tigers are hard to paint, but their bones are even harder to paint. 画龙画虎难画骨, 知人知面不知心[488] means 'In drawing a dragon or a tiger, you show its skin, not its bones; in knowing a man, you can only know his name and face, not his heart,' or 'there is no way to really know a person,' to put it simply.

---

484 跪着听的音乐 [-著聽--樂] guìzhe tīng de yīnyuè (kneel–*ing*-listen-'s-music)

485 此曲只应天上有, 人间能得几回闻 [---應---, -間--幾-聞] (this-song-only-should-heaven-have, human-world-can-get-how many-time-heard)

486 画鬼最容易 [畫----] huà guǐ zuì róngyì (draw-ghost-most-easy)

487 丈山尺树, 寸马分人 [---樹-馬--] zhàngshān chǐshù, cùnmǎ fēnrén (10 feet-mountain-foot-tree-1/10 foot-horse-1/100-man)

488 画龙画虎难画骨, 知人知面不知心 [畫龍畫-難畫-,-] huà lóng huà hǔ nán huà gǔ, zhī rén zhī miàn bù zhī xīn (draw-dragon-draw-tiger-hardly-draw-bone, know-people-know-face-hardly-know-heart/mind)

5 Social relations, family, women, education (社会关系, 家庭, 女人, 教育)

164. Human relations (人际关系) 5

关系 (connections) play an extremely important role in Chinese society, particularly given that people's concept of social hierarchy is still strong and equal rights have not been fully implemented. A person not knowing 人情世故[489] (worldly wisdom) is considered immature. One value expressed in folk culture is to be friendly with everyone (与人为善).[490] However, humans are wicked (人心险恶[491]) and a man cannot help but to go with the tide (人在江湖, 身不由己).[492] The Thick Black Theory (厚黑学[493]) has been popular ever since its birth in 1911. The key concepts of this theory include 脸皮厚[494] (face-skin-thick, shameless) and 心黑[495] (heart-black, cruel). In most cases, worldly wisdom lies in choosing a side to stand with (站队).[496] If you are lucky to be on the winning side, your life will be much easier.

- #19 Oneself and others (人与己); #26 Not standing out (不出头); #135 Find a happy medium (折中); #136 Individual vs. group (一人与一群); #145 To one's face and in his back (当面与背后); #165 Social hierarchy (等级); #196 Friends and friendship (朋友, 友谊)

165. Social hierarchy (等级) 10

In both ancient and modern China, people have been divided into various grades and ranks, so the official titles and job titles have been very important. Chinese people were divided roughly into four classes: 士[497] (shì, officials/scholars); 农 (nóng, farmers/peasants); 工 (gōng, artisans); and 商 (shāng, merchants) throughout history. Once, the Yuan dynasty (1271–1368) had ten levels/castes: (1) 官[498] (guān, high officials/bureaucrats); (2) 吏 (lì, petty officials); (3) 僧 (sēng, Buddhist monks); (4) 道 (dào, Taoists priests); (5) 医 (yī, physicians); (6) 工 (gōng, artisans); (7) 匠 (jiàng, carpenters/workers); (8) 娼 (chāng, prostitutes); (9) 儒 (rú, Confucian scholars); and (10) 丐 (gài, beggars). A dysphemism 臭老九[499] (chòulǎojiǔ, Stinking Old Ninth) was coined thereafter to refer to

---

489 人情世故 [-] rén qíng shì gù (human-feeling-world-norm)
490 与人为善 [與-爲-] yǔ rén wéi shàn (with-others-be-kind)
491 人心险恶 [--險惡] rénxīn xiǎn'è (people-heart-treacherous-vicious)
492 人在江湖, 身不由己 [-] rén zài jiānghú, shēn bù yóu jǐ (people-at-wild world, one-not-by-oneself)
493 厚黑学 [--學] hòu hēi xué (thick-black-theory)
494 脸皮厚 [臉--] liǎnpí hòu (face-skin-thick)
495 心黑 [-] xīn hēi (heart-black)
496 站队 [-隊] zhànduì (join-side)
497 士农工商 [-農--] see in-text
498 官吏僧道医工匠娼儒丐 [----醫-----] see in-text
499 臭老九 [-] chòu lǎo-jiǔ (stinky-no.-nine)

Social relations, family, women, education 63

educators and Confucian scholars and was unfortunately widely used even in the 1960s and 1970s during the Cultural Revolution. Actually, the Book of Han (completed in 82) divided all famous people before the Han dynasty into nine grades, with the first three being sages (圣人), benevolent people (仁人) and wise men (智人), and the last being fools (愚人). Hierarchy was and still is highly valued by Chinese society. This is reflected in a saying 官大一级压死人,[500] which means 'officials one rank superior overpower the inferior.' 高人一等[501] (be a head taller than others) and 人上人[502] (upper class) are still some Chinese people's dream.

- #23 Who do you think you are? (你算老几啊?); #135 Find a happy medium (折中); #164 Human relations (人际关系); #166 Rulers and the ruled, ancient and present (社会的两极); #188 Sub-ministerial level universities (副部级大学); #198 Boss (老板)

166. Rulers and the ruled, ancient and present (社会的两极) 3

Simply put, there are two kinds of people. They are at the two extremes of the social hierarchy. The following is a rough classification: (1) 劳心者 (those who work with their brains) vs. 劳力者 (those who work with their muscles/hands), as in Mencius's saying 劳心者治人, 劳力者治于人[503] (those who work with their brains govern and those who work with their muscles/hands are governed); (2) 肉食者 (meat-eater, the carnivorous) vs. 吃草的 (grass-eater). 肉食者 is from the *Zuo Commentary of The Spring and Autumn Annals*, and 吃草的 is the contemporary form of expression; (3) 官 (officials) vs. 民 (the people), as in 官逼民反 (official exploitation drives the people to rebellion); (4) 光脚的 (those who are barefoot) vs. 穿鞋的 (those who wear shoes), as in a proverb 光脚的不怕穿鞋的[504] (those with nothing do not fear those with power, he who is down need fear no fall); (5) 喝咖啡的 (coffee-drinker) vs. 吃大蒜的 (garlic-eater). The saying '一个吃大蒜的怎么可以和一个喝咖啡的在一起呢' (how can a person who loves eating garlic stand together with a person who loves drinking coffee) was used by Shanghai stand-up comedian Zhou Libo in 2013 to describe the difference between Chinese southern and northern cultures in a metaphorical way. This contrast can be applied to social disparity; (6) 赵家人 (the Zhao family) vs. 非赵家人 (non-Zhao family). 赵家人 refers to Chinese dignitaries. The phrase was from Lu Xun's *The True Story of Ah Q* (1921–1922).

- #129 Rich and powerful (富贵); #132 Poor (穷); #165 Social hierarchy (等级)

167. Ancestors (祖宗) 5

Ancestors were very important to ancient Chinese people whose ultimate glory was 光宗耀祖[505] (to reflect glory on one's ancestors) and whose most basic duty was 传宗接代[506] (to produce a male heir to carry on the family line). If one person became famous or prominent, he would try hard to attach glories to his ancestry even if there were not any. As a

---

500 官大一级压死人 [---级壓--] guān dà yì jí yā sǐ rén (rank/post-higher-one-level-crush-dead-people)
501 高人一等 [-] gāo rén yì děng (higher-people-one-level)
502 人上人 [-] rén shàng rén (people-above-person)
503 劳心者治人, 劳力者治于人 [勞----, 勞--於-] láoxīnzhě zhìrén, láolìzhě zhìyú rén (work-brain-people-govern-others, work-strength-people-govern-by-others)
504 光脚的不怕穿鞋的 [-]guāngjiǎodebúpàchuānxiéde(bare-foot-people-not-fear-wear-shoe-people)
505 光宗耀祖 [-] guāng zōng yào zǔ (glorify-clan-show off-ancestor)
506 传宗接代 [傳---] chuán zōng jiē dài (pass on-clan-continue-generation)

64 *Social relations, family, women, education*

result, the ancestor of a famous Chinese person was 不是名儒, 便是名臣[507] (either a famous Confucian scholar or a famous minister/official) (from '*On Damn It*' by Lu Xun, 1925). People would condemn a person who had brought humiliation to his family as a 不肖子孙[508] (unworthy descendant). An even worse curse than 'fuck your mom' is 操你祖宗八代[509] (fuck your ancestors of eight generations).

- #168 Filial (孝)

168. Filial (孝) 10

Filial piety has been promoted throughout Chinese history. The Han and Ming dynasties even claimed that they ruled the country by 孝 (filial piety). Almost all emperors of the Han dynasty had the word 孝 in their posthumous titles, such as 孝文皇帝 (Emperor Wen of Han, 207 BCE–157 BCE). In cultural terms, *孝经*[510] (*Classic of Filial Piety*) is one of the Thirteen Classics of Confucianism, and 二十四孝图[511] (*The Twenty-four Filial Exemplars*) was one of the most popular readers in the Chinese history. The maxim 百善孝为先[512] was coined in the Qing dynasty; however, the Classic of Filial Piety quoted the Confucian words '罪莫大于不孝[513]' (there is not a worse crime than not being filial). Besides rulers, the common people also wanted their children to be filial, but what if they were not? Use sticks according to a saying, 棍棒底下出孝子[514] (spare the rod, spoil the child). Being filial is not easy all the time, therefore, 久病床前无孝子[515] (if ill for long in bed, you won't be watched and fed). Confucianists associated 'loyal' with 'filial,' but ironically, the founding emperor of the Han dynasty (206 BCE–220 CE) Liu Bang was notorious for being unfilial. When his enemy Xiang Yu threatened to boil his father alive, Liu Bang laughed and asked Xiang Yu to spare him a cup (分一杯羹).[516] Another time, when Liu Bang was being hunted down by Xiang Yu's army, he kicked his children off the cart several times, to save his own skin.

- #33 Benevolence and justice (仁与义); #164 Human relations (人际关系); #169 Parents (父母); #170 Parents and children (父母与子女)

169. Parents (父母) 10

In English, the conventional order of mentioning one's parents is Mom and Dad, but the Chinese way is the opposite, 父母 (father and mother). In ancient China, children were bound to their parents from birth to burial. Children's basic filial piety to parents is 身体发肤, 受之父母, 不敢毁伤, 孝之始也[517] (our bodies, to every hair and bit of skin, are received from our parents,

---

507 不是名儒, 便是名臣 [-] búshì míng rú, biàn shì míng chén (not-be-famous-Confucian scholar, then-be-famous-minister)

508 不肖子孙 [-] bú xiào zǐsūn (not-alike-descendant)

509 操你祖宗八代 [-] cào nǐ zǔzōng bā dài (fuck-your-ancestor-8-generation)

510 孝经 [-經] xiàojīng (filial piety-classic)

511 二十四孝图 [----圖] èrshísì xiào tú (24-filial piety-drawing)

512 百善孝为先 [---為-] bǎi shàn xiào wéi xiān (100-virtue-filial piety-is-first)

513 罪莫大于不孝 [---於--] zuì mò dàyú bú xiào (crime-no-bigger-than-not-filial)

514 棍棒底下出孝子 [-] gùnbàng dǐxia chū xiàozǐ (rod-under-come-filial-child)

515 久病床前无孝子 [--牀-無--] jiǔ bìng chuāngqián wú xiàozǐ (long-ill-bed-side-no-filial-child)

516 分一杯羹 [-] fēn yì bēi gēng (spare-one-cup-broth)

517 身体发肤, 受之父母, 不敢毁伤, 孝之始也 [-體髮膚, -, --毁傷, -] shēntǐ fà fū, shòu zhī fùmǔ, bùgǎn huǐ shāng, xiào zhī shǐ yě (body-hair-skin, received-it-(from) parents, not-dare-destroy-harm, filial piety-'s-beginning-*marker of affirmation*)

Social relations, family, women, education   65

and we must not presume to injure or wound them. This is the beginning of filial piety), which explains why very few ancient Chinese had tattoos on their bodies. Children are made from father's sperm and mother's egg. Every part of a human body is from them, so one has to cherish it. According to the *Romance of the Three Kingdoms*, in 192, Xiahou Dun (155–220), a mighty general, was hit on his left eye by an arrow, but he pulled the eye out and ate it, saying '父精母血, 不可弃也'[518] (it is from father's sperm and mother's blood, I cannot discard it). A person's marriage would be arranged by his parents (父母之命,[519] parents' order). One should not move too far from home if his parents are alive (父母在, 不远游).[520] If one's father has died, he should quit his job to live near his father's tomb and restrain from any entertainment for three years. This is called 服丧[521] (mourning). Children should always obey their parents' orders since 天下无不是的父母[522] (all parents in the world cannot be wrong). Existence of both parents (父母双全[523]) was considered a fortune for a person in ancient China.

- #170 Parents and children (父母与子女)

170. Parents and children (父母与子女) 5

All parents love their children (可怜天下父母心,[524] mercy is the feelings all parents under heaven have toward their offspring), but children will not understand this until they become parents themselves (养儿方知父母恩,[525] only when one raises a child can one know the kindness of his parents). Usually, 儿行千里母担忧, 母行千里儿不愁[526] (a mother's thought follows her son from wherever he goes, but a son never worries about her mother no matter where she goes), and even worse, 久病床前无孝子[527] (a parent of prolonged illness finds no filial children at the bedside).

- #169 Parents (父母); #195 Respecting teachers (尊师)

171. Families: exemplary and satisfactory (家庭: 令人羡慕的和令人满意的) 5

Big families were praised by the government in ancient China, so 四世同堂[528] (four generations live in the same house) was viewed as being an exemplary family. For such families, the most desirable scenario was to have 儿孙绕膝[529] (sons and grandsons are playing around parents and grandparents). After the Song and Yuan dynasties, upper-class families would like to boast that their families did not have males who violated the law in three generations or females who remarried in five generations (三世无犯法之男, 五世无再婚之女).[530] For northern rural families, their

---

518 父精母血, 不可弃也 [-, --棄-] fù jīng mǔ xuè, bùkě qì yě (father's-sperm-mother's-blood, not-can-abandon- *marker of affirmation*)

519 父母之命 [-] fùmǔ zhī mìng (parents-'s-order)

520 父母在, 不远游 [-] fùmǔ zài, bù yuǎn yóu (parents-alive, not-far-travel)

521 服丧 [-喪] fúsāng (observe-mourning)

522 天下无不是的父母 [--無-----] tiānxià wú búshì de fùmǔ (world-no-not-correct-'s-parents)

523 父母双全 [--雙-] fùmǔ shuāng quán (parents-both-alive)

524 可怜天下父母心 [-] kělián tiānxià fùmǔ xīn (pitiful-world-parent-heart)

525 养儿方知父母恩[養兒-----]yǎngérfāngzhīfùmǔēn(raise-child-onlywhen-know-parent-kindness)

526 儿行千里母担忧, 母行千里儿不愁 [兒----擔憂, ----兒--] ér xíng qiān lǐ mǔ dānyōu, mú xíng qiān lǐ ér bù chóu (child-travel-1,000-*li*-mother-worry, mother-travel-1,000-*li*-child-not-worry)

527 久病床前无孝子 [--牀-無--] jiǔ bìng chuánqián wú xiàozǐ (long-ill-bed-side-no-filial-child)

528 四世同堂 [-] sì shì tóng tang (4-generation-same-house)

529 儿孙绕膝 [兒孫繞-] érsūn rào xī (children-grandchildren-around-knee)

530 三世无犯法之男, 五世无再婚之女 [--無----, --無----] sān shì wú fànfǎ zhī nán, wǔ shì wú zàihūn zhī nǔ (3-generation-no-violate-law-'s-male, 5-generation-no-again-marry-'s-female)

66 *Social relations, family, women, education*

ideal was 三十亩地一头牛, 老婆孩子热炕头,[531] which means 'it is good enough if a man has 30 acres (mu) of land, one cow, one wife, children and a warm kang (a heatable clay bed).'

- #170 Parents and children (父母与子女); #172 Rule the roost (当家)

172. Rule the roost (当家) 1

当家 or 当家作主 means 'to be the head of the family, manage the house, rule the roost.' The big boss is 大当家的, and the one only next to him is 二当家的. Managing a family is not easy, and it requires responsibility (不当家不知柴米贵,[532] literally 'if one does not keep the house, he does not know how expensive the charcoals and rice are'), so some people would like to be a hands-off leader (甩手掌柜).[533] Children of the poor know the hardships of life sooner (穷人的孩子早当家).[534] The goal of the Chinese Communist Party is to let the people 'be the masters of the country' (当家作主).[535]

173. Husband and wife: good (夫妻: 关系好) 10

Marriage is tied together by a thread of luck (千里姻缘一线牵[536]) and knotted by the god of marriage (月下老人,[537] literally 'old man under the moon.') Before marriage, the couple had to experience the karma of a thousand years (百年修得同船渡, 千年修得共枕眠).[538] After being married, the couple had different roles in life. The husband was the breadwinner and the wife the housemaker (男主外, 女主内),[539] but they worked together harmoniously and respected each other, as in 你耕田来我织布, 我挑水来你浇园[540] (you plow the land and I weave cloth; I carry water and you irrigate the garden), 举案齐眉[541] (husband and wife treating each other with courtesy) and 夫唱妇随[542] (the husband sings and the wife echoes). The couple might have disagreements, but they would reconcile before the next day since 夫妻没有隔夜的仇[543] (there is no overnight feud between husband and wife) and 床头吵架床尾和[544] (a couple's quarrels are quickly mended).

- #50 Share weal or woe? (同甘还是共苦); #174 Husband and wife: bad (夫妻: 关系差)

---

531 三十亩地一头牛, 老婆孩子热炕头 [----頭-, ----熱-頭] sānshí mǔ dì yì tóu niú, lǎopo háizi rè kàngtóu (30-acre-land-one-*measure word*-cow, wife-children-hot-heated clay bed-warmer end)

532 不当家不知柴米贵 [-當-----貴] bù dāngjiā bù zhī cháimǐ guì (not-manage-house-not-know-charcoal-rice-expensive)

533 甩手掌柜 [---櫃] shuǐ shǒu zhǎngguì (off-hand-manager)

534 穷人的孩子早当家 [窮-----當-] qióngrén de háizi zǎo dāngjiā (poor-people-child-early-manage-house)

535 当家作主 [當---] dāngjiā zuòzhǔ (manage-house-be-master)

536 千里姻缘一线牵 [---缘-綫牽] qiān lǐ yīn yuán yí xiàn qiān (1,000-li-predestined marriage-one-thread-tie)

537 月下老人 [] yuè xià lǎorén (moon-under-old-man)

538 百年修得同船渡, 千年修得共枕眠 [-] bǎi nián xiū dé tóng chuán dù, qiān nián xiū dé gòng zhěn mián (100-year-practice-get-same-boat-cross, 1,000-year-practice-get-together-pillow-sleep)

539 男主外, 女主内 [-] nán zhǔ wài, nǚ zhǔ nèi (husband-in charge of-outside, wife-in charge of-inside)

540 你耕田来我织布, 我挑水来你浇园 [---來-織-, ---來-澆園] nǐ gēngtián lái wǒ zhībù, nǐ tiāoshuǐ lái wǒ jiāo yuán (you-plow-land-*filler*-I-weave-cloth, I-carry-water-*filler*-you-irrigate-garden)

541 举案齐眉 [舉-齊-] jǔ àn qí méi (hold-wooden tray-level to-eyebrow)

542 夫唱妇随 [--婦隨] fū chàng fù suí (husband-sing-wife-echo)

543 夫妻没有隔夜的仇 [-] fūqī méiyǒu géyè de chóu (husband and wife-not-have-overnight-'s-feud)

544 床头吵架床尾和 [牀頭--牀--] chuángtóu chǎojià chuángwěi hé (bed-head end-quarrel-bed-tail end-reconcile)

Social relations, family, women, education 67

174. Husband and wife: bad (夫妻: 关系差) 3

Husband and wife do not always live harmoniously; they may quarrel, break and betray each other: 夫妻本是同林鸟, 大难临头各自飞[545] (the husband and wife should be birds of the same forest, but each flies at the sight of great disasters). Husbands may treat their wives as objects (兄弟如手足, 妻子如衣服,[546] brothers are like hands and feet, but wives are like clothing – you can change clothes whenever you want, by Liu Bei (161–223), founder of the State of Shu Han). Women may despise their husbands, 父一而已, 人尽可夫[547] (you have only one father, but every man could be your husband). According to *Zuo Zhuan, The Chronicle of Zuo*, in 697 BCE, Duke Li of Zheng schemed with a minister, Yong Jiu to kill Yong Jiu's father-in-law, a minister in power. Yong Jiu's wife knew the plan and asked her mother what to do. Her mother said: 人尽夫也, 父一而已, 胡可比也? (Every man could be your husband, but you have only one father. The two are not comparable). Then Yong Jiu's wife told her father; her father killed Yong Jiu, and Duke Li was exiled. A man could have many wives (三妻四妾[548]), and a wife could enjoy the advantageous sides of two men as attested by the story, 东食西宿[549]: A girl in the State of Qi is marriageable age and two families propose. The man of the family in the east is ugly but rich, and the man of the family in the west is handsome but poor. The girl's parents cannot decide and ask the girl to decide by herself. If she likes the man in the east family, she will bare her left arm, and vice versa. The girl bares both of her arms and her parents ask why. The girl says: I want to eat with the east family and sleep with the west family (东食西宿).

- #50 Share weal or woe? (同甘还是共苦); #173 Husband and wife: good (夫妻: 关系好)

175. Children (孩子) 5

Chinese people find that the possessions of other families are better, but their own children are always the best (东西是别人的好, 孩子是自己的好).[550] You can tell what a child of three years old is going to be when he is old (三岁看到老,[551] child is father of the man). Since like father like son (有其父必有其子),[552] and dragons will bear dragons and mice are born experts in digging holes (龙生龙, 凤生凤, 老鼠的儿子会打洞).[553] No one likes their foes and debtees, except for two kinds of people, spouse and children (夫妻是前世的冤家, 孩子是前世的债主).[554] All Chinese people agree that daughters are

---

545 夫妻本是同林鸟, 大难临头各自飞 [------鸟, -難臨頭--飛] fūqī běn shì tóng lín niǎo, dànǎn líntóu gèzì fēi (husband and wife-essentially-is-same-woods-bird, great-disaster-arrive-upon-each-oneself-fly)

546 兄弟如手足, 妻子如衣服 [-] xiōngdì rú shǒuzú, qīzi rú yīfu (brothers-like-hand-foot, wife-like-clothes)

547 父一而已, 人尽可夫 [-, -盡--] fù yī éryǐ, rén jìn kě fū (father-one-and only, people-all-can be-husband)

548 三妻四妾 [-] sān qī sì qiè (3-wife-4-concubine)

549 东食西宿 [東---] dōng shí xī sù (east-dine-west-sleep)

550 东西是别人的好, 孩子是自己的好 [東------, -] dōngxi shì biérén de hǎo, háizi shì zìjǐ de hǎo (things-is-other-'s-better, child-is-oneself-'s-better)

551 三岁看到老 [-岁---] sān suì kàn dào lǎo (3-years old-see-through-old)

552 有其父必有其子 [-] yǒu qí fù bì yǒu qí zǐ (have-that-father-must-have-that-son)

553 龙生龙, 凤生凤, 老鼠的儿子会打洞 [龍-龍, 鳳-鳳, ---兒-會--] lóng shēng lóng, fèng shēng fèng, lǎoshǔ de érzi huì dǎdòng (dragon-bear-dragon, phoenix-bear-phoenix, mouse-'s-son-good at-dig-hole)

554 夫妻是前世的冤家, 孩子是前世的债主 [-, ------债-] fūqī shì qiánshì de yuānjiā, háizi shì qiánshì de zhàizhǔ (husband and wife-is-last-life-'s-foe, child-is-last-life-'s-creditor)

68 *Social relations, family, women, education*

small cozy cotton-padded jackets (女儿是父母贴心的小棉袄),[555] but they have not yet reached a consensus what their sons are.

- #170 Parents and children (父母与子女)

176. Cousins (表亲) 2

表亲 refers to second generation kinship. Since Chinese families were populous throughout history, there is a saying 一表三千里, which means 'you can easily find a second generation relative in an area of thousands of square miles' or 'you can connect by a certain kinship with anyone in an area of thousands of square miles.' There is another saying 一代亲, 二代表, 三代就完了, which means 'the first generation kinships are real, the second are not close and the third are gone.'

- #167 Ancestors (祖宗)

177. **Women, regarding sex and marriage** (忠, 贞, 烈的女人) 5

With regard to sex and marriage, Chinese women in history were required to possess three virtues: loyalty (忠), chastity (贞) and martyrdom (烈). When a woman's husband was alive, she should only be loyal to him (从一而终, be faithful to husband until death), no matter what he was like (嫁鸡随鸡, 嫁狗随狗,[556] follow the man you marry, be he fowl or cur). After a woman's husband died, she should not remarry (烈女不嫁二夫,[557] a chaste woman does not marry two husbands). If a girl's fiancé died before the marriage ceremony, she would be encouraged to be a widow (望门寡,[558] literally 'seeing-gate-widow.') If a widow committed suicide for her late or betrothed husband, she would be entitled to have a biography included in 烈女传[559] (biographies of martyrs) in the historical records and to have a chastity memorial arch (贞节牌坊[560]) ordered by the emperor. It was the ideal of many Chinese women to be with their husbands not only in bed but also in the tomb (生要同衾, 死要同穴).[561]

- #180 Women and their names in ancient China (女人的名字); #186 Heroines (女英雄)

178. **Women, unlucky** (倒霉的女人) 5

For a woman, being born in ancient China was a tragedy, from birth to death. From birth, a woman was called 赔钱货[562] (literally 'lose-money-goods'). When she grew up, she did not need to get any talent since 女子无才便是德[563] (a woman is virtuous if she lacks talent, ignorance is a woman's virtue). If she was lucky enough to be beautiful, she would then be considered ominous (红颜祸水).[564] Before marriage, she had her own name, but after the arranged marriage

---

555 女儿是父母贴心的小棉袄 [-兒---贴----襖] nǚ'ér shì fùmǔ tiēxīn de xiǎo mián'ǎo (daughter-is-parents-'s-close to-heart-'s-small-cotton-padded jacket)

556 嫁鸡随鸡, 嫁狗随狗 [-鷄随鷄, --随-] jià jī suí jī, jià gǒu suí gǒu (marry-cock-follow-cock, marry-dog-follow dog)

557 烈女不嫁二夫 [-] liènǚ bú jià èr fū (chaste-woman-not-marry-two-husband)

558 望门寡 [-門-] wàng mén guǎ (see-gate-widow)

559 烈女传 [--傳] liènǚ zhuàn (chaste-woman-biography)

560 贞洁牌坊 [貞潔--] zhēnjié páifang (chastity-memorial arch)

561 生要同衾, 死要同穴 [-] shēng yào tóng qín, sǐ yào tóng xuè (alive-want-same-quilt, dead-will be-same-tomb)

562 赔钱货 [賠錢貨] péiqián huò (lose-money-goods)

563 女子无才便是德 [--無----] nǚzǐ wú cái biàn shì dé (woman-no-talent-then-is-virtue)

564 红颜祸水 [紅顏禍-] hóngyán huòshuǐ (rosy-cheek-ominous-water)

(包办婚姻[565]), she lost her first name and would be called by her husband's last name with the surname marker '氏.' She had to follow the Three Obediences (三从),[566] namely 'obey her father as a daughter, obey her husband as a wife, and obey her sons in widowhood' (未嫁从父, 既嫁从夫, 夫死从子[567]). As a wife, her husband would likely to treat her cruelly as demonstrated in sayings such as 打到的媳妇揉到的面[568] (taming a wife is like kneading a dough, the harder you hit her, the more obedient she will be). She was not trusted to be a good head of the family, since 女人当家, 房倒屋塌[569] (if women control their families, the house will collapse). After she died, her name could not be written in the genealogy of either her father or her husband. Ordinary people did not respect women, and neither Confucius, who once said 唯女子与小人为难养也, 近之则不逊, 远之则怨[570] (Only women and mean persons are hard to get along with. If you get familiar with them, they lose their humility; if you are distant, they resent it).

- #179 Discrimination of women (女人干坏事); #181 Women and goods (女人与货); #183 Earthquakes and women (地震与女人); #184 Wives, housewives and brooms (妻子, 妇女与扫帚)

179. Discrimination of women (女人干坏事) 3

For a long time, younger sisters were called 女弟 (literally 'female younger brother') in Chinese history. 奸 originally meant 'evil, wicked, treacherous,' and it is related to 女 (woman) and 干 (do). This character had two variants, 姧 and 姦, both of which are more closely related to women.

- #178 Women, unlucky (倒霉的女人); #183 Earthquakes and women (地震与女人)

180. Women and their names in ancient China (女人的名字) 3

Chinese women did not have equal status as men throughout imperial history. Even most empresses and princesses did not have names, let alone ordinary women. For example, we only know that the empress of the third emperor of the Ming dynasty had a surname 徐 (xú, Empress Xu). She was well educated. Ironically, in 1404, she compiled a reader 内训 (Women's Code of Conduct), which along with other three books 女诫 (Nǚjiè), 女论语 (Nǚ Lúnyǔ), and 女范捷录 (Nǚfàn Jiélù) are called 女四书 (Women's Four Books). The book would be more valuable if she had appealed for the right for women to have their names.

- #181 Women and goods (女人与货); #182 Prostitutes, other names of (妓女的别称)

181. Women and goods (女人与货) 10

货 (huò) means 'goods, merchandise.' In ancient China, women were discriminated against and associated with 货, for example, 贱货 (jiànhuò, literally 'cheap-goods,' contemptible wretch); 浪货 (lànghuò, literally 'dissolute-goods,' loose woman); 骚货 (sāohuò, literally

---

565 包办婚姻 [-辦--] bāobàn hūnyīn (arrange-marriage)
566 三从 [-從] sān cóng (3-obedience)
567 未嫁从父, 既嫁从夫, 夫死从子 [--從-, --從-, --從-] wèi jià cóng fù, jì jià cóng fū, fū sǐ cóng zǐ (not-married-obedient-father, already-married-obedient-husband, husband-dead-obedient-son)
568 打到的媳妇揉到的面 [----婦---麵] dǎ dào de xífù róu dào de miàn (beat-thoroughly-'s-wife-knead-thoroughly-'s-dough)
569 女人当家, 房倒屋塌 [--當-, -] nǚrén dāngjiā, fáng dǎo wū tā (woman-manage-household, house-collapse-room-sink)
570 唯女子与小人为难养也, 近之则不逊, 远之则怨 [---與--為難養-, --則--, 遠-則-] wéi nǚzǐ yǔ xiǎorén wéi nán yǎng yě, jìn zhī zé bù xùn, yuǎn zhī zé yuàn (only-women-and-mean person-is-hard-accommodate, close to-them-then-not-modest, stay away from-them-then-resent)

70 *Social relations, family, women, education*

'coquettish-goods,' lascivious woman, tart); 二手货 (èrshǒuhuò, literally 'second-hand-goods,' divorced woman); and 赔钱货 (péiqiánhuò, literally 'lose-money-goods,' girl) etc.

- #180 Women and their names in ancient China (女人的名字); #184 Wives, housewives and brooms (妻子, 妇女与扫帚)

182. Prostitutes, other names of (妓女的别称) 2

Prostitution is arguably the oldest profession in the world, including in China where it was officially banned in 1949. Needless to say, underground prostitution does exist and seems to be flourishing. Someone collected terms for prostitutes and got 106 names, including those used in local areas. Actually, the number can be doubled if a little more research were to be conducted. The following are some commonly known terms for prostitutes listed according to their vulgarity from being genteel to being insulting: 青楼女子 (blue-mansion-woman), 风尘女子 (wind-dust-woman), 烟花女子 (smoky-flower-woman), 失足女 (lost-stand-woman), 性工作者 (sex worker, above being genteel or neutral and below vulgar or insulting), 援交妹(compensated-dating-girl, used in Taiwan or related to Japan), 小姐 (miss), 站街女 (stand-street-woman), 妓女 (prostitute), 娼妓 (whore-prostitute), 鸡[571] (chicken, prostitute), 野鸡 (wild-chicken, lowly prostitute), 婊子 (bitch), 破鞋[572] (worn-shoe, whore), 公共汽车 (bus, used in Beijing dialect).

- #178 Women, unlucky (倒霉的女人); #181 Women and goods (女人与货)

183. Earthquakes and women (地震与女人) 3

On September 17, 1303, Shanxi in China experienced the first recorded earthquake with a magnitude of 8.0. It was also one of the deadliest earthquakes of all time, with an estimated 200,000 casualties. The emperor asked for the cause of the catastrophe, and an official replied: 地为阴而主静, 妻道, 臣道, 子道也, 三者失其道, 则地为之弗宁, meaning 'the earth belongs to *yin* and is in charge of peace, which is just like the way of being a wife, a subject of a king, or a son. Now the three ways are all wrong, therefore the earth could not keep the peace.' This is understandable if said by a pedantic scholar, but it was said by 齐履谦 (Qi Lüqian, 1263–1329) who was a famous mathematician and astronomer.

- #58 Heavenly principles (天理); #178 Women, unlucky (倒霉的女人); #179 Discrimination of women (女人干坏事)

184. Wives, housewives and brooms (妻子, 妇女与扫帚) 5

妇 (婦) means 'woman,' especially a 'married woman.' 妻 means 'wife.' Both characters are composed of two major parts, 女 (woman) and 帚 (broom). They show the ancient Chinese mindset that a woman was closely associated with a broom and therefore housework.

- #2 Chinese characters and way of thinking (汉字与思维); #178 Women, unlucky (倒霉的女人)

185. Rosy cheeks (红颜) 5

红颜 literally means 'red-cheeks' and is a synonym for woman, or beautiful woman. Although it sounds like a beautiful word, it has a sad connotation. For example, 红颜知己[573]

---

571 鸡 [鷄] jī (chicken, prostitute)
572 破鞋 [-] pòxié (worn-shoe)
573 红颜知己 [紅顏--] hóngyán zhījǐ (woman-soulmate)

Social relations, family, women, education 71

means 'pretty young lady bosom friend' but carries a connotation that the man loves her but they can only be friends. 红颜薄命[574] means 'beautiful women usually have an unfortunate life.' Even worse, 红颜 is associated with scourges (红颜祸水,[575] beauty if the root of the scourge). The downfall of the Ming dynasty was blamed on a beauty, Chen Yuanyuan (1624–1681), a concubine of Wu Sangui whose surrender to the Qing army caused the Ming dynasty collapse immediately (冲冠一怒为红颜,[576] a burst of anger was just for a beauty).

- #127 Beauty (美女); #197 Soulmates (知己)

186. Heroines (女英雄) 2

Ancient Chinese women wore headdresses (巾帼), so heroines are called 巾帼英雄,[577] for example, 巾帼不让须眉[578] (women are as excellent as their male counterparts). The most famous Chinese heroine known in the West is Mulan (花木兰) who was a woman of true prowess (女中豪杰). Mao Zedong praised women, saying, '女人能顶半边天'[579] (women can hold up half the sky). Nowadays, capable women are called 女强人 (iron lady, superwoman) or 女汉子[580] (tough girl, cowgirl).

- #17 Times and heroes (时势与英雄)

187. The true. . . (真. .). 1

Chinese, like many other historically extensively used languages, is filled with complimentary words. For instance, 教授 (jiàoshòu, professor) is not as flattering a title as a hundred years ago. How does one express the true/real person in an acclamation? Professor and historian 陈寅恪 (Chén Yínkè, or Chén Yínquè, 1890–1969), was a 教授的教授 (professors' professor). The Yuan dynasty Prime Minister 廉希宪 (Lián Xīxiàn, 1231–1280) was revered as 宰相中真宰相, 男子中真男子 (the true prime minister among prime ministers, and a true man among men).

188. Sub-ministerial level universities (副部级大学) 5

It is obvious that Chinese higher education is bureaucratized (教育行政化) since there are currently 31 sub-ministerial level universities (副部级大学),[581] which include Peking University, Tsinghua University, Renmin University of China, Beijing Normal University, etc. Party secretaries (书记) and presidents (校长) of these colleges are appointed by the Organization Department (组织部) of the Central Committee of the Communist Party of China, not by the Ministry of Education (教育部).

- #165 Social hierarchy (等级); #190 Education: importance, content (教育: 重要性和内容)

---

574 红颜薄命 [紅顏--] hóngyán bómìng (beautiful woman-short-life)
575 红颜祸水 [紅顏禍-] hóngyán huòshuǐ (beautiful woman-disastrous-water)
576 冲冠一怒为红颜 [衝冠--為紅顏] chōngguān yí nù wèi hóngyán (pop up-crown-great-anger-for-beautiful woman)
577 巾帼英雄 [-幗--] jīnguó yīngxióng (headdress-hero)
578 巾帼不让须眉 [-幗-讓鬚-] jīnguó bú ràng xūméi (female-not-inferior-male)
579 女人能顶半边天 [---頂-邊-] nǚrén néng dǐng bàn biān tiān (woman-can-hold-half-side-sky)
580 女汉子 [-漢-] nǚ hànzi (female-man)
581 副部级大学 [--級-學] fù-bùjí dàxué (vice-ministerial-level-university)

72   *Social relations, family, women, education*

189. Innovation and Chinese college mottos (大学校训与创新) 3

More than 60 Chinese colleges have roughly, if not exactly, the same motto: 严谨, 勤奋, 求实, 创新,[582] which means 'rigorous, diligent, realistic and innovative.' The colleges include Beijing Medical University, Beijing Institute of Technology, Donghua University (formerly China Textile University), etc. If so many colleges use the same motto, they are not innovative, especially because this motto arguably belongs to and originates from Peking University, the best university in China.

- #39 Old or new (新与旧); #191 Education: learning methods (教育: 学习方法); #192 Learning methods (学习方法)

190. Education: importance, content (教育: 重要性和内容) 5

The most important content found in Chinese education focuses on 'virtue' (德, dé). In ancient China, knowledge could be categorized into two groups, 大学 (great learning) and 小学 (small learning). The purpose of 大学 (great learning) was to cultivate one's virtue. This is reflected in the very first sentence of one of the *Four Books* of Confucianism, *Great Learning*, 大学之道, 在明明德.[583] . . (The way of great learning consists in manifesting one's bright virtue,. .). On the other hand, 小学 (small learning) consisted of three subjects, 文字, 音韵 and 训诂 (philology, phonology and exegesis). Clearly, 'small learning' is not as important as 'great learning.' What did Confucian teach his disciples? 礼乐射御书数[584] (rite, music, archery, driving (a cart), calligraphy and mathematics). 礼 (rite) was the most important. The guidelines in mainland China set forth that the goals of education are 德智体, 德智体美劳,[585] 德智体美 roughly in Mao's era, Deng's era and in the 21st century, respectively. 德 means 'virtue.' 智 means 'intelligence, mental powers.' 体 'PE,' 美 means 'aesthetics,' and 劳 means 'work (ethic).' In the Republic of China, the main educational goals are 德智体群美 with 群 being 'concept of community, collectivism.' In summary, 德 (virtue) is a priority of Chinese education, ancient and modern. Education is so important that one of the worst insults is to say somebody 有娘生, 没爹教[586] (has a mother who gave birth to him, but does not have a father to educate him). While 德 (virtue) should have been able to maintain its high status in education, it lost to the reality of the 1980s and after. There was a saying at that time, 学好数理化, 不如有个好爸爸[587] (to have a rich daddy is better than to study well on math, physics and chemistry).

- #191 Education: learning methods (教育: 学习方法); #193 Value and joy of learning (读书的价值和快乐)

191. Education: learning methods (教育: 学习方法) 3

The method of learning or educating is simply: reading. If you do not know the meaning of something, read it, since 书读百遍, 其义自见/现[588] (when a book is read a hundred times,

---

582 严谨, 勤奋, 求实, 创新 [嚴謹, -奮, -實, 創-] yánjǐn, qínfèn, qiúshí, chuàngxīn (rigorous, diligent, realistic, innovative)

583 大学之道, 在明明德 [-學--, -] dà xué zhī dào, zài míng dé (great-learning-'s-way, consist in-manifest-bright-virtue)

584 礼乐射御书数[禮樂--書數]lǐyuèshèyùshūshù(rite-music-archery-driving-calligraphy-mathematics)

585 德智体美劳 [--體-勞] dé zhì tǐ měi láo (virtue-intelligence-PE-arts-work ethic)

586 有娘生, 没爹教 [-] yǒu niáng shēng, méi diē jiào (have-mother-give birth to, no-father-educate)

587 学好数理化, 不如有个好爸爸 [學-數--, ---個---] xué hǎo shùlǐhuà, bùrú yǒu gè hǎo bàba (learn-well-mathematics-physics-chemistry, not as good as-have-a-good-father)

588 书读百遍, 其义自见/现 [書讀--, -義-見/現] shū dú bǎi biàn, qí yì zì jiàn/xiàn (book-read-100-time, its-meaning-self-appear)

Social relations, family, women, education 73

its meaning naturally becomes clear). If you do not know how to write an essay, read books, since 读书破万卷, 下笔如有神[589] (after you have read more than 10,000 volumes, you will find it easy to write as if God were there helping you). If you cannot write a poem, read poetry, since 熟读唐诗三百首, 不会作诗也会吟[590] (if you have read the *Three Hundred Tang Poems* enough times, you will definitely be able to recite some even if you cannot write one). Is reading fun? Not at all. All children in ancient China had to read one of the *Four Books*, 中庸 (the *Doctrine of the Mean*). However, that book is so hard to read that there was a saying among children, 中庸中庸, 屁股打得通红[591] (or 打得屁股通红), which means 'the *Doctrine of the Mean*? Oh No! My butt is still very red after being spanked.' Most people did not know how to read because they just read without thinking (好读书不求甚解,[592] love reading but make no effort to understand the real meaning). Even if students wanted to know further details, they were not allowed because their teachers/masters almost unanimously followed the way set by the forefather of Chinese education, Confucius, 不能极问[593] (not allowed to ask for details and why). In this way, reading is tiresome, but one has to be diligent (书山有路勤为径, 学海无涯苦作舟,[594] up the mountain of books, there is a path of diligence; across the boundless sea of learning, there is a boat made from hard work). There are many exemplary stories of studying hard, for example, 囊萤映雪[595] (read by the light of bagged fireflies or the reflected light of snow) and 凿壁偷光[596] (bore a hole in the wall to get some light from a neighbor's home). Are reading and grades really important? Yes, since 考考考, 老师的法宝; 分分分, 学生的命根[597] (exam, exam, exam, the teacher's magic weapon; grade, grade, grade, the student's very life).

- #192 Learning methods (学习方法)

192. Learning methods (学习方法) 1

The Chinese people are good copycats (照猫画虎,[598] copy something without catching its spirit), but in the realm of arts, a prominent Chinese painter, Qi Baishi (1864–1957) had a famous saying, 学我者生, 似我者死[599] (those who would try to grasp my spirit will survive, but those who just copy my techniques will not).

- #191 Education: learning methods (教育: 学习方法)

---

589 读书破万卷, 下笔如有神 [讀書-萬-, -筆---] rúshū pò wàn juàn, xiàbǐ rú yǒu shén (read-book-exceeding-10,000-volume, begin-write-as-have-god)

590 熟读唐诗三百首, 不会作诗也会吟 [-讀-詩---, -會-詩-會-] shú dú Tángshī sānbǎi shǒu, búhuì zuòshī yě huì yín (proficiently-read-Tang-poem-300-*measure word*, not-able to-compose-poem-still-can-chant)

591 中庸中庸, 屁股打得通红 [-, -----紅] Zhōngyōng Zhōngyōng, pìgǔ dǎ de tōnghóng (Doctrine of the Mean-Doctrine of the Mean, butt-beaten-very red)

592 好读书不求甚解[-讀書----]hào dúshū bù qiú shèn jiě(love-reading-not-seek-deep-understanding)

593 不能极问 [--極問] bùnéng jí wèn (not-allowed-extremely-ask)

594 书山有路勤为径, 学海无涯苦作舟 [書----為徑, 學-無----] shū shān yǒu lù qín wéi jìng, xué hǎi wú yá kǔ zuò zhōu (book-mountain-have-road-diligence-be-trail, learning-sea-no-boundary-endurance-be-boat)

595 囊萤映雪 [-螢--] náng yíng yìng xuě (bag-firefly-reflect-snow)

596 凿壁偷光 [鑿---] záo bì tōu guāng (bore-wall-steal-light)

597 考考考, 老师的法宝; 分分分, 学生的命根 [-, -師--寶; -, -學----] kǎo kǎo kǎo, lǎoshī de fǎbǎo; fēn fēn fēn, xuéshēng de mìnggēn (exam-exam-exam, teacher-'s magic weapon; score-score-score, student-'s-lifeblood)

598 照猫画虎 [--畫-] zhào māo huà hǔ (model-cat-draw-tiger)

599 学我者生, 似我者死[學---,-]xuéwǒzhěshēng, sìwǒzhěsǐ(study-me-person-survive, imitate-me-person-die)

74 *Social relations, family, women, education*

193. **Value and joy of learning** (读书的价值和快乐) 5

Reading Confucian books and competing in the Imperial Examinations (科举考试) could change a person's life completely, because 书中自有黄金屋, 书中自有颜如玉[600] (in books are sumptuous houses and fair ladies, learning brings everything) and even could bring about a miracle 朝为田舍郎, 暮登天子堂[601] (literally 'a country boy in the morning can be a minister in imperial court in the evening'). Feudal rules preached that 万般皆下品, 唯有读书高[602] (learning is above all trades) and 满朝朱紫贵, 尽是读书人[603] (all ministers in splendid costumes in the imperial court are diligent learners). Is reading fun? It depends on your determination and will. A prominent poet of the Southern Song dynasty, Lu You (1125–1210) wrote a couplet for his study room, 万卷古今消永日, 一窗昏晓送流年 (literally '10,000 books, past and present, can steal a whole day easily, and reading by the window, day and night, ages you quickly.')

- #190 Education: importance, content (教育: 重要性和内容)

194. **Teacher and student, master and apprentice** (师生, 师徒) 5

Teacher and student, or master and apprentice was probably the most important human relationship beyond the basic five, i.e., ruler and subject (君臣), father and son (父子), husband and wife (夫妇), brothers (兄弟) and friends (朋友). Teachers, along with Heaven, Earth, monarchy and parents, were worshipped in ancient China. The relationship between a master and apprentice, or teacher and student, is similar to that of a father and son (师徒如父子),[604] and a teacher for one day is a father for a lifetime (一日为师, 终身为父).[605] Students/apprentices must follow their teacher's/master's instructions (萧规曹随[606]) and could not ask endless questions (不能极问).[607] However, some ingenious scholars encouraged students excel beyond their teachers. Xunzi (313 BCE–238 BCE) said, 'the student surpasses the master' (青出于蓝而胜于蓝[608]), and Han Yu (768–824) said in his well-known essay, *师说*[609] (On teachers), 'the student need not be inferior to the teacher' (弟子不必不如师).[610]

- #195 Respecting teachers (尊师)

---

600 书中自有黄金屋, 书中自有颜如玉 [書------, 書---颜--] shū zhōng zì yǒu huángjīn wū, shū zhōng zì yǒu yán rú yù (book-inside-naturally-have-gold-room, book-inside-naturally-have-beauty)

601 朝为田舍郎, 暮登天子堂 [-] zhāo wéi tiánshè láng, mù dēng tiānzǐ tang (morning-is-country-boy, evening-ascend to-emperor-court)

602 万般皆下品, 唯有读书高 [萬----, --讀書-] wàn bān jiē xiǎpǐn, wéi yǒu dúshū gāo (10,000-profession-all-low-rank, only-learning-high)

603 满朝朱紫贵, 尽是读书人 [滿---貴, 盡-讀書-] mǎn cháo zhūzǐ guì, jìn shì dúshū rén (whole-court-red-purple-noble, all-are-learned-people)

604 师徒如父子 [師----] shītú rú fùzǐ (master and disciple-like-father and son)

605 一日为师, 终身为父 [--為師, 終-爲-] yī rì wéi shī, zhōngshēn wéi fù (one-day-as-teacher, whole-life-as-father)

606 萧规曹随 [蕭規-隨] Xiāo guī Cáo suí (Xiao He-set rules-Cao Shen-follow)

607 不能极问 [--極問] bùnéng jí wèn (not-allowed-extremely-ask)

608 青出于蓝而胜于蓝 [--於藍-勝於藍] qīng chū yú lán ér shèng yú lán (indigo-out-of-blue-but-exceed-than-blue)

609 师说 [師說] shī shuō (teacher-commentary)

610 弟子不必不如师 [------師] dìzǐ búbì bùrú shī (disciple-not-necessary-not-as good as-teacher)

Social relations, family, women, education 75

195. Respecting teachers (尊师) 5

In ancient China and some contemporary East Asian countries, teachers and their teaching are highly valued (尊师重道).[611] Teachers are usually models of virtue for others (为人师表).[612] Teachers, along with Heaven, Earth, the monarchy and ancestors (天地君亲师[613]), would be offered sacrifices at least once a year by every family. In Taiwan, Teacher's Day (教师节[614]) is on September 28, which is also Confucius' birthday. In mainland China, Teacher's Day is September 10.

- #194 Teacher and student, master and apprentice (师生, 师徒)

196. Friends and friendship (朋友, 友谊) 5

Friends (朋友) constitute one of the five human relationships in Confucian ethics, and the basic requirement for being friends is 'trust' (信). Childhood sweethearts (青梅竹马[615]) are intimate (两小无猜).[616] Girls' bosom friends are called 闺密[617]/闺蜜, and men's sworn friends are 铁哥们儿,[618] who would shed blood for friends (为朋友两肋插刀,[619] literally 'be stabbed in a friend's stead'). Men should not take advantage of the wives of the friends (朋友妻, 不可欺).[620] It is true that the more friends you have, the more options you have (多个朋友多条路),[621] but people following different paths won't consult each other (道不同不相为谋).[622] Westerners say that friendship lasts forever (友谊地久天长,[623] Auld Lang Syne), but the Chinese say 君子之交淡如水[624] (the friendship between gentlemen is as pure as water). The extremely popular American television sitcom *Friends* is translated as 老友记 in Chinese.

- #164 Human relations (人际关系); #197 Soulmates (知己)

197. Soulmates (知己) 5

It is said in the West that one can have only three to five close friends at a time. Three to five may be small; however, it is still much larger than the number a Chinese person can have, which is one. Lu Xun excerpted two lines of verse and made up a couplet 人生得一知己足矣, 斯世当以同怀视之,[625] which means 'one should feel blessed to

---

611 尊师重道 [-師--] zūn shī zhòng dào (respect-teacher-value-moral)
612 为人师表 [為-師-] wéi rén shī biǎo (serve as-people's-teacher-model)
613 天地君亲师 [---親師] tiān dì jūn qīn shī (heaven-earth-monarchy-parents-teacher)
614 教师节 [-師節] jiàoshī jié (teacher-day)
615 青梅竹马 [---馬] qīngméi zhú mǎ (green-plum-bamboo-horse)
616 两小无猜 [--無-] liǎng xiǎo wú cāi (two-little children-no-suspicion)
617 闺密 [閨-] guīmì (lady's chamber-close friend)
618 铁哥们儿 [鐵-們-] tiěgēménr (alloyed/inseparable-buddy)
619 为朋友两肋插刀 [為------] wèi péngyou liǎnglèi chā dāo (for-friend-both-rib-stab-knife)
620 朋友妻, 不可欺 [-] péngyou qī, bùkě qī (friend's-wife, not-allowed-take advantage)
621 多个朋友多条路 [-個---條-] duō ge péngyou duō tiáo lù (more-measure word-friend-more-measure word-way)
622 道不同不相为谋 [-----為謀] dào bùtóng bù xiāng wéi móu (path-not-same-not-each other-do-consult)
623 友谊地久天长 [-誼---長] yǒuyì dìjiǔ tiāncháng (friendship-last forever)
624 君子之交淡如水 [-] jūnzi zhī jiāo dàn rú shuǐ (gentlemen-'s-socialization-pure-like-water)
625 人生得一知己足矣, 斯世当以同怀视之 [-,--當--懷視-] rénshēng dé yī zhījǐ zú yǐ, sī shì dāng yǐ tóng huái shì zhī (life-get-one-soulmate-enough-*marker of affirmation*, that-life-should-use-same-heart-view-it)

76 *Social relations, family, women, education*

have a soulmate, and he should cherish this friendship for the rest of his life.' A soulmate is someone who you can open your heart to (交心, literally 'exchange heart/mind') and who is appreciative of your talents and soul (知音, literally 'appreciate-music.') The word '知音'[626] originated from a touching story from early Warring States period: Boya was good at playing Chinese zither (qin), and Zhong Ziqi was good at appreciating music. When Boya was playing and thinking of high mountains, Ziqi would say, 'how towering like Mount Tai!' When Boya was playing and thinking of flowing water, Ziqi would say, 'how vast like rivers!' When Ziqi died, Boya broke his zither and never played again. Since then, 高山流水[627] (high mountains and flowing water) became a synonym for appreciation and 知音 a soulmate. A gentleman can die for his soulmate (士为知己者死).[628] Bosom friends are like close neighbors even though they may be poles apart (海内存知己, 天涯若比邻).[629] When they meet, a thousand toasts are only a few (酒逢知己千杯少[630]) since bosom friends are so few, who else can really appreciate you (知音少, 弦断有谁听,[631] a line in a verse by Yue Fei).

- #185 Rosy cheeks (红颜); #196 Friends and friendship (朋友, 友谊)

198. Boss (老板) 2

The Chinese Communist Party advocates using 同志 (comrade) as a common term of address among party members. However, government officials actually use 老板 (boss) to refer to senior officials. This was definitely influenced by the business world. Using 老板 instead of 同志 shows government officials have 江湖气 (sly in the ways of the world), which is generally contrary to how the laws regulate.

- #164 Human relations (人际关系); #165 Social hierarchy (等级)

199. Bo Le (伯乐) 2

For a Chinese, the greatest fortune he could ever have is to come across Bo Le (伯乐, 680 BCE–610 BCE), a horse tamer whose name became synonymous with 'a good judge of (especially hidden) talent' as demonstrated in a Chinese idiom 伯乐相马[632] (literally 'Bo Le looks over a horse) and a famous saying 千里马常有, 而伯乐不常有[633] (talents are everywhere, however, the people who can recognize them are rare). If you are lucky enough to have met one, he is your 贵人[634] (literally 'respectable person') or 人生导师 (life advisor), to use a

---

626 知音 [-] zhīyīn (appreciate-music)

627 高山流水 [-] gāoshān liúshuǐ (high-mountain-flowing-water)

628 士为知己者死 [-] shì wèi zhījǐ zhě sǐ (gentleman-for-soulmate-people-die)

629 海内存知己, 天涯若比邻 [-, ----鄰] hǎinèi cún zhījǐ, tiānyá ruò bǐlín (world-inside-exist-soulmate, end of the world-like-neighbor)

630 酒逢知己千杯少 [-] jiǔ féng zhījǐ qiān bēi shǎo (drinking-meet-soulmate-1,000-cup-too less)

631 知音少, 弦断有谁听 [-, -斷-誰聽] zhīyīn shǎo, xián duàn yǒu shéi tīng (soulmate-less, string-broken-have-somebody-tell)

632 伯乐相马 [-樂-馬] Bólè xiàng mǎ (Bo Le-look over-horse)

633 千里马常有, 而伯乐不常有 [--馬--, --樂---] qiānlǐmǎ cháng yǒu, ér Bólè bù cháng yǒu (talent-often-have, but-Bo Le-not-often-have)

634 贵人 [貴-] guìrén (respectable-person)

Social relations, family, women, education 77

more contemporary expression. If one is talented but not lucky enough to have met a Bo Le, he 怀才不遇[635] (has unrecognized talents).

- #138 Flunky vs. talent (奴才vs. 人才)

200. Middlemen (中间人) 2

Chinese people lack business sense and drive. Guangdong Province is known for being the birthplace of Chinese foreign trade after the economic reforms of the late 1970s. However, there is a popular saying among Cantonese people, 不做中, 不做保, 不做媒人三世好,[636] which means 'do not be a middleman, do not be a guarantor, do not be a match-maker, and you will be free of any trouble for three generations.'

- #164 Human relations (人际关系)

201. Experienced and inexperienced (内行与外行) 2

Some say that the Chinese people 内斗内行, 外斗外行[637] (are experienced at internal strife, inexperienced/indifferent in fighting their real external enemies). 内行 and 外行 people see differently. 内行看门道, 外行看热闹 means 'The dilettante watches the scene of bustle, the adept guard the entrance.'

202. Copycatting culture (山寨文化) 2

'Copycatting culture' (山寨文化[638]) has a strong base in China since many hold the opinion that the world owes a lot to China since it has greatly benefitted from the Four Great Inventions (四大发明) of China in history but had not paid any patent fee to China. Now it is time for China to even the score.

- #44 Shortcuts (捷径)

203. Foreign and rustic (洋与土) 2

洋 (foreign), the word itself and the things it is associated with, leaves mixed impressions for most Chinese people. They could be positive, such as 洋气 (stylish) and 洋楼 (beautiful single house), or more likely, negative, such as 洋鬼子 (foreign devil) and 崇洋媚外[639] (idolize foreign things). Foreign-brown-nosers say 外国的月亮比中国的圆[640] (the moon in foreign countries is rounder than it is in China). The absolute acceptance or refusal to

---

635 怀才不遇 [懷---] huái cái bú yù (have-talent-not-met)
636 不做中, 不做保, 不做媒人三世好 [-] bú zuòzhōng, bú zuòbǎo, bú zuò méirén sān shì hǎo (not-be-middleman, not-be-guarantor, not-be-matchmaker-3-generation-good)
637 内斗内行, 外斗外行 [-鬥--, -鬥--] nèidòu nèiháng, wàidòu wàiháng (internal-fight-expert, external-fight-inexperienced)
638 山寨文化 [-] shānzhài wénhuà (mountain-fortress-culture)
639 崇洋媚外 [-] chóng yáng mèi wài (worship-overseas-toady to-foreign)
640 外国的月亮比中国的圆 [-國-----過--] wàiguó de yuèliang bǐ Zhōngguó de yuán (foreign-country-'s-moon-compared with-China-'s-round)

78 *Social relations, family, women, education*

foreign things is not good either, and the best way might be to 洋为中用[641] (adapt foreign things for Chinese use) or 中学为体, 西学为用[642] (utilize Chinese learning for fundamental principles and Western learning for practical uses), which is a principle advocated by Zhang Zhidong (1837–1909), a very influential official and reformer during the late Qing dynasty.

- #37 Stress the past, not the present (厚古薄今); #202 Copycatting culture (山寨文化); #204 Foreign and imported goods (洋货)

204. **Foreign and imported goods** (洋货) 1

When China was forced to open its doors to the Western countries from mid-1800s to mid-1900s, foreign merchandise (洋货) was introduced to China, usually with a 洋 (foreign) included in their names, such as 洋火 (火 means 火柴, match); 洋胰子 (胰子 means 香皂, soap); and 洋装 (foreign attire). Along with the foreign trade arose a mixed language, namely 洋泾浜 (Chinese Pidgin English). The Shanghai International Settlement (上海公共租界, 1863–1941) was known for being bustling and prosperous, and was also called 十里洋场.[643] Now the treaties had been dissolved long time before, but the word '十里洋场' survived and carries a tone of slight compliment. It seems people only remember the prosperity of that place, but ignore the history of humiliation.

- #202 Copycatting culture (山寨文化); #203 Foreign and rustic (洋与土)

---

641 洋为中用 [-為--] yáng wéi Zhōng yòng (foreign-by-China-use)
642 中学为体, 西学为用 [-學為體, -學為-] Zhōng xué wéi tǐ, xīxué wéi yòng (Chinese-learning-as-fundamental, Western-learning-for-use)
643 十里洋场 [---場] shílǐ yángchǎng (ten-mile-foreign-place)

6   Nature, animals, language (自然, 动物, 语言)

205. Blue mountains (青山) 1

Mountains are a part of objective reality, and blue mountains (青山) are a symbol of it in Chinese culture. 青山绿水 (blue mountains and green waters) is a synonym for beautiful scenery. We hope friendship lasts forever, just like the blue mountains never grow old and the green waters always flow on (青山不老, 绿水长流).[644] If you failed, a Chinese would comfort you with a saying 留得青山在, 不怕没柴烧[645] (keep to the blue mountains and you don't have to worry about where to get firewood, while there is life, there is hope).

- #206 Water (水)

206. Water (水) 3

Water is vital to human beings. However, when the word 'water' (水) is combined with other words and thus has an extended meaning, the meaning is usually negative, for example, 最水状元 (worst first-round pick, for example, in the NBA draft), 水很深[646] (there is too much non-public information that outsiders cannot get), 泼冷水[647] (pour cold water on, discourage), 泼脏水[648] (throw mud at, slander) and women are 红颜祸水[649] (beauty is the root of the scourge).

- #205 Blue mountains (青山); #207 Water and fire/soil/wind (水火/水土/风水)

207. Water and fire/soil/wind (水火/水土/风水) 2

Water and fire are incompatible (水火不容).[650] If two people are enemies or foes, they are 势如水火 (like fire and water). If one's situation is terribly miserable, he is in 水深火热[651] (an abyss of suffering). Be cautious of flood or fire since they have no mercy for anyone (水火无情).[652] If you did not feel very well at a new place, old people would say that you are 水土不服[653] (not

---

644 青山不老, 绿水长流 [-, 綠-長-] qīngshān bù lǎo, lǜshuǐ cháng liú (blue-mountain-never-grow old, green-waters-always-flow)

645 留得青山在, 不怕没柴烧 [-, ----烧] liú dé qīngshān zài, búpà méi chái shāo (keep-get-green-mountain-exist, not-worry-no-charcoal-burn)

646 水很深 [-] shuǐ hěn shēn (water-very-deep)

647 泼冷水 [潑--] pō lěngshuǐ (pour-cold-water)

648 泼脏水 [潑髒-] pō zāngshuǐ (throw-dirty-water)

649 红颜祸水 [紅顏禍-] hóngyán huòshuǐ (rosy-cheek-perilous-water)

650 水火不容 [-] shuǐhuǒ bùróng (water-fire-not-compatible)

651 水深火热 [---熱] shuǐ shēn huǒ rè (water-deep-fire-hot)

652 水火无情 [--無-] shuǐ huǒ wú qíng (flood-fire-no-mercy)

653 水土不服 [-] shuǐ tǔ bù fú (water-soil-not-acclimatized)

80 *Nature, animals, language*

used to the water and soil), and their suggestion would be to bring a bag of dirt from your hometown and take it to wherever you go. If you do not feel well, add some dirt into the water since 一方水土养一方人[654] (the unique features of a local environment always give special characteristics to its inhabitants, you are where you live). The geomancy of the place you live in is 风水 (feng shui). It is said that Xi'an, Nanjing, Luoyang and Beijing are places of excellent geomantic quality (风水宝地).[655] Practicing feng shui (看风水) is not a legal profession but actually pays very well. It is not easy to be a convincing feng shui master (风水先生).[656]

- #206 Water (水)

208. Super 'wind' (超级风) 1

The wind (风, fēng) is a natural phenomenon. It is suitable to combine 风 with words of other natural phenomena, and 风 is always in front of other words, for example, 风云 (wind-cloud, stormy or unstable situations); 风雨 (wind-rain, trials and hardships); 风霜 (wind-frost, hardships of a journey or in one's life); 风雪 (wind-snow, snowstorm); 风雷 (wind-thunder, tempest); 风浪 (wind-tide, storm);风潮 (wind-tide, unrest) etc.

209. Flowers and willows (花柳) 2

Flowers are beautiful, and willows are tender, and in combination, they are a symbol of women, often a more negative one, for example, 花街柳巷 (red-light district), 寻花问柳 (visit brothels), 墙花路柳 (woman of the street), 残花败柳[657] (fallen woman) and 花柳病[658] (venereal disease) etc. The literal and immediate extended meanings are still seen in words such as 花红柳绿 (profusion of garden flowers) and 柳暗花明[659]/花明柳暗 (beauteous scene).

- #210 Flowers, grass, trees (花草木)

210. Flowers, grass, trees (花草木) 1

When 花 (flower) and 草 (grass) are used in a pattern together, they often refer to 'women,' for example, 拈花惹草[660] (fool around with women) and 墙花路草[661]/柳 (woman of the street). When 草 (grass) and 木 (tree) are used in the same pattern, they often refer to all (nonhuman) things, for example, 一草一木[662] (every little thing); 草木皆兵[663] (literally 'grass and trees are all soldiers,' a state of extreme nervousness); and 人非草木, 孰能无情[664] (men are human and none are heartless).

- #209 Flowers and willows (花柳)

---

654 一方水土养一方人 [----養---] yī fāng shuǐtǔ yǎng yī fāng rén (one-place-water and soil-raise-one-place-people)
655 风水宝地 [風-寶-] fēngshuǐ bǎodì (feng shui-treasure-place)
656 风水先生 [風---] fēngshuǐ xiānsheng (feng shui-master)
657 残花败柳 [殘-敗-] cán huā bài liǔ (withered-flower-dead-willow)
658 花柳病 [-] huāliǔbìng (flower-willow-disease)
659 柳暗花明 [-] liǔ àn huā míng (willow-obscure-flower-bright)
660 拈花惹草 [-] niān huā rě cǎo (pick-flower-stir-grass)
661 墙花路草 [墙---] qiáng huā lù cǎo (wall-flower-road-grass)
662 一草一木 [-] yì cǎo yí mù (one-grass-one-tree)
663 草木皆兵 [-] cǎomù jiē bīng (grass-tree-all-soldier)
664 人非草木, 孰能无情 [-] rén fēi cǎomù, shú néng wúqíng (people-not-grass-tree, who-can-not have-emotion)

Nature, animals, language 81

211. Flowers and unfaithfulness (花与不忠) 2

The original and the main contemporary meaning of 花 is 'flower,' which is usually positive; however, in the following words, especially when duplicated, 花 has a negative connotation: 花心 (fickle), 花花世界 (world of sensual pleasures), 花花公子 (playboy), 花花太岁 (ancient Chinese playboy) and 花花肠子 (flower-flower-intestine, scheme). We can say, '在这个花花世界, 中国的花花太岁和外国的花花公子都是花心, 对女人都有花花肠子,' which requires no further explanation as long as you add up the individual meanings.

- #209 Flowers and willows (花柳)

212. Peonies and prosperous (牡丹和富贵) 2

The peony is widely regarded as the national flower of the People's Republic of China. There are two adjectives closely associated with the peony: 雍容华贵[665] (be poised and stately) and 国色天香[666] (peerlessly beautiful and unsurpassably fragrant). In China, the peony is called 花中之王 (king of the flower) and is a symbol of prosperity. Many people gift a new home or company a painting of peonies (花开富贵[667]) to wish a prosperous future. The most famous species of Chinese peony is 洛阳牡丹 (Luoyang peony).

- #129 Rich and powerful (富贵)

213. Four Noblemen (四君子) 2

Four kinds of flowers or plants are considered to be 'four noblemen' of all flowers by ancient Chinese literati. They are plum (梅, méi), orchid (兰, lán), bamboo (竹, zhú), and chrysanthemum (菊, jú). Paintings and poetry of these plants were a major literary phenomena in ancient China. Interestingly enough, all of the four characters come with the second tone in Mandarin Chinese. In Korea, the order of the Four Noblemen is 梅兰菊竹, slightly different from the Chinese 梅兰竹菊.

- #34 Refined and popular (雅俗)

214. Tigers (老虎) 2

In Chinese culture, tigers are seen as powerful and auspicious, so 虎 is often mentioned with dragon (龙) in this regard, for example, 龙争虎斗 (a fierce battle between two giants), 生龙活虎 (full of vigor and vitality), 藏龙卧虎 (hidden talents) and 龙骧虎步 (an imposing air). Tigers are also fierce and dangerous, so the word 虎 in proverbs tends to carry a negative connotation, for example, 一山不容二虎 (two tigers cannot share one mountain); 不入虎穴, 焉得虎子 (nothing good comes without risk); and 虎毒不食子 (even a monster would not hurt its own children).

215. Dogs (狗) 5

As man's best friend, dogs only began to be given their due respect and fair treatment in China recently. However, the Chinese language has a very long history. This being said, the word/character '狗' (dog) in the Chinese language carries a negative connotation in almost

---

665 雍容华贵 [--華貴] yōngróng huáguì (graceful-gorgeous)
666 国色天香 [國---] guósè tiānxiāng (national-beauty-celestial-fragrance)
667 花开富贵 [-開-貴] huākāi fùguì (flower-blossom-rich-powerful)

82 *Nature, animals, language*

all compound words and phrases, for example, 狗东西[668] (damn thing), 狗崽子 (puppy, son of a bitch), 走狗[669] (lackey), 狗腿子[670] (henchman), 狗咬狗[671] (dogfight), 狗改不了吃屎[672] (the fox may grow gray, but never good), 狗眼看人低[673] (be damned snobbish) and 狗嘴里吐不出象牙[674] (what can you expect from a hog but a grunt), to name only a few. The only exception is 儿不嫌母丑, 狗不嫌家贫[675] (a child will not loathe his mother however ugly, and a dog will not shun a home however poor).

- #216 Dogs and chicken/pigs (鸡犬/猪狗)

216. Dogs and chicken/pigs (鸡犬/猪狗) 2

鸡 (rooster, hen or chick) and 狗 (dog) are important poultry and domestic animals that were vital to the lives of ancient Chinese people, who in return developed a profound affection for them. However, when the two words are used together, they will usually convey a negative connotation, for example, 鸡飞狗跳[676] (chicken-fly-dog-jump, in turmoil) and 鸡犬升天[677] (chicken-dog-ascend-heaven, relatives and followers of a high official were promoted after him) etc. There is even a superstition 鸡狗不到头[678] that means the marriage of a couple born in the year of rooster and the year of the dog cannot last. The combination of 猪 (pig) and 狗 is even worse, for example, 猪狗不如[679] (worse than pigs and dogs, lower than low).

- #215 Dogs (狗)

217. Cows (牛) 1

Cattles (牛) are known for their strength to plow field and they were so important for Chinese agriculture that every Chinese administration in history protected cows from being slaughtered without a good reason. Basically, phrases with 牛 are not negative except 吹牛拍马 (chuīniú pāimǎ, to boast and to flatter,) 对牛弹琴 (duìniú tánqín, to play thither to a cow, to cast pearls before swine,) and some modern ones. The two most famous and positive sayings about cows and calves are 初生牛犊不怕虎 (chūshēng niúdú bú pà hǔ, youth knows no fear) and (横眉冷对千夫指,) 俯首甘为孺子牛[680] (head-bowed, like a willing ox I serve the children) which is a line of verse from Lu Xun's poem '自嘲' (self-satire) written in 1932.

- #218 Symbolism of goats (羊的象征意义)

---

668 狗东西 [-東-] gǒudōngxi (dog-creature)
669 走狗 [-] zǒu gǒu (walking-dog)
670 狗腿子 [-] gǒutuǐzi (dog-leg-man)
671 狗咬狗 [-] gǒu yǎo gǒu (dog-bite-dog)
672 狗改不了吃屎 [-] gǒu gǎi bùliǎo chīshǐ (dog-change-not-able to-eat-poop)
673 狗眼看人低 [-] gǒu yǎn kàn rén dī (dog-eye-look at-people-low)
674 狗嘴里吐不出象牙 [--裏-----] gǒu zuǐ lǐ tǔ bù chū xiàngyá (dog-mouth-inside-spit-not-out-elephant tusk)
675 儿不嫌母丑, 狗不嫌家贫 [兒---醜, ----貧] ér bù xián mǔ chǒu, gǒu bù xián jiā pín (son-not-loathe-mother-ugly, dog-not-loathe-home-poor)
676 鸡飞狗跳 [鷄飛--] jī fēi gǒu tiào (chicken-fly-dog-jump)
677 鸡犬升天 [鷄---] jī quǎn shēng tiān (chicken-dog-ascend-heaven)
678 鸡狗不到头 [鷄---頭] jī gǒu bú dào tóu (chicken-dog-not-arrive-end)
679 猪狗不如 [-] zhū gǒu bù rú (pig-dog-not-equal to)
680 俯首甘为孺子牛 [---爲---] fǔshǒu gān wéi rúzǐniú (bow-head-willing-be-children-calf)

Nature, animals, language   83

218. Symbolism of goats (羊的象征意义) 2

Many emperors of ancient China offered a goat, among many other treasures such as jade, maps and household registration books, when they surrendered to their enemies. Goats (羊) are a symbol of auspiciousness (祥, xiáng), docility or submission. Therefore, presenting a goat (献羊) is a symbol of wishing the winner 'auspicious' fortune while the presenter is submissive and his fate is at the winner's discretion.

219. Monkeys (猴子) 2

Human beings and monkeys, such as rhesus macaques, share 97.5% of their DNA, and Chinese people thought human beings evolved from monkeys before knowledge of the gene was known to the public. However, the Chinese word 猴 (monkey) carries a negative connotation in almost all fixed expressions. For example, an ugly guy is described as 尖嘴猴腮[681] (having pointed mouth and monkey's cheek) and a worthless person in imposing attire is 沐猴而冠[682] (a rhesus with a hat on, mule in horse harness). Monkeys are mocked for not being intelligent (猴子捞月,[683] monkeys rescue the moon, an empty effort) and scared by a chicken being killed on the spot (杀鸡骇猴,[684] beat the dog before the lion). Days that will never come are called 猴年马月[685] (year of the monkey and month of the horse). Monkeys finally hold their heads high, but only when the tigers are absent (山中无老虎, 猴子称大王,[686] when the cat's away, the mice will play).

220. Bats (蝙蝠) 2

Bats (蝙蝠, biānfú) are ugly mammals, but their gloomy image in the Chinese mind is reversed by the sound of their name, which is associated with an auspicious Chinese word 福 (fú, fortune, fortunate). Fortune (福) is abstract, but bats (蝙蝠) are concrete, so on Chinese auspicious paintings bats are commonly used as a symbol of fortune. For example, 多福多寿[687] (live long and prosper) was a common blessing in ancient China, and the common image of this blessing is many (usually five) bats (蝙蝠) above a tree full of peaches.

- #121 Custom (风俗); #264 Homophonic puns (谐音双关)

221. Fish and meat (鱼与肉) 1

Fish and meat were both luxury foods in ancient China, so when the two words are used in conjunction, they mean 'sumptuous diet, square meal.' Rulers were addicted to abundant fish and meat (大鱼大肉), but this also had the meaning of 'the fat of the people.' Therefore, rulers were like the knife and cutting board, and the people were like fish (人为刀俎, 我为鱼肉),[688] destined to be cruelly oppressed (鱼肉百姓).

---

681 尖嘴猴腮 [-] jiān zuǐ hóu sāi (pointy-mouth-monkey-cheek)
682 沐猴而冠 [-] mùhóu ér guàn (rhesus-monkey-but-crown)
683 猴子捞月 [--捞-] hóuzi lāo yuè (monkey-fishing-moon)
684 杀鸡骇猴 [殺鷄駭-] shā jī hài hóu (kill-chicken-threaten-monkey)
685 猴年马月 [--馬-] hóu nián mǎ yuè (monkey-year-horse-month)
686 山中无老虎, 猴子称大王 [--無--, --稱--] shān zhōng wú lǎohǔ, hóuzi chēng dàwáng (mountain-in-no-tiger, monkey-claim-king)
687 多福多寿 [---壽] duō fú duō shòu (more-fortune-longer-longevity)
688 人为刀俎, 我为鱼肉 [-為--, -為魚-] rén wéi dāozǔ, wǒ wéi yú ròu (others-be-knife-chopping board, I-be-fish-meat)

84   *Nature, animals, language*

222. Eyebrows and urgency (眉毛与紧急) 1

It might be that since 眉毛/眉 (eyebrows) are close to the eyes they can see immediate urgency, 眉毛/眉 is often involved in expressing 'urgency,' for example, 火烧眉毛 (extremely urgent), 燃眉之急[689] (matter of great urgency) and 迫在眉睫 (pressing).

223. Hands and feet (手和脚) 1

When 手 (hand) and 脚 (foot) are used in a phrase, the words carry a negative meaning, for example, 碍手碍脚 (be in the way), 大手大脚 (to spend with a free hand), 毛手毛脚 (clumsy or be flustered with movement), 束手束脚 (timid and hesitant), 动手动脚 (to get fresh with somebody). Aside from the four-character idioms, even phrases that are not fixed such as 做手脚 (to play a trick) and 动手脚 (to manipulate, fight) have negative meanings as well.

224. Wok (锅) 2

Woks are an essential cookware for Chinese people, and they are often associated with food. They thus symbolize 'life,' usually a hard one, for example, 等米下锅[690] (wait for rice to be put in the pot, live from hand to mouth, in strained circumstances); 揭不开锅[691] (have nothing in the pot, run out of food); and 砸锅卖铁[692] (smash one's pots and pans and sell the iron, offer all one has). Because China had large populations almost throughout its history, Chinese woks/pots were usually large, so 锅 (wok) has a connotation of 'large, entirety,' for example, 吃着碗里，看着锅里[693] (eat what's in one's bowl while eyeing the pot, be unsatisfied with what one has); 大锅饭[694] (large wok food, indiscriminate egalitarianism), 连锅端 or 一锅端[695] (whole pot removed, to be wiped out all at once); and 一马勺坏一锅[696] or 一粒老鼠屎，坏了一锅粥[697] (one bad apple spoils the barrel). Woks are usually black and hot when cooking, so the word 锅 sometimes has a negative stemming from the words 'black' or 'hot,' for example, 背黑锅[698] (carry on a black pot, be left holding the bag) and 热锅上蚂蚁[699] (ants on a hot pan, like cats on hot bricks).

- #225 Chinese cooking methods (中国菜的做法)

225. Chinese cooking methods (中国菜的做法) 2

Because the Chinese like to eat hot foods, most of their cooking methods are related to fire, for example (红) 烧 (braise), 烤 (bake, roast), 炖 (stew), 炒 (stir-fry), 炸 (fry), 烹 (quick fry),

---

689 燃眉之急 [-] ránméi zhījí (burn-eyebrow-'s-urgency)
690 等米下锅 [---鍋] děng mǐ xiàguō (wait for-rice-be put in-wok)
691 揭不开锅 [--開鍋] jiē bùkāi guō (uncover-not-open-wok)
692 砸锅卖铁 [-鍋賣鐵] zá guō mài tiě (smash-wok-sell-iron)
693 吃着碗里，看着锅里 [-著-裏，-著鍋裏] chīzhe wǎn lǐ, kànzhe guō lǐ (eat-bowl-inside, look-wok-inside)
694 大锅饭 [-鍋飯] dà guō fàn (large-wok-food)
695 一锅端 [-鍋-] yī guō duān (whole-wok-remove)
696 一马勺坏一锅 [---壞-鍋] yì mǎsháo huài yī guō (one-big-ladle-spoil-one-wok)
697 一粒老鼠屎，坏了一锅粥 [-, 壞--鍋-] yī lì lǎoshǔ shǐ, huài le yī guō zhōu (one-bit-mouse-poop, spoil-ed-one-wok-porridge)
698 背黑锅 [--鍋] bēi hēi guō (carry on the back-black-pot)
699 热锅上的蚂蚁 [熱鍋--螞蟻] règuō shàng de mǎyǐ (hot-wok-in-'s-ant)

Nature, animals, language 85

煎 (fry, simmer), 煮 (boil), 熬 (cook on a slow fire), 蒸 (steam), 热 (heat), all listed above and having 'fire' (火) on the left part of the characters or in the lower part (灬).

- #122 Food and drink (饮食)

226. Buns or dumplings (包子) 2

Slang that includes buns or dumplings (包子) usually have a negative connotation, for example, 土包子 (country bumpkin), 草包 (good-for-nothing), 骚包 (attention whore) and 熊/怂包 (coward).

- #122 Food and drink (饮食)

227. Bone (骨头) 1

The human skeleton is composed of 206 bones. In the Chinese language, bones (骨头) usually symbolize humans, for example, 软骨头[700] (soft bone, spineless person, coward); 硬骨头 (hard bone, person of indomitable will); and 贱骨头 (cheap bone, miserable wretch, self-imposed sufferer). To nitpick is 鸡蛋里挑骨头[701] (to find quarrel in a straw). If a person is too cruel and brutal, he 吃人不吐骨头[702] (devours a person without spitting out the bones – be extremely ruthless and cruel to people).

228. Color and lust (色) 1

色 originally means 'reflection of the cheeks (颜, yán).' Since women's cheeks are rosy (红颜), 色 refers to a beautiful woman, for example, 美色 (beauty), 好色 (lust) and 色狼 (lecher).

- #155 Colors and culture (颜色与文化)

229. Gold and jade (金玉) 5

Gold (金) and jade (玉) are rare in nature, precious for people, and thus carrying a connotation of 'noble' in Chinese language. For example, an emperor's words are 金口玉言[703] (golden mouth and pearly words, words from the authority), and an emperor's daughters are 金枝玉叶[704] (gold branches and jade leaves, female descendants of imperial lineage). Words or sayings with the pattern 金/玉 have a connotation of 'perfect, wonderful,' for example, 金科玉律 (golden rule), 金玉良言 (invaluable advice), 金玉良缘 (perfect couple), 金童玉女[705] (young man and woman with good looks and talents) and 金玉其外, 败絮其中[706] (shining on the outside but rotten inside). The normal form of this pattern is 金 in front of 玉, not the other way round.

- #230 Metals, precious and non-precious (金银铜铁); #231 More precious than gold (比金子还贵)

---

700 软/硬/贱骨头 [軟/-/賤-頭] ruǎn/yìng/jiàn gútou (soft/hard/cheap-bone)
701 鸡蛋里挑骨头 [鷄-裏--頭] jīdàn lǐ tiāo gútou (egg-inside-pick-bone)
702 吃人不吐骨头 [-----頭] chīrén bù tǔ gútou (eat-people-not-spit-bone)
703 金口玉言 [-] jīn kǒu yù yán (gold-mouth-jade-words)
704 金枝玉叶 [---葉] jīn zhī yù yè (gold-branch-jade-leave)
705 金童玉女 [-] jīn tóng yù nǚ (gold-boy-jade-girl)
706 金玉其外, 败絮其中 [-, 敗---] jīn yù qí wài, bài xù qí zhōng (gold-jade-its-outside, worn-cotton-its-inside)

86 *Nature, animals, language*

230. Metals, precious and non-precious (金银铜铁) 1

金 (jīn, gold) and 银 (yín, silver) are naturally rare metals, so this characteristic is also reflected in language. For example, 真金白银 means 'real money.' 铜 (tóng, copper) and 铁 (tiě, metal) are base metals (贱金属, literally 'cheap-metal,') so is there a phrase 破铜烂铁 (pòtóng làntiě) that means 'scrap metal.'

231. More precious than gold (比金子还贵) 2

Which is more precious, gold (黄金), diamond (钻石), pearl (珍珠) or jade (玉)? For Chinese, especially those who are rich and well educated, the answer is 玉 (yù, jade). They think 玉 has five virtues, namely 仁 (benevolent), 义 (just), 智 (wise), 勇 (brave) and 洁 (pure) many of which are virtues esteemed by Confucius.

- #229 Gold and jade (金玉)

232. Importance of tools (工具的重要性) 2

There are two Chinese sayings that emphasize the importance of tools. One is 工欲善其事, 必先利其器[707] (if a worker wants to do a good job, he must first sharpen his tools, good tools are prerequisite to success). The other is 巧妇难为无米之炊[708] (you cannot make something out of nothing; one cannot make a silk purse out of a sow's ear). The Chinese god of builders and contractors is 鲁班 (Lu Ban, 507 BCE–444 BCE) who invented the 锯 (saw) and even a wooden magpie that could fly in the sky for three days, according to some legends. If one displays his slight skill before an expert, it is 班门弄斧[709] or 鲁班门前耍大斧.[710]

- #44 Shortcuts (捷径)

233. Needle (针) 1

Needles are tiny, and it is not easy to hand make one. But as long as you work hard enough, you can grind an iron rod into a needle (只要功夫深, 铁杵磨成针,[711] with time and patience), to find it (大海捞针,[712] look for a needle in a haystack). Some people say women's hearts are just like a needle lost in the seabed (女人心, 海底针,[713] a woman's heart is unpredictable). Needles are pointy and sharp. Comments can also be sharp (一针见血,[714] let blood with a single prick of the needle, hit the nail on the head) or disguisedly strong (绵里藏针,[715] needle hidden in silk floss, an iron fist in a velvet glove). Needles are also worthless. The Chinese Communist Party won the hearts of the masses in her early stage of growth by claiming they 不拿群众一针一线[716] (would never take any

---

707 工欲善其事, 必先利其器 [-] gōng yù shàn qí shì, bì xiān lì qí qì (worker-want-better-his-work, must-first-sharpen-his-tool)

708 巧妇难为无米之炊 [-婦難爲無---] qiǎofù nán wéi wúmǐzhīchuī (skillful-housewife-hard-make-without-rice-'s-cooking)

709 班门弄斧 [-門--] Bānmén nòngfǔ (Lu Ban-gate-show off-axe)

710 鲁班门前耍大斧 [鲁-門----] Lǔ Bān ménqián shuǎ dà fǔ (Lu Ban-gate-front-show off-big-axe)

711 只要功夫深, 铁杵磨成针 [-, 鐵---針] zhǐyào gōngfu shēn, tiěchǔ mó chéng zhēn (as long as-effort-deep, iron-rod-grind-into-needle)

712 大海捞针 [--撈針] dàhǎi lāo zhēn (deep-sea-search for-needle)

713 女人心, 海底针 [-, --針] nǚrén xīn, hǎidǐ zhēn (woman-heart, sea-bed-needle)

714 一针见血 [-針--] yī zhēn jiàn xiě (one-needle-see-blood)

715 绵里藏针 [綿裏-針] mián lǐ cáng zhēn (soft-inside-hide-needle)

716 不拿群众一针一线 [---衆-針-綫] bù ná qúnzhòng yī zhēn yī xiàn (not-take-ordinary people-one-needle-one-thread)

Nature, animals, language 87

tiny piece of property from the masses). Was this true? Don't 给个棒槌就当针[717] (regard a wooden club as a needle, take it too seriously).

234. Nails (钉子) 2

Nails are small but useful, so 烂船还有三斤钉[718] (the body of a starved camel is still bigger than that of a living horse) and 板上钉钉[719] (be finalized). They are also hard, and the metaphorical meaning of 钉子 is something hard to deal with, for example, 眼中钉, 肉中刺[720] (eyesore, a stone in your shoe), 软钉子[721] (polite snub), 拔掉这个钉子 (get rid of this troublemaker) and 钉子户[722] (nail household, a family who refuses to move).

235. Wall (墙) 3

Walls are a symbol of separation of the inside and outside. 兄弟阋于墙, 而外御其侮[723] means 'brothers may quarrel at home, but will join forces against attacks from the outside.' Fence-sitters are 墙头草.[724] If something comes out of the wall, or there is something outside the wall, the word usually carries a negative connotation, for example, 红杏出墙[725] (literally 'red apricot blossom reaches over the wall, a woman is unfaithful to her husband'); 墙里开花墙外香[726] (one's accomplishments are easily known outside his own unit); and 隔墙有耳[727] (walls have ears). Although Chinese people usually need the wall, when it is really going to collapse, everyone gives it a push (墙倒众人推).[728]

236. Boats (舟和船) 1

Both 舟 (zhōu) and 船 (chuán) mean 'boat,' but 船 has been more commonly used since the Han dynasty. 舟 is more archaic and preserved in idioms such as 破釜沉舟 (pòfǔ chénzhōu, break the pots and sink the boats, burn one's bridges); 同舟共济 (tóngzhōu gòngjì, cross the river together in the same boat, overcome difficulties together); and 刻舟求剑 (kèzhōu qiújiàn, to inscribe boat for sword, to act foolishly without regard to changed circumstances) etc.

237. Roads and ways (道和路) 1

道 means 'way' and 路 'road.' In ancient China, 道 were usually one way, so there is a saying '一条道跑到黑' (to go down a road until its end, be single-minded, be as stubborn as a mule). 路 were usually two ways and much broader than 道, so is there a rendered saying 条条大路通罗马 (all roads lead to Rome).

---

717 给个棒槌就当针 [給個---當針] gěi ge bàngchui jiù dāng zhēn (given-wooden club-then-regard as-needle)

718 烂船还有三千钉 [爛-還---釘] làn chuán hái yǒu sān qiān ding (rotten-boat-still-have-3,000-nail)

719 板上钉钉 [--釘釘] bǎn shàng dìng ding (board-on-strike-nail)

720 眼中钉, 肉中刺 [--釘, -] yǎn zhōng dīng, ròu zhōng cì (eye-inside-nail, body-inside-thorn)

721 软钉子 [軟釘-] ruǎn dīngzi (soft-nail)

722 钉子户 [釘--] dīngzihù (nail-household)

723 兄弟阋于墙, 而外御其辱 [--鬩於, --禦--] xiōngdì xì yú qiáng, ér wài yù qí rǔ (brothers-quarrel-within-wall, but-outside-defend-their-insult)

724 墙头草 [墙頭-] qiángtóu cǎo (wall-top-grass)

725 红杏出墙 [紅--墙] hóng xìng chū qiáng (red-apricot-outside-wall)

726 墙里开花墙外香 [墙裏開-墙--] qiáng lǐ kāihuā qiáng wài xiāng (wall-inside-blossom-flower-wall-outside-fragrant)

727 隔墙有耳 [-墙--] gé qiáng yǒu ěr (cross-wall-have-ear)

728 墙倒众人推 [墙-衆--] qiáng dǎo zhòngrén tuī (wall-collapse-massive-people-push)

88   *Nature, animals, language*

238. Quality and rice (质量与大米) 2

Many Chinese words on 'quality' are related to the radical 米 ('rice'), for example, 精 (fine, refined), 粗 (coarse), 糙 (rough, crude, unrefined), 糟 (rotten, bad, poor), 糟糕 (terrible), 糟粕 (dross, waste) etc. It denotes a strong connection between food and quality.

- #2 Chinese characters and way of thinking (汉字与思维)

239. Medicine (药) 2

Generally speaking, Chinese people eat considerably less medicine than Americans do. They believe 是药三分毒[729] (any medicine has its side effect) and 三分药，七分养[730] (good aftercare works much better than medicine). Sometimes you have to take medicines although they taste bitter (良药苦口利于病,[731] good medicine is bitter to the taste, but beneficial for your health). Never take wrong medicine or be considered to have taken wrong medicine (吃错药,[732] literally 'take wrong medicine') since it means 'someone is weird.'

240. East . . . west. . . (东/西) 1

Idioms with the pattern '东/西' (east . . . west) are usually colloquial and have a (slightly) negative connotation, such as 'disorderly' and 'in hardship.' For example, 东张西望 (glance this way and that), 东奔西走 (run about busily), 东拉西扯 (talk aimlessly), 说东道西 (chat of everything under the sun) and 声东击西 (aim at a pigeon and shoot at a crow) etc.

- #241 South . . . north. . . (南/北); #248 Things (东西不是南北)

241. South . . . north. . . (南/北) 1

Idioms with the pattern '南/北' (south . . . west) sometimes have a (slightly) negative connotation, such as 'wrongly,' for example, 南辕北辙 (try to go south by driving the chariot north – act in a way that defeats one's purpose), 南腔北调 (with mixed accents), 南征北战 (fight the north and south on many fronts) and 走南闯北 (journey north and south), among others.

- #240 East . . . west. . . (东/西)

242. I was here (到此一游) 1

Before the 2000s, Chinese tourists were notorious for drawing or inscribing their names and the phrase '到此一游'[733] (literally 'arrived here for a visit,' I was here) at tourist sites, both domestic and foreign. This disrespectful practice might originate from Sun Wukong, the Monkey King in the famous novel *Journey to the West* (Xiyouji), who wrote '到此一游' with his urine on the middle finger of the right hand of the Tathagata. Have Chinese people always been so disrespectful since ancient times? The answer is no. Educated people used to write a poem pertaining to his mood at the tourist site. For example, when the great poet Li Bai (Li Po) visited the Yellow Crane Tower in Wuhan, Hubei Province, he wanted to write a poem. However, when he saw a poem by another poet Cui Hao, he gave up the idea and left only half of a verbal

---

729 是药三分毒 [-藥---] shì yào sānfēn dú (any-medicine-3–1/10-poisonous)
730 三分药, 七分养 [--藥, --養] sānfēn yào, qīfēn yang (3–1/10-medicine, 7–1/10-aftercare)
731 良药苦口利于病 [-藥-----]liángyào kǔkǒu lìyú bìng(good-medicine-bitter-mouth-benefit-to-illness)
732 吃错药 [-錯藥] chī cuò yào (take-wrong-medicine)
733 到此一游 [-] dào cǐ yì yóu (arrived-here-once-tour)

Nature, animals, language 89

poem, 眼前好景道不得, 崔颢题诗在上头 (how disappointing that I could not write a poem on the beautiful scenery just before my eyes! Cui Hao's poem is already there).

• #34 Refined and popular (雅俗)

243. Foreign countries with '国' in their Chinese names (*国) 2

Only seven foreign countries are called *国 in Chinese. They are 英国 (England, UK), 法国 (France), 德国 (Germany), 俄国 (Russia), 美国 (America, U.S.), 泰国 (Thailand) and 韩国 (S. Korea). The first five were very influential in China in the 19th century, and the last two names are from their original or native written forms in Chinese.

244. Warning, mild (温和的警告) 1

Chinese people are known for often speaking in a roundabout way. If one rejects or warns you mildly, he may say 你好自为之[734] (look out for yourself), 你看着办吧[735] (you are on your own) or 你要想清楚 (think twice before you act). On a side note, the accompanying intonation matters too!

245. The worst curse word (贼) 3

In ancient China, the worst curse did not involve sexual references or the person's ancestors. It was the word 贼 (zéi), which originally means 'cruelly injure or kill.' Before the relatively new meaning 'thief,' 贼 usually meant 'traitor.' For example, 民贼 (traitor to the people), 独夫民贼 (autocrat and traitor to the people), 乱臣贼子 (traitors and usurpers), 奸贼 (conspirator), 卖国贼 (traitor), 反贼 (rebel, traitor), 叛贼 (renegade, traitor), and 认贼做父 (take the foe for one's father), etc. In 1968, Chinese President Liu Shaoqi (1898–1969) was denounced as 工贼 (traitor to the working class) and subsequently tortured to death in the following year. 贼 was used on those who had betrayed orthodox morals or values. That being said, betrayal to original beliefs was condemned most heavily in China.

• #91 Emperors, kings, generals, ministers (帝王将相)

246. Not afraid (不怕) 1

If one is strong and/or ignorant enough, he is fearless. For example, true gold fears no fire (真金不怕火炼,[736] a person of integrity can stand severest tests) and a newborn calf is not afraid of tigers (初生牛犊不怕虎,[737] young people are bold). There is a useful pattern to describe that you are only afraid of one thing: 天不怕, 地不怕, 就怕,[738] for example, 天不怕, 地不怕, 就怕老外说中国话 (nothing is more dreadful than a foreigner who speaks Chinese) and 天不怕, 地不怕, 就怕流氓有文化 (the worst is hooligans are also well educated). One should always be prepared for the one risk in a million (不怕一万, 就怕万一[739]) and keep his hopes up (留得青山在, 不怕没柴烧,[740] keep the green mountains and you don't have to

---

734 你好自为之 [---為-] nǐ hǎozìwéizhī (you-well-oneself-conduct-it)
735 你看着办吧 [--著辦-] nǐ kànzhe bàn ba (you-consider-it-do-then)
736 真金不怕火炼 [-----煉] zhēn jīn búpà huǒ liàn (real-gold-not-fear-fire-temper)
737 初生牛犊不怕虎 [---犢---] chūshēng niúdú búpà hǔ (newly-born-cow-calf-not-fear-tiger)
738 天不怕, 地不怕, 就怕 . . . [-] tiān búpà, dì búpà, jiù pà . . . (heaven-not-afraid, earth-not-afraid, only-afraid. . .)
739 不怕一万, 就怕万一 [---萬, --萬-] búpà yīwàn, jiù pà wànyī (not-afraid-10,000, only-afraid-1 in 10,000)
740 留得青山在, 不怕没柴烧 [-, ----烧] liú dé qīngshān zài, búpà méi chái shāo (keep-get-green-mountain-exist, not-worry-no-charcoal-burn)

90 *Nature, animals, language*

worry about where to get firewood – while there is life, there is hope). The Communist Party claims it is not to be scared off (不怕邪,[741] be unafraid of evil forces).

- #109 Boldest proclamation of reform (三不足)

247. More bad guys (坏人多) 5

The Chinese language was more concerned with negative words, and the Chinese has lexicon catalogued much more negative words than positive ones. For example, according to *A Thesaurus of Modern Chinese* (现代汉语分类词典, edited by Su Xinchun et al., 2013), there are 22 words in 5 categories to describe a 'good man (好人),' whereas there are 424 words in 53 categories to describe a 'person of bad acts (劣迹者).'

- #1 Chinese language and culture: Negative tendency (中国语言的负面倾向)

248. Things (东西不是南北) 2

There is no universally accepted answer. One explanation is that in the Eastern Han dynasty, there were two capitals, the eastern capital in Luoyang and the western capital in Chang'an. Businessmen went to buy from either Luoyang or Chang'an (买东 or 买西), therefore 东西 became synonymous with 'things.' The second explanation is that, in the Tang dynasty, the capital Chang'an had two markets, 东市 and 西市, and 东西 became synonymous with things. The third explanation is related to the 'Five Elements' of which the phase of the south (南) is 'fire' (火) and the north (北) 'water' (水). 水 and 火 (water/flood and fire) are not good for one's home, but the phase of 东 (木, wood) and 西 (金, gold) are good for one's home. Therefore, 东西, not 南北 became a synonym for things.

- #240 East . . . west. . . (东/西)

249. Juxtaposed antonyms meaning 'category' or 'scope' (并列反义词表范围) 5

If two antonyms are used in a compound word, it could mean a category that the two antonyms fall under, for example, 好坏 means 'good' and 'bad' individually but 'quality' as a compound. Other words of this kind include 上下 (above-below, about); 大小 (big-small, size); 长短 (long-short, length, distance); 高低 (high-low, height); 宽窄 (broad-narrow, width, breadth); 粗细 (thick-thin, size); 深浅 (deep-shallow, dark-light, depth, shade); 轻重 (light-heavy, weight); 难易 (hard-easy, difficulty); 得失 (gain-loss, result); and 优劣 (superior-inferior, quality, level) etc.

- #250 Juxtaposition of male and female (连绵词: 雌雄)

250. Juxtaposition of male and female (连绵词: 雌雄) 1

凤凰/鳳凰 (phoenix), 鸳鸯/鴛鴦 (mandarin duck) and 麒麟 (kirin) are each composed of a male and female. Usually the male is before the female. For example, 凤 (fèng) is a male phoenix and 凰 (huáng) a female one.

- #284 Binomal words (连绵词)

---

741 不怕邪 [-] búpà xié (not-fear-evil)

Nature, animals, language 91

251. Spatial-temporal metaphors (时空比喻) 5

In terms of spatial-temporal metaphors, the dimension of 'year (年)' and 'day (天)' is mainly horizontal, for example, 明天 (tomorrow), 明年 (next year), 来年 (the incoming year), 后天 (literally 'after-day,' the day after tomorrow), 后年 (literally 'after-year,' the year after next), 昨天 (yesterday), 去年 (last year), 前天 (the day before yesterday), 前年 (the year before last). For 'month (月)' and measure words for verbs such as '次 (time)' and '回 (time),' the dimension is vertical. For example, 上个月 (literally 'up-month,' last month), 下个月 (literally 'down-month,' next month), 上次/回 (last time) and 下回/次 (next time). Interestingly, 'year (年)' and 'day (天) cannot be modified with measure word '个' but 'month (月)' can.

252. Modal verb serial (能愿动词的连用) 1

Modal verbs can sometimes be used together to express a complex mode. Remember two typical strings, and you will get used to others. (1) 可能应该可以. For example: Daughter: 妈妈, 我能用一下爸爸的手机吗? (Mommy, may I use my daddy's cellphone for a while?) Mom: 可能应该可以. It literally means 'probably you are entitled to be allowed.' 可能 means 'probably, not 100% sure,' 应该 'ought to' (since daddy is not using it), and 可以 'allowed.' (2) 可能会愿意. For example: A. 你觉得那位小姐会接受那个老头子的求婚吗? (Do you think that young lady will accept that old man's marriage proposal?) B: 可能会愿意 (因为那个老头子是个亿万富翁). Probably, she will be willing to accept it (since that old man is a billionaire). 可能 means 'probably,' 会 means 'will' and 愿意 means 'to be willing.'

253. 'And' vs. 和 (和与 'and') 3

The English word 'and' has about 13 equivalents in Chinese. If you always translate 'and' into 和, the chance of error is high; however, if you translate it into '还有,' the chance of error reduces significantly. Nevertheless, using '还有' should be the last resort. You need to learn as many as synonyms to sound like a native.

- #256 Chinese equivalent of the English word 'do' (弄)

254. The meaning of yìsi ('意思'的意思) 5

The main meaning of 意思 is 'meaning,' but the usage of 意思 is much more than that. The following is a widespread play on language:
小王给局长 (bureau director) 送红包 (red envelope).

局长: '你这是什么意思?
小王: '没什么, 意思意思.'
局长: '你这就不够意思了.'
小王: '小意思, 小意思.'
局长: '你这人真有意思.'
小王: '其实也没别的意思.'
局长: '那我就不好意思了.'
小王: '是我不好意思了.'

92 *Nature, animals, language*

Xiao Wang sends a red envelope (containing money) to a bureau director.

Director: What do you *mean?*
Xiao Wang: Nothing, *a token* (of appreciation).
Director: You *make me feel embarrassed.*
Xiao Wang: Just *a small token.*
Director: You are *interesting.*
Xiao Wang: Actually, I *had no other intentions.*
Director: Then I will take it *with guilty feeling.*
Xiao Wang: It's me who should *feel guilty* (since the money is not much).

255. I'll think about it (研究研究) 2

At the beginning of Chinese economic reform, if a government official said he needed to 研究研究[742] (literally 'I'll think about it') when requested to do a favor, street-smart people would know that he was probably hinting that you should give him some presents like 烟酒 (cigarettes and liquor) since 烟酒烟酒 (yānjiǔ yānjiǔ) and 研究研究 (yánjiu yánjiu) are almost homophones. Nowadays, in a similar scenario, cigarettes and liquor could scarcely settle the matter unless the wine and cigars are from top brands, worthy of royalty.

- #123 Liquor and drinking (酒, 喝酒)

256. Chinese equivalent of the English word 'do' (弄) 2

弄 (nòng) functions as the English colloquial word 'to make' or 'to do.' For example, 中午我弄俩菜, 你弄瓶白酒, 咱俩好好聊聊 (At noon I'll make two dishes, and you get a bottle of alcohol, the two of us have a good chat). Another example is 我的电脑让我弄坏了, 然后我就修, 结果我弄来弄去也弄不明白到底哪儿出了问题 (My computer is down and I tried to repair it, but I tried again and again and am still unable to figure out what's the problem).

- #253 'And' vs. 和 (和与 'and')

257. Classics (经) 3

经 (經, jīng) originally means 'longitudinal threads (of a piece of cloth)' from which evolved meanings such as 'principle,' 'classics' and 'often.' Since 经 has a meaning 'often, periodical,' menstruation or menses is called 月经 (literally 'month-periodically') in Chinese. Many ancient classics are called 经, among which are 诗经 (Shījīng, *Shih-ching*, the *Classic of Poetry*, or *Book of Songs*); 易经 (Yìjīng, *I Ching*, the *Classic of Changes*); and 心经 (Xīnjīng, the *Heart Sutra*) etc. A common word 经济 (jīngjì, economy) is derived from the phrase 经世济民 (jīngshì jìmín, literally 'govern-world-help-people') meaning 'govern and benefit the people.' Also in traditional Chinese medicine (TCM), the meridian system is called 经 (络).

- #95 Master (*子)

258. Heavenly Stems and Earthly Branches to compute time (天干地支纪年) 5

The ten Heavenly/Celestial Stems are 甲, 乙, 丙, 丁, 戊, 己, 庚, 辛, 壬, 癸 (jiǎ, yǐ, bǐng, dīng, wù, jǐ, gēng, xīn, rén, guǐ), and the twelve Earthly Branches are 子, 丑, 寅, 卯, 辰, 巳,

---

742 研究研究 [-] yánjiu yánjiu (research-*reduplication*)

午, 未, 申, 酉, 戌, 亥 (zǐ, chǒu, yín, mǎo, chén, sì, wǔ, wèi, shēn, yǒu, xū, hài). In combination, they can form a sexagenary cycle to record years, months, days and hours – the main way to reckon time in ancient China until the establishment of the Republic of China in 1912 remaining in use in some fields. For example, January 1st, 2020, can be estimated as 己亥年丙子月癸卯日.

- #285 Chinese ordinal numbers (汉语顺序号)

259. Idioms with 'heaven/earth' (带'天/地'的成语) 3

Among the 50,000 Chinese idioms the pattern using '天/地' is the most productive one, yielding about 200 idioms. Since 天 and 地 have the largest difference in the Chinese perceptive, the idioms with this pattern carry a connotation of 'extremely.' For example, the two idioms 翻天覆地 and 震天动地 mean 'huge change' and 'extremely shocking,' respectively. Likewise, 天寒地冻 means 'extremely/bitterly cold,' and 天经地义 means 'absolutely/perfectly justified' since '经' (classics) are unalterable.

260. Language games (文字游戏) 2

Chinese language games are not 语言游戏 (language game), but 文字游戏 (literally 'character game'), which denotes that games are played primarily with characters, not words. Some examples include 字谜 (riddle about a character); 灯谜 (riddle written on a lantern); 绕口令 (tongue twister); 对联 (antithetical couplet); 顶针续麻 (dǐngzhēn xùmá, anadiplosis, especially 成语接龙 relay of idioms); 回文诗 (palindromic poem); 藏头诗 (cángtóushī, acrostic); 飞花令 (a drinkers' wager game with a specific character); the superstitious 生辰八字 (birth chart); and so on.

- #107 Ignorant young ladies (无知少女); #261 Language play on internet (网络上的语言游戏); #277 White Bone Spirit (白骨精)

261. Language play on internet (网络上的语言游戏) 2

Chinese netizens created many ways to avoid censorship or express attitudes toward celebrities and certain events. For example, the U.S. President Donald Trump is called 床铺 (bedding, chuángpù, a Chinese pronunciation similar to the English pronunciation 'Trump'); the former U.S. President Obama is called 'O8' since '8' is pronounced 'ba,' exactly the same as the 'ba' in 'Obama'; China is called 西朝鲜 (literally 'west Korea'); and June 4th is called May 35th.

- #35 Humorous (幽默); #260 Language games (文字游戏)

262. Euphemisms for 'to die' ('死'的委婉语) 5

Generally, the Chinese people lack calm when facing death at an old age, so 'longevity' (寿 shòu, or 长寿) was the most important theme in auspicious wishes and folk arts in ancient China. Euphemisms are vital for learners of Chinese to grasp in order to communicate with the Chinese in their way. Here are some major euphemisms for 'to die,' 'dead' or 'death': (1) 走了 (left) or 没了 (gone), for example, 他昨天走了, 她是哪天没的? (2) 永别了 (forever-parted), for example, 他跟我们永别了, (3) 百年 (100-years) or 千古 (1,000-ages), for example, '我百年之后, 你. . . .' '千古' is usually seen on the memorial ceremony, (4) 断气了 (stop-breathing), 出事了 (something happened), (5) 见阎王爷 (jiàn Yánwángyé, see King of

94 *Nature, animals, language*

Hell), 上西天 (go the Western Paradise), 见马克思 ((of a CCP member) goes see Karl Marx) etc. Still several dozen expressions, however, are rather difficult for learners of Chinese.

- #51 Life and death (生死); #55 Die, death (死); #56 Chinese condolences (节哀顺变)

263. Euphemisms for 'sexual intercourse' ('做爱'的委婉语) 5

Generally, the Chinese people are very roundabout when mentioning 'sexual intercourse' in public. Some main euphemisms include: (1) 上床 (go to-bed); (2) 睡觉 (sleep); (3) 那种事 (that kind of thing); (4) 房事 (room-thing); (5) 嘿咻 (hēixiu, originated from Taiwan); (6) 造人 (make-baby); (7) 交公粮 (surrender-state-tax grain, used in mainland China for a man's reluctance to make love with his wife); and (8) 啪啪啪 (onomatopoeic) etc. Recently a previously vulgar word '打炮' (to fire – a gun, cannon) has become less or not vulgar for young adults.

264. Homophonic puns (谐音双关) 3

Chinese is a monosyllabic language and has a large number of homophonous syllables. Homophonic puns are a rhetoric device, which can make the language lively and witty. For example, Chinese people have a tradition to display large '福' (fortune) upside down (倒了) on their gates on the spring festival. 福倒了 (fortune is 'upside down') is a homophonic pun of 福到了[743] (fortune 'has arrived') since '倒' (upside down) and '到' (arrive) are homophonous (dào). For another example, spring festival pictures of 年年有鱼 (literally 'every year has fish') imply 年年有余 (literally 'every year has surplus') since 鱼 (fish) and 余 (surplus) are homophonous (yú). 算了 (suànle) means 'forget (about) it.' The author of this book once came across a pun with 'suànle.' When his wife asked him give her some scallions (葱, cōng) for cooking, he said, '没葱了' (no scallions). Then, she said, 'méi cōng jiù suàn le,' but he was at a loss and had to ask her for clarification since it could mean two things. One is 没葱就算了 (if there are no scallions then forget it), and the other is 没葱就蒜了 (if there are no scallions, then use garlic).

- #220 Bats (蝙蝠); #265 Fish and 'surplus' (鱼和余); #266 Prosperity and prostitution (繁荣'娼'盛)

265. Fish and 'surplus' (鱼和余) 1

Why do Chinese people like 鱼 (fish)? Because 鱼 and 余 (餘) are homophones of yú, and 余 (餘) has an auspicious meaning, 'surplus,' which was understandably welcomed in old times when food was scare. Therefore, many Chinese people eat fish and paste pictures of fish on the wall on Chinese New Year.

- #221 Fish and meat (鱼与肉); #264 Homophonic puns (谐音双关)

266. Prosperity and prostitution (繁荣'娼'盛) 1

繁荣昌盛 (fánróng chāngshèng) means 'prosperous and flourishing,' which is supposed to be a very positive word; however, sometimes it is purposely used as 繁荣娼盛 with the third

---

743 福到了 [-] fú dàole (fortune-arrived)

Nature, animals, language 95

character 娟 being different from the original one, 昌. 娟 means 'prostitute, bitch.' This is a case of homophonic puns.

- #124 Bad habits (恶习); #264 Homophonic puns (谐音双关)

267. Dilution of vulgar words (傻*) 1

'傻*' is a typical word of Mandarin Chinese profanity, meaning 'stupid person' with 傻 being 'stupid' and '* (bī)' here a vulgar word for vagina. It was a very vulgar word before the era of internet; however, it has become less vulgar since you can often hear it from men or women, in private or in public. This is a small piece of evidence that in recent years, the impact of the Chinese language can deteriorate.

268. The most heartbreaking vows (最让人心碎的誓言) 5

发誓 (fāshì) means 'to swear, to vow.' We all swear, but the most heartbreaking vows in the whole of Chinese history were made by 窦娥 (竇娥, Dòu É), a character in Guan Hanqing's famous drama *Dou E Yuan* (*Injustice to Dou E*, 1291): 血溅白练 (xuě jiàn bái liàn, blood will fly onto her white clothes but not drip onto the ground after she was beheaded); 六月飞雪[744] (there comes a heavy snow to cover her dead body in Chuzhou of southern China in the lunar month of June); and 大旱 (hàn) 三年 (there will be a drought in Chuzhou, a city next to the fourth largest freshwater lake in China). All three events happened after Dou E's death.

- #58 Heavenly principles (天理); #66 Retribution, karma (报应)

269. Choice of Chinese characters for foreign place names (外国地名中的汉字的选择) 2

To avoid confusion between names of foreign persons or places and Chinese words, Xinhua News Agency, China's state news agency stipulated that names of foreign persons or places should be rendered with uncommon Chinese characters. For example, deriving meaning from the characters that make up the name Palestine (巴勒斯坦, Bālèsītǎn) and Ethiopia (埃塞俄比亚, Áisàiébǐyà) is impossible or meaningless.

- #2 Chinese characters and way of thinking (汉字与思维)

270. Classical translation of movie titles (电影片名经典翻译) 2

Translation is an art of language. The following are classical translation of foreign movies: *Waterloo Bridge* (1940) is 魂断蓝桥 (Húnduàn Lánqiáo, literally 'soul-broken/lost (at)-blue-bridge'). 蓝桥 (blue-bridge) is a legendary place for true lovers to meet. *Ghost* (1990) is 人鬼情未了 (rén guǐ qíng wèi liǎo, literally 'human-ghost-love-not-ended.') 情未了 is a line from a famous Five Dynasties poem. *Gone with the Wind* (1939) is 乱世佳人 (Luànshì Jiārén, literally 'chaotic-time-beautiful-woman.') 佳人 is also the title of a poem by the greatest Chinese poet Du Fu (712–770). *The Wizard of Oz* (1939) is 绿野仙踪 (Lǜyě Xiānzōng, literally 'green-pasture-fairy-trace'), which definitely attracts children's interests. Interestingly enough, most of the best translated movies were shot around 1939.

---

744 六月飞雪 [--飛-] liùyuè fēixuě (June-fly-snow)

96　*Nature, animals, language*

271. Forget-me-not (勿忘我) 1

The forget-me-not flower symbolizes true and undying love. It is translated as 勿忘我 (not-forget-me, wù wàng wǒ), beautiful both in meaning and in alliteration (w-w-w).

272. Vegetables introduced to China (传入中国的蔬菜) 1

Throughout the history of China, many foreign vegetables were introduced to China and their names left some marks, for example, 胡 was a people who lived in Central Asia and 胡萝卜 (carrot) and 黄瓜 (see the next note for details) were introduced. From there, 洋 means 'foreign,' and thus, 洋葱 (onion) and 洋芹 (celery) got their names, 西 means 'Western,' thus 西兰花 (broccoli), 西红柿 (tomato), 西瓜 (watermelon) and 西芹 (celery) got their names.

- #122 Food and drink (饮食); #203 Foreign and rustic (洋与土); #204 Foreign and imported goods (洋货)

273. Chinglish, updated (新中式英语) 1

Before when the word 'Chinglish' was mentioned, we would instantly think of sayings such as 好久不见 (long time no see), 人山人海 (people mountain people sea) etc. The list now must be updated to include internet memes such as, 'you can you up' (你行你上), which means 'if you can do it, then you should go up and do it,' and 'no zuo no die' (不作死就不会死 or 不作不死), which means 'one would not be in trouble had he not asked for it.'

274. Brothers' names and radicals (兄弟人名的汉字与部首) 3

Chinese men were supposed to carry on the family name and lineage, so brothers typically shared a same character in the given names. If there were only one character in the given name, a same radical might be shared in the character. For example, Emperor Wu of Liang (梁武帝萧衍, Xiao Yan, 464–549) named his eight sons 统, 综, 纲, 绩, 续, 纶, 绎 and 纪, which share the same radical 纟 (mì, silk). This may be the first case that this naming practice occurred. The founding emperor of the Ming dynasty, Hongwu Emperor (1328–1398) named all of his current and future male offspring for 20 generations. For example, 高瞻祁见祐, 厚载翊常由, 慈和怡伯仲 and 简靖迪先猷. However, this practice was terminated at the 10th generation '由' by the Qing dynasty in 1644. Wu xing (五行, The Five Elements), namely, 金木水火土 (metal, wood, water, fire, earth), had a profound influence in the naming system.

- #2 Chinese characters and way of thinking (汉字与思维)

275. Forms of address: respectful, honorific and modest (尊称, 敬称, 谦称) 2

Respectful and honorific forms of address are used to respect and elevate others. For example, 高* (high, as in 高见 'your brilliant idea'), 台* (archaic in mainland China but current in some other Chinese communities worldwide. You, your, as in **台鉴 'Attention to **'), 垂* (as in 垂询 'deign to inquire into something'), 赐* (as in 赐教 'condescend to instruct'), 奉* (as in 无可奉告 'No comments'), etc. Modest forms of address are used to belittle or depreciate oneself or his family members. Some examples include 小* (little, as in 小人 'I, me, person of low position'), 愚* (foolish, as in 愚见 'my humble opinion'), 拙* (clumsy, as in 拙见 'my humble opinion' and 拙著 'my poor writing'), 鄙* (remote, vulgar, as in 鄙人 'I, me, your humble servant'),

Nature, animals, language 97

敝* (worn-out, ragged, as in 敝公司 'my company'), 寡* (few, scant, as in 寡人 '(of an emperor) I, me), 贱* (cheap, as in 贱内 'my humble wife'), etc. Perhaps to many Westerners' surprise, 家* (family) and 舍* (home) are not to be honored, but to be downgraded, for example, '家父[745]' (my father) and '舍弟' (my younger brother). If one's family and home were not to be respected or honored, then what was worth respecting? It was the government and officials.

- #34 Refined and popular (雅俗); #52 'Death penalty' and modesty (死罪死罪); #149 Civilities (客套)

276. Southern Chinese names and 阿* (南方人名中的'阿') 1

阿 is widely added to the last characters of Southern Chinese's given names or names of relatives to show endearment, for example, 阿娇 (A'Jiao, the first empress of Emperor Wudi of Han), 阿珂 (A'Ke, in Jin Yong's novel *The Deer and the Cauldron*), 阿Q (Ah Q, in Lu Xun's fiction 'The True Story of Ah Q'), 阿公 (grandpa), 阿婆 (grandma), 阿爸阿妈 (mommy and daddy), 阿母 (mom), 阿姨 (aunt) and 阿大 (the eldest child) etc. 阿猫阿狗 is an exception, which means 'Tom, Dick and Harry.'

- #121 Custom (风俗)

277. White Bone Spirit (白骨精) 1

白骨精 (báigǔjīng) is known as the role of White Bone Spirit, a demon in the classic Chinese mythological novel *Journey to the West*. Now in the job market it refers to three kinds of people, 白领 (báilǐng, white-collar), 骨干 (gǔgàn, backbone) and 精英 (jīngyīng, elite).

- #107 Ignorant young ladies (无知少女); #260 Language games (文字游戏)

278. Circle of. . . (*坛/界) 2

Both **界 (jiè) and *坛 (tán) mean 'professor/circle of,' but generally speaking, modifiers of 界 are disyllabic and those of 坛 monosyllabic, for example, 音乐界 vs. 乐坛 (music world/circles), 体育界 vs. 体坛 (sports world/circles), 电影界 vs. 影坛 (movie circles), 足球界 vs. 足坛 (football world/circles) etc. However, 政界 vs. 政坛 (political circles) and a few more pairs are exceptions.

279. To speak eloquently (能说) 3

Confucius despised people who were eloquent. He said 巧言令色鲜矣仁 (Honey words and flattering looks seldom speak of human-heartedness). But in the Warring States Period (475 BCE–221 BCE), there was the School of Diplomacy (纵横家, Zònghéngjiā) whose members such as Su Qin (?–284 BCE) and Zhang Yi (373? BCE–309 BCE) were truly eloquent. Zhang Yi was once suspected to have stolen a precious jade and was bitterly beaten as punishment. His wife mocked him, 'Had you not learned and lobbied the dukes, would you have been humiliated like this?' Zhang Yi did not answer but asked his wife, 'Check to see whether my tongue is still there (视吾舌尚在否)?' His wife laughed and said yes. Then Zhang Yi said, 'That's enough (足矣).' Eloquent people 巧舌如簧 (talk glibly), 口若悬河

---

745 家父 [-] jiāfù (family-father)

98 *Nature, animals, language*

(speak with torrential eloquence), and can even 把死人说活了 (talk to the dead and make them come back to life).

- #42 Silence (沉默); #280 To talk nonsense (胡说)

280. To talk nonsense (胡说) 1

When someone talks nonsense, he 胡说八道 (shoots one's mouth off), 信口开河 (has a loose tongue), 信口雌黄 (flaps one's tongue too freely), or even 满嘴跑火车 (blows smoke/is full of it).

- #279 To speak eloquently (能说)

281. Difficulty levels of Chinese rhyme (韵脚的难易) 2

Li Bai (Li Po, 李白, 701–762) was one of the greatest poets in all of Chinese history. His poem '静夜思,'[746] is probably the most cited Chinese poem. It reads: 床前明月光,[747] 疑是地上霜. 举头望明月, 低头思故乡. This poem is so popular because of Li Bai's fame and artistry. However, people often neglect the fact that this poem rhymes 'ang,' which has many possible characters. Another easy sound to rhyme is 'an.' If you want to challenge a person with a Chinese rhyme, ask him to write a poem with the rhyme 'üe' as in 雪 (xuě, snow).

- #161 Antithetical couplets (对联)

282. Chinese characters composed of 人 (比, 从, 北, 化) 2

比, 从, 北 and 化 all look quite different, especially considering the left portions of them. However, their meanings are all derived from the relative position of their parts, two people. 比 depicts two men standing side by side, thus its meaning 'to compare.' 从 depicts a man following another, thus its meaning 'to follow, with.' 北 depicts two men back to back, thus meaning 'opposite.' 化 depicts one man straight up and one man upside down, thus meaning 'change.'

- #2 Chinese characters and way of thinking (汉字与思维)

283. Synonyms (近义词) 5

Almost every single Chinese character is a word in itself. In total, there are about 50,000 to 80,000 characters in the history of the Chinese language. Characters in combination can also form compound words. There are about 400,000 words in the history of the Chinese language thus far. Taking this into account, how many synonyms can a Chinese word/character have? Reading dictionaries of synonyms, including the oldest surviving Chinese dictionary, *Erya* (尔雅, 3rd century BCE) can overwhelm you. However, by analyzing this question from a new perspective, one can draw the conclusion that there are typically no more than three synonyms for Chinese words. Suppose there are many seemingly synonymous characters, A, B, C, D, E. . . . If they are true and nearly exchangeable synonyms, then their combinations such as AB, AC, AD, AE, BC, BD, BE, CD, CE, DE . . . or reverse ones such as BA, CA . . . are likely to be words as well. However, the actual combination of seemingly synonymous characters is usually limited to a mere three. For example, 贺 (hè, congratulate); 庆 (qìng,

---

746 静夜思 [静--] Jìngyèsī (quiet-night-long for)
747 床前明月光 [-] chuángqián míngyuè guāng (bed-front-bright-moon-light)

Nature, animals, language 99

celebrate); and 祝 (zhù, wish) can form only three combinations: 庆祝, 庆贺 and 祝贺. We can also find that the sequence of combination is right-spreading, starting from 庆, then to 祝 and finally to 贺. Ample examples can be found in *A Thematic Dictionary of Contemporary Chinese*, compiled by Liwei Jiao et al. in 2019.

- #236 Boats (舟和船); #237 Roads and ways (道和路)

284. Binomal words (连绵词) 3

Don't be scared when you see two juxtaposed and seemingly hard characters, since there is a great chance that they are binomes of animals, birds, worms or reptiles, for example, 凤凰 (phoenix); 鸳鸯 (mandarin duck); 鹦鹉 (parrot); 骆驼 (camel); 蜥蜴 (lizard); 蝙蝠 (bat); 蟾蜍 (toad); 蛤蟆 (toad); and 麒麟 (kirin, qilin, a mythical animal) etc.

- #250 Juxtaposition of male and female (连绵词: 雌雄)

285. Chinese ordinal numbers (汉语顺序号) 3

Besides the numeral numbers 一二三四 . . . (1, 2, 3, 4. . .), the following methods were used to mark ordinal numbers: (1) 天干地支[748] (Heavenly Stems and Earthly Branches) can count numbers from 1 to 60. They were widely used in counting years. (2) 伯仲叔季[749] were used to name brothers in sequence. (3) 元亨利贞 were used mainly to name brothers in sequence. (4) 三字经 (*Three Character Classic*), 百家姓 (*Hundred Family Surnames*) and 千字文 (*Thousand Character Classic*) are three popular children's books. They were used to count large numbers. For example, the Jiangnan Examination Hall (江南贡院, 1168–1905) was the largest examination hall in the history of China, with 20,644 rooms at its peak. The rooms were numbered according to 千字文.

- #258 Heavenly Stems and Earthly Branches to compute time (天干地支纪年)

286. Three and four (*三*四) 2

Idioms with this structure usually have a connotation of 'uncertainty, chaos,' for example, 说三道四 (literally 'speak-3-say-4,' to carp, make irresponsible comments), 颠三倒四 (incoherent), 朝三暮四 (blow hot and cold, chop and change), 不三不四 (neither fish nor fowl), 丢三落四 (scatterbrained), 挑三拣四 (pick and choose) and 推三阻四 (give the runaround) etc.

287. Lucky numbers (6和8) 5

Chinese people are superstitious about some numbers. For instance, 6 and 8 are considered lucky and 4 unlucky, because the Cantonese pronunciation of 8 sounds similar to 发 (in 发财, get rich). On the other hand, the Mandarin pronunciation of 4 sounds similar to 死 (die). The opening ceremony of the Beijing Summer Olympic Games started officially on August 8th, 2008 at 8 pm. Long one of the richest Chinese, Sir Ka-shing Li (李嘉诚, 1928–) retired officially on March 16th, 2018 at 16:36. Numbers with more 6 or 8 are considered lucky. For example, wedding photography often costs 8,888 RMB.

- #121 Custom (风俗)

---

748 天干地支 [-] tiāngàn dìzhī (heavenly-stem-earthly-branch)
749 伯仲叔季 [-] bó zhòng shū jì ((of brothers) eldest-second-third-youngest)

100 *Nature, animals, language*

288. Five buttons (五颗扣子) 1

The Yat-Sen Suit (中山装) or the Mao Suit has five front buttons, supposedly to avoid the numbers 4 or 6, which in combination could have a very negative meaning in words such as 四六不懂[750] (basically ignorant and uncivilized). One explanation is that 天, 地, 父 and 母 (Heaven, Earth, father and mother) are basic concepts and ethics. It happens that 天 and 父 have four strokes each, and 地 and 母 six strokes each. If a person is regarded as 四六不懂, he is blamed not knowing 天地 (thus ignorant) and 父母 (thus uncivilized).

289. 73 and 84 (七十三, 八十四) 1

Many old people in the rural areas often say 七十三, 八十四, 阎王不请自己去[751] (73 or 84, one will die even if the King of Hell does not call you) because Confucius lived 73 years (from 551 BCE–479 BCE) and Mencius lived 84 years (from 372 BCE–289 BCE). On a side note, ancient Chinese people counted ages using the nominal age, which is usually one year older than the real age.

- #95 Master (*子)

290. Three hundred (三百) 1

Chinese literary works favor the number 300. For example, the *Classic of Poetry* (诗经) is also called 诗三百 (literally 'poems 300'). The most popular reader of Chinese poetry is 唐诗三百首 (*Three Hundred Tang Poems*).

- #156 Representatives of Chinese literature (中国文学的代表)

---

750 四六不懂 [-] sì liù bù dǒng (4–6-not-know)

751 七十三, 八十四, 阎王不请自己去 [-, -, 閻--請---] qīshísān, bāshísì, yánwáng bù qǐng zìjǐ qù (73–84, king of hell-not-call-oneself-go)

Appendix 1
English index of entries

73 and 84 #289

Ancestors #167
'And' vs. 和 #253
Antithetical couplets #161
Attitude to life #120
Auditory impression of the Chinese language #4
Auspicious signs and the color white #61

Bad habits #124
Bats #220
The battle of Chinese character forms: traditional, simplified or pinyin? #3
Beauty #127
Benevolence and justice #33
Binomal words #284
Blessing and the unfortunate Song dynasty #78
Blue mountains #205
Boats #236
Boldest proclamation of reform #109
Bo Le #199
Bone #227
Boss #198
Brothers' names and radicals #274
Buddha and monks #68
Buddhism and emperors with a posthumous title of 武 #67
Buddhist texts and knife #69
Buns or dumplings #226

Change #10
Change #12
Change, in the wrong way #13
Children #175
Chinese characters and way of thinking #2
Chinese characters composed of 人 #282
Chinese condolences #56
Chinese cooking methods #225

102 *English index of entries*

Chinese emperors should thank historians. #100
Chinese equivalent of the English word 'do' #256
Chinese language and culture: Negative tendency #1
Chinese literary works with the richest culture #160
Chinese ordinal numbers #285
Chinglish, updated #273
Choice of Chinese characters for foreign place names #269
Circle of. . . #278
Civilities #149
Classical translation of movie titles #270
Classics #257
Collectivism #108
Color and lust #228
Colors and culture #155
Common lengths of forms in Chinese literature #157
Confucius says #158
Copycatting culture #202
Correctness of names #82
Courage #16
Cousins #176
Cows #217
Custom #121

'Death penalty' and modesty #52
Debt #133
Deterioration #154
Die, death #55
Difficulty levels of Chinese rhyme #281
Dilution of vulgar words #267
Discrimination of women #179
Discuss in an open manner #113
Dogs #215
Dogs and chicken/pigs #216
Dream #126
Dusts and the human world #72

Earthquakes and women #183
East . . . west. . . #240
Education: importance, content #190
Education: learning methods #191
Electricity and Chinese idioms #8
Emperors, kings, generals, ministers #91
Euphemisms for 'sexual intercourse' #263
Euphemisms for 'to die' #262
Experienced and inexperienced #201
Eyebrows and urgency #222

Face and dignity #148
Fairness #63

English index of entries 103

Fame and fortune #31
Families: exemplary and satisfactory #171
Fawn #141
Feudal #88
Filial #168
Find a happy medium #135
Find fault #151
The first thing to do after a new emperor ascended the throne in ancient China #74
Fish and 'surplus' #265
Fish and meat #221
Five buttons #288
Flowers and unfaithfulness #211
Flowers and willows #209
Flowers, grass, trees #210
Flunky vs. talent #138
Fondness for children #128
Food and drink #122
Foreign and imported goods #204
Foreign and rustic #203
Foreign countries with '国' in their Chinese names #243
Forget-me-not #271
Forms of address: respectful, honorific and modest #275
Four magnificent characters and the declination of the Northern Song #77
Four Noblemen #213
Friends and friendship #196

Gain extra advantage and suffer losses #134
Gamble #125
Getting rich and building roads #9
Gifted scholars and beautiful women #159
Gifts to avoid giving #146
Given names: taboo and honor #87
'Go drink tea' #71
Gold and jade #229
Good or bad #36
Greedy #45

Hands and feet #223
Hatred #144
Heavenly principles #58
Heavenly Stems and Earthly Branches to compute time #258
Heroines #186
The history and a young girl #117
Homophonic puns #264
Human relations #164
Humorous #35
Husband and wife: bad #174
Husband and wife: good #173

104 *English index of entries*

I was here #242
I'll think about it #255
Idioms with 'heaven/earth' #259
Idioms with markers of simile #7
Ignorant young ladies #107
Importance of tools #232
Individual vs. group #136
Innovation and Chinese college mottos #189
Integrity in one's later years #48
Integrity vs. ability #32

Japanese era names feature common Chinese characters #115
Juxtaposed antonyms meaning 'category' or 'scope' #249
Juxtaposition of male and female #250

Keeping the emperor company #92
Kick someone to the curb #28
Kindness #143
Kindness and hatred #142

Language games #260
Language play on internet #261
The last bit of an emperor's dignity #101
Laws #60
Learning methods #192
Legacy #47
Life and death #51
Liquor and drinking #123
Little * #105
Locations of the four temples in Beijing #62
Long live #102
Louis Cha Leung-yung #139
Loyal and martial #98
Lu Xun #40
Lucky numbers #287

Mandate of Heaven, or God's will #59
Master #95
Mean person #137
The meaning of yìsi #254
Medicine #239
Men vs. ghosts #64
Men's three treasures #54
Mental balance #29
Metals, precious and non-precious #230
Middlemen #200
Ministry of Rites and its importance #99
Mirrors #147

English index of entries 105

Modal verb serial #252
Model of all Chinese #96
Monkeys #219
More bad guys #247
More precious than gold #231
The most heartbreaking vows #268
Music one gets to kneel down when listening #162
Mystic Dragon Cult Leader #140

Nails #234
Naming taboo #86
Needle #233
No principles #25
Noble temperament #130
Nonverbal love #49
North Korea and South Korea #116
Not afraid #246
Not even recognize cows and goats #93
Not flip flop #110
Not standing out #26

Old or new #39
One Belt One Road Initiative #114
One man #103
Oneself and others #19
Onlookers #41
Open and aboveboard #81
Ordinary Chinese people's dream, now and then #119
Outstanding statecraft and brilliant military exploits #73

Painting #163
Parents #169
Parents and children #170
Partial and impartial #21
Party, the #106
Peaceful and chaotic #89
Penitential decrees and letters of self-criticism #90
Peonies and prosperous #212
People, the #14
Poor #132
Posthumous titles #83
The pride of a great empire and the reluctance to lose power #80
Prime ministers must be chosen from Confucian scholars #76
Prosperity and prostitution #266
Prostitutes, other names of #182
Purpose of life #118

Quality and rice #238

106 *English index of entries*

Refined and popular #34
Repent #46
Representatives of Chinese literature #156
Respecting teachers #195
Retribution, karma #66
Rich and powerful #129
Roads and ways #237
Rosy cheeks #185
Rule the roost #172
Rulers and the ruled, ancient and present #166
Rumor #150

Sages and men of virtue #94
Same and different #57
Savior #104
Seek others for help #153
Share weal or woe? #50
Sharp-witted remarks #70
Shortcuts #44
Silence #42
Snobbish #24
Social hierarchy #165
Sophistication #27
Soulmates #197
Sound and culture #5
South . . . north. . . #241
Southern Chinese names and 阿* #276
Spatial-temporal metaphors #251
Speculative #22
Standpoint #15
Stay foolish #43
Stress the past, not the present #37
Sub-ministerial level universities #188
Success and failure #30
Super 'wind' #208
Suspicious #152
Symbolism of goats #218
Synonyms #283

Teacher and student, master and apprentice #194
Temple names and achievements of emperors #85
Temple names of emperors #84
Temporal sequence #6
Things #248
Thoughtcrimes #112
Three and four #286
Three hundred #290
Three Immortal Deeds #97

English index of entries   107

Tigers #214
Times and heroes #17
To one's face and in his back #145
To speak eloquently #279
To survive by all possible means #53
To take or decline the throne #79
To talk nonsense #280
Tolerant #18
The true. . . #187

Unrestrained #131
Utilitarianism #20

Value and joy of learning #193
Vast land and abundant natural resources #38
Vegetables introduced to China #272
The verse that changed China the most #11

Wall #235
Warning inscription on a stone #111
Warning, mild #244
Water #206
Water and fire/soil/wind #207
What was needed to rule China? #75
White Bone Spirit #277
Who do you think you are? #23
Wives, housewives and brooms #184
Wok #224
Women and goods #181
Women and their names in ancient China #180
Women, regarding sex and marriage #177
Women, unlucky #178
The worst curse word #245

Yin and yang #65

Appendix 2
Alphabetical index of Chinese entries

白骨精 #277

包子 #226

报应 #66

北韩与南朝鲜 #116

北京四坛的方位 #62

比, 从, 北, 化 #282

比金子还贵 #231

避讳 #86

蝙蝠 #220

变差 #154

变坏 #13

表亲 #176

并列反义词表范围 #249

伯乐 #199

不出头 #26

不能送的礼物 #146

不怕 #246

不折腾 #110

才子佳人 #159

超级风 #208

尘与世 #72

沉默 #42

成语中的电 #8

吃茶去 #71

仇 #144

传入中国的蔬菜 #272

吹捧 #141

大学校训与创新 #189

带'天/地'的成语 #259

带比喻词的成语 #7

当家 #172

当面与背后 #145

党 #106

倒霉的女人 #178

到此一游 #242

Alphabetical index of Chinese entries 109

道和路 #237
德与才 #32
等级 #165
地大物博 #38
地震与女人 #183
帝国不愿舍弃的荣光 #80
帝王将相 #91
电影片名经典翻译 #270
钉子 #234
东/西 #240
东西不是南北 #248
读书的价值和快乐 #193
赌 #125
对联 #161
恶习 #124
恩 #143
恩仇 #142
法 #60
繁荣'娼'盛 #266
'丰亨豫大'与北宋的衰败 #77
风流 #131
风俗 #121
封建 #88
佛教与'*武帝' #67
佛经与刀 #69
佛与和尚/僧 #68
夫妻: 关系差 #174
夫妻: 关系好 #173
父母 #169
父母与子女 #170
副部级大学 #188
富贵 #129
富含中国文化的文艺作品 #160
改变 #12
改名 #87
工具的重要性 #232
公道 #63
公与私 #21
功利主义 #20
功名 #47
狗 #215
骨头 #227
光明正大 #81
贵族气质 #130
跪着听的音乐 #162
锅 #224
*国 #243

110　*Alphabetical index of Chinese entries*

孩子 #175
汉语的听觉印象 #4
汉语顺序号 #285
汉字与思维 #2
汉字之争 #3
和与 'and' #253
河清海晏与岁月静好 #119
红颜 #185
猴子 #219
厚古薄今 #37
胡说 #280
花草木 #210
花柳 #209
花与不忠 #211
化 #10
画画 #163
怀疑 #152
坏人多 #247
皇帝最后的尊严 #101
回头 #46
活着 #53
机锋 #70
鸡犬/猪狗 #216
集体主义 #108
几种中国文学体裁的长度 #157
妓女的别称 #182
家庭: 令人羡慕的和令人满意的 #171
见牛羊亦不识 #93
教育: 学习方法 #191
教育: 重要性和内容 #190
节哀顺变 #56
捷径 #44
戒石铭 #111
金银铜铁 #230
金庸, Jin Yong #139
金玉 #229
近义词 #283
经 #257
镜子 #147
酒, 喝酒 #123
救星 #104
看客 #41
客套 #149
宽容 #18
老板 #198
老虎 #214
礼部的地位 #99

Alphabetical index of Chinese entries 111

历史与小姑娘 #117
立场 #15
连绵词 #284
连绵词: 雌雄 #250
脸, 面子 #148
恋童 #128
灵活 #27
流言 #150
6和8 #287
鲁迅 #40
眉毛与紧急 #222
美女 #127
梦 #126
庙号 #84
庙号与成就 #85
名利 #31
名正言顺 #82
牡丹和富贵 #212
南/北 #241
南方人名中的'阿' #276
难得糊涂 #43
内行与外行 #201
能说 #279
能愿动词的连用 #252
你算老几啊? #23
牛 #217
农民的三宝 #54
弄 #256
奴才 vs. 人才 #138
女人的名字 #180
女人干坏事 #179
女人与货 #181
女英雄 #186
朋友, 友谊 #196
七十三, 八十四 #289
妻子, 妇女与扫帚 #184
墙 #235
青山 #205
穷 #132
求人 #153
劝进与固辞 #79
人际关系 #164
人民 #14
人与鬼 #64
人与己 #19
仁与义 #33
日本年号中的汉字 #115

112 *Alphabetical index of Chinese entries*

如何治理中国? #75
三百 #290
三不朽 #97
三不足 #109
*三*四 #286
色 #228
傻* #267
山寨文化 #202
社会的两极 #166
神龙教主 #140
生活的目的 #118
生活态度 #120
生死 #51
圣贤 #94
胜负, 成败 #30
师生, 师徒 #194
时间顺序 #6
时空比喻 #251
时势与英雄 #17
势利眼 #24
谥号 #83
手和脚 #223
水 #206
水火/水土/风水 #207
思想罪 #112
死 #55
'死'的委婉语 #262
死罪死罪 #52
四君子 #213
宋朝年号与'祐' #78
贪婪 #45
*坛/界 #278
天干地支纪年 #258
天理 #58
天命, 天意 #59
条目汉语顺序
同甘还是共苦 #50
同与异 #57
投机 #22
外国地名中的汉字的选择 #269
晚节 #48
万岁 #102
网络上的语言游戏 #261
妄议 #113
温和的警告 #244
文治武功 #73
文字游戏 #260

Alphabetical index of Chinese entries 113

无言的爱 #49
无原则 #25
无知少女 #107
五颗扣子 #288
勿忘我 #271
祥瑞与白色 #61
小 #105
小人 #137
孝 #168
谐音双关 #264
卸磨杀驴 #28
心理平衡 #29
新皇继位后做的第一件事 #74
新与旧 #39
新中式英语 #273
兄弟人名的汉字与部首 #274
学习方法 #192
雅俗 #34
研究研究 #255
颜色与文化 #155
羊的象征意义 #218
洋货 #204
洋与土 #203
药 #239
一带一路 #114
一人 #103
一人与一群 #136
'意思'的意思 #254
阴阳 #65
饮食 #122
影响中国最大的一句话 #11
勇气 #16
优劣 #36
幽默 #35
鱼和余 #265
鱼与肉 #221
与大人物相处 #92
语音与文化 #5
韵脚的难易 #281
宰相须用读书人 #76
贼 #245
债 #133
占便宜与吃亏 #134
找借口 #151
折中 #135
针 #233
真 . . . #187

114 *Alphabetical index of Chinese entries*

知己 #197
质量与大米 #238
治与乱 #89
致富与修路 #9
中国菜的做法 #225
中国皇帝应该感谢史官 #100
中国人的楷模 #96
中国文学的代表 #156
中国语言的负面倾向 #1
中间人 #200
忠, 贞, 烈的女人 #177
忠武 #98
舟和船 #236
*子 #95
子曰 #158
祖宗 #167
最让人心碎的誓言 #268
罪己诏与检讨书 #90
尊称, 敬称, 谦称 #275
尊师 #195
'做爱'的委婉语 #263

Appendix 3

Alphabetical index of Chinese expressions in footnotes

Note: The 500 culturally rich idioms, proverbs and maxims are numbered.

八卦 [-] 458
白日梦 [--夢] 332

1. 白首为功名 [--為--] 140
2. 百年修得同船渡, 千年修得共枕眠 [-] 538
3. 百善孝为先 [---為-] 512
4. 班门弄斧 [-門--] 709

板上钉钉 [--釘釘] 719

5. 半部论语治天下 [--論語---] 225
6. 伴君如伴虎 [-] 235
7. 邦有道, 贫且贱焉, 耻也; 邦无道, 富且贵焉, 耻也 [-, 貧-賤-, 恥-; -無-, --貴-, 恥-] 363

包办婚姻 [-辦--] 565
报仇雪恨[報---] 431

8. 杯酒释兵权 [--釋-權] 237

北韩 [-韓] 281

9. 背黑锅 [--鍋] 698
10. 背后捅刀子 [-後---] 442
11. 本来无一物, 何处惹尘埃 [--無--, -處-塵-] 216
12. 闭门谢客读书 [閉門謝-讀書] 149
13. 别丢父母的脸 [-----臉] 453

伯乐相马 [-樂-馬] 632

14. 伯仲叔季 [-] 749
15. 不出头 [--頭] 397
16. 不打勤, 不打懒, 专打不长眼 [-, --懶, 專--長-] 67
17. 不当第一 [-當--] 62
18. 不当家不知柴米贵 [-當-----貴] 532
19. 不得妄议国政 [---議國-] 279
20. 不看僧面看佛面 [-] 210
21. 不拿群众一针一线 [---衆-針-綫] 716

116 *Alphabetical index of Chinese expressions in footnotes*

22. 不能极问 [--極問] 593, 607

不怕邪 [-] 741

23. 不怕一万, 就怕万一 [---萬, --萬-] 739

不偏不倚 [-] 392

24. 不是名儒, 便是名臣 [-] 507
25. 不谈工作 [-談--] 150
26. 不肖子孙 [-] 508
27. 不以成败论英雄 [---敗論--] 77
28. 不在沉默中爆发, 就在沉默中灭亡 [------發, -----滅-] 116

不择手段 [-擇--] 46

29. 不占白不占 [-] 388
30. 不折腾 [--騰] 273
31. 不重生男重生女 [-] 49
32. 不撞南墙不回头 [---墙--頭] 134
33. 不自由, 毋宁死 [-, -寧-] 160
34. 不作为 [--為] 63
35. 不做中, 不做保, 不做媒人三世好 [-] 636
36. 残花败柳 [殘-敗-] 657
37. 操你祖宗八代 [-] 509
38. 草木皆兵 [-] 663

沉默是金 [-] 115

39. 沉鱼落雁, 闭月羞花 [-魚--, 閉---] 345
40. 吃茶去 [-] 214

吃错药 [-錯藥] 732

41. 吃得苦中苦, 方为人上人 [-] 284
42. 吃喝嫖赌抽 [---賭-] 320

吃苦 [-] 285

43. 吃亏是福 [-虧--] 390
44. 吃了上顿没下顿 [---頓--頓] 370

吃人 [-] 352

45. 吃人不吐骨头 [-----頭] 702
46. 吃着碗里, 看着锅里 [-著-裏, -著鍋裏] 129, 693
47. 痴人说梦 [癡-説夢] 334
48. 冲冠一怒为红颜 [衝冠--為紅顔] 576
49. 崇洋媚外 [-] 639

仇深似海 [-] 435

50. 丑妻薄田破棉袄 [醜-----襖] 161
51. 臭老九 [-] 499

出世 [-] 291

Alphabetical index of Chinese expressions in footnotes   117

52. 出头的椽子先烂 [-頭----爛] 58
53. 初生牛犊不怕虎 [---犢---] 737

　　雏妓 [雛-] 348

54. 楚王好细腰, 宫中多饿死 [---細-, ---餓-] 48
55. 传宗接代 [傳---] 506
56. 床前明月光 [-] 747
57. 床头吵架床尾和 [牀頭--牀--] 544

　　吹鼓手 [-] 410

58. 吹喇叭, 抬轿子 [-, 擡轎-] 411
59. 春秋大梦 [---夢] 341
60. 此曲只应天上有, 人间能得几回闻 [---應---, -間--幾-聞] 485
61. 从一而终 [從--終] 14
62. 存天理, 去人欲 [-] 170
63. 打到的媳妇揉到的面 [----婦---麵] 568
64. 大成至圣先师文宣王 [---聖-師---] 230

　　大恩大德 [-] 428
　　大恩难报, 不如杀之 [--難報, --殺-] 420

65. 大恩如大仇 [-] 419

　　大富大贵 [---貴] 360

66. 大锅饭 [-鍋飯] 694

　　大海捞针 [--撈針] 712

67. 大梦谁先觉 [-夢誰-覺] 342
68. 大上有立德 [-] 246
69. 大树底下好乘凉 [-樹----涼] 23
70. 大学之道, 在明明德 [-學--, -] 583

　　戴高帽 [-] 413

71. 戴绿帽 [-綠-] 444
72. 单丝不成线, 独木不成林 [單絲--綫, 獨----] 266
73. 但见新人笑, 哪闻旧人哭 [-見---, -聞舊--] 102

　　淡泊名利 [-] 82
　　当家作主 [當---] 535

74. 当面教子, 背后教妻 [當---, -後--] 443
75. 当面一套, 背后一套 [當---, -後--] 438
76. 党, 国家和人民 [黨, 國----] 17
77. 党啊, 亲爱的妈妈 [黨-, 親愛-媽媽] 262
78. 党妈 [黨媽] 263
79. 到此一游 [-] 733
80. 道不同不相为谋 [-----為謀] 622

　　得寸进尺 [--進-] 125
　　得过且过 [-過-過] 298

118 *Alphabetical index of Chinese expressions in footnotes*

81. 得陇望蜀 [-隴--] 126
82. 得饶人处且饶人 [-饒-處-饒-] 34
83. 德才兼备 [---備] 89
84. 德智体美劳 [--體-勞] 585

　　等米下锅 ［---鍋］690

85. 弟子不必不如师 [------師] 610
86. 点水之恩当涌泉相报 [點---當湧--報] 427

　　钉子户 ［釘--］722

87. 丢脸 [-臉] 449

　　丢人 ［-］451

88. 东食西宿 [東---] 549
89. 东西是别人的好, 孩子是自己的好 [東------, -] 550
90. 独乐乐不如众乐乐 [獨樂樂--衆樂樂] 256
91. 读书破万卷, 下笔如有神 [讀書-萬-, -筆---] 589

　　赌场得意, 情场失意 [賭場--, -場--] 328
　　赌场失意, 情场得意 [賭場--, -場--] 72

92. 赌场无父子 [賭場無--] 325

　　赌近盗 ［賭-盜］327

93. 对酒当歌, 人生几何 [對-當-, --幾-] 310
94. 多福多寿 [---壽] 687
95. 多个朋友多条路 [-個---條] 621
96. 多行不义必自毙 [---義--斃] 203
97. 躲得过初一, 躲不过十五 [--過--, --過--] 382
98. 恶人自有恶人磨 [惡---惡-] 202
99. 饿死事极小, 失节事极大 [餓--極-, -節-極-] 171, 306

　　恩公 ［-］425

100. 恩将仇报 [-將-報] 418
101. 恩客 [-] 426

　　恩师 ［-師］424

102. 儿不嫌母丑, 狗不嫌家贫 [兒---醜, ----貧] 55, 675
103. 儿行千里母担忧, 母行千里儿不愁 [兒----擔憂, ----兒--] 526

　　儿孙绕膝 ［兒孫繞-］529

104. 尔俸尔禄, 民膏民脂, 下民易虐, 上天难欺 [爾-爾-, -, -, --難-] 275
105. 二十四孝图 [----圖] 511
106. 二手货 [--貨] 106

　　法不责众 ［--責衆］398

107. 放下屠刀, 立地成佛 [-] 211

Alphabetical index of Chinese expressions in footnotes 119

108. 飞鸟尽, 良弓藏; 狡兔死, 走狗烹 [飛鳥儘, -; -, -] 69

　　非富即贵 [---貴] 359

109. 分一杯羹 [-] 516
110. 粪土当年万户侯 [糞-當-萬--] 247
111. 丰亨豫大 [豐---] 226

　　风流才子 [風---] 367
　　风水宝地 [風-寶-] 655
　　风水先生 [風---] 656
　　封建思想 [-] 233

112. 夫唱妇随 [--婦隨] 542
113. 夫妻本是同林鸟, 大难临头各自飞 [------鳥, -難臨頭--飛] 545
114. 夫妻没有隔夜的仇 [-] 543
115. 夫妻是前世的冤家, 孩子是前世的债主 [-, ------債-] 554

　　服丧 [-喪] 521

116. 福到了 [-] 743

　　俯首甘为孺子牛 [---爲---] 680

117. 父精母血, 不可弃也 [-, --棄-] 518

　　父母双全 [--雙-] 523

118. 父母在, 不远游 [-] 520

　　父母之恩 [-] 422
　　父母之命 [-] 519

119. 父一而已, 人尽可夫 [-, -盡--] 547

　　父债子还 [-債-還] 381
　　附庸风雅 [--風-] 94

120. 副部级大学 [--級-學] 581
121. 富不过三代 [--過--] 365

　　富贵病 [-貴-] 358

122. 富贵不还乡, 如锦衣夜行 [-貴-還鄉, -錦---] 361
123. 富贵险中求 [-貴險--] 356
124. 腹诽 [-誹] 276, 468
125. 盖棺定论 [蓋--論] 147

　　赶尽杀绝 [趕盡殺絕] 36

126. 高处不胜寒 [-處-勝-] 255

　　高人一等 [-] 501

127. 高山流水 [-] 627
128. 歌功颂德 [--頌-] 222
129. 隔墙有耳 [-墙--] 727

120 *Alphabetical index of Chinese expressions in footnotes*

130. 给个棒槌就当针 [給個---當針] 717
131. 工欲善其事, 必先利其器 [-] 707
132. 公道世间惟白发, 贵人头上不曾饶 [---間--髮, 貴-頭---饒] 188
133. 公道自在人心 [-] 186
134. 功高震主 [-] 236

　　功名利禄 〔-〕 81

135. 苟富贵, 无相忘 [--貴, 勿--] 362

　　狗东西 〔-東-〕 668

136. 狗改不了吃屎 [-] 672

　　狗腿子 〔-〕 670

137. 狗眼看人低 [-] 673

　　狗咬狗 〔-〕 671

138. 狗嘴里吐不出象牙 [--裏-----] 674
139. 古来圣贤皆寂寞, 唯有饮者留其名 [-來聖賢---, --飲----] 245
140. 官大一级压死人 [---級壓--] 500
141. 官吏僧道医工匠娼儒丐 [----醫-----] 498
142. 光脚的不怕穿鞋的 [-] 504
143. 光宗耀祖 [-] 505

　　闺密 [闈-] 617
　　鬼子 [-] 190
　　贵人 [貴-] 634

144. 跪着听的音乐 [-著聽--樂] 484
145. 棍棒底下出孝子 [-] 514

　　国恨家仇 [國---] 433
　　国色天香 [國---] 666

146. 过河拆桥 [過--橋] 70
147. 海内存知己, 天涯若比邻 [-, ----鄰] 629
148. 含饴弄孙 [-飴-孫] 148

　　寒号鸟 [-號鳥] 299
　　好话说尽 [-話說盡] 439

149. 好了歌 [-] 86
150. 好马不吃回头草 [-馬---頭-] 135
151. 好人不长寿, 祸害一千年 [---長壽, 禍----] 205

　　好人有好报 〔----報〕 201

152. 好死不如赖活着 [----賴-著] 159
153. 好心没好报 [----報] 204
154. 好大喜功 [-] 218
155. 好读书不求甚解 [-讀書----] 592

　　和事佬 〔-〕 25, 394

Alphabetical index of Chinese expressions in footnotes   121

156. 河清海晏 [-] 288

黑手党 [--黨] 259

157. 红杏出墙 [紅--墙] 725
158. 红颜薄命 [紅顔--] 574
159. 红颜祸水 [紅顔禍-] 564, 575, 649

红颜知己 [紅顔--] 573

160. 猴年马月 [--馬-] 685

猴子捞月 [--捞-] 683

161. 厚古薄今 [-] 98
162. 厚黑学 [--學] 493

花开富贵 [-開-貴] 357, 667
花柳病 [-] 658

163. 花天酒地 [-] 316
164. 化悲痛为力量 [---為--] 4
165. 化腐朽为神奇 [---為--] 6
166. 化干戈为玉帛 [---爲--] 5

画鬼最容易 [畫----] 486

167. 画鬼最易 [畫---] 192
168. 画龙画虎难画骨, 知人知面不知心 [畫龍畫-難畫-, -] 488

怀才不遇 [懷---] 635
坏事做绝 [壞--絕] 441
黄赌毒 [-賭-] 322, 329

169. 黄粱一梦 [---夢] 335
170. 回头再说 [-頭-说] 456

活着 [-著] 287

171. 和稀泥 [-] 26, 395

鸡 [鷄] 571

172. 鸡蛋里挑骨头 [鷄-裏--頭] 465, 701

鸡飞狗跳 [鷄飛--] 676

173. 鸡狗不到头 [鷄---頭] 678

鸡犬不宁 [鷄--寧] 221

174. 鸡犬升天 [鷄---] 677
175. 鸡犬之声相闻, 民至老死不相往来 [雞--聲-聞, -------來] 295
176. 既无外债, 也无内债 [-無-債, -無-債] 384
177. 家父 [-] 745
178. 嫁鸡随鸡, 嫁狗随狗 [-鷄随鷄, --随-] 556

122 *Alphabetical index of Chinese expressions in footnotes*

179. 尖嘴猴腮 [-] 681

　　见机行事 〔見機--〕 64

180. 见牛羊亦不识 [見----識] 238
181. 见什么人说什么话, 到什么山唱什么歌 [見-麼-說-麼話, --麼---麼-] 65
182. 脚上没鞋穷半截 [----穷--] 372

　　教师节 [-師節] 614
　　揭不开锅 [--開鍋] 691

183. 节哀顺变 [節-順變] 168
184. 结草衔环 [結-銜環] 429
185. 巾帼不让须眉 [-幗-讓鬚-] 578

　　巾帼英雄 〔-幗--〕 577

186. 今朝有酒今朝醉 [-] 296
187. 金口玉言 [-] 703
188. 金童玉女 [-] 705
189. 金玉其外, 败絮其中 [-, 敗---] 706

　　金枝玉叶 〔---葉〕 704

190. 竟无一人是男儿 [-無----兒] 28
191. 敬而远之 [--遠-] 402
192. 静夜思 [靜--] 746
193. 久病床前无孝子 [--牀-無--] 515, 527
194. 久赌必输 [-賭-輸] 323
195. 酒不醉人人自醉 [-] 312

　　酒逢知己千杯少 〔-〕 630

196. 酒逢知己千杯少, 话不投机半句多 [-, 話--機---] 309

　　酒后乱性 〔-後亂-〕 314

197. 酒后吐真言 [-後---] 313

　　酒肉朋友 〔-〕 315

198. 旧的不去, 新的不来 [舊---, ---來] 103
199. 救急不救穷 [----窮] 376
200. 救救孩子 [-] 353
201. 举案齐眉 [舉-齊-] 541
202. 举头三尺有神灵 [舉頭----靈] 176, 198
203. 聚沙成塔, 集腋成裘 [-] 267
204. 绝圣弃智 [絕聖棄-] 243
205. 君子报仇, 十年不晚 [--報-, -] 436
206. 君子之交淡如水 [-] 624
207. 开弓没有回头箭 [-----頭] 133
208. 看热闹的不嫌事大 [-熱鬧-----] 113
209. 看人下菜碟 [-] 52
210. 考考考, 老师的法宝; 分分分, 学生的命根 [-, -師--寶; -, -學----] 597

Alphabetical index of Chinese expressions in footnotes 123

211. 可怜天下父母心 [-] 524
212. 苦海无边, 回头是岸 [--無邊, -頭--] 130
213. 烂船还有三千钉 [爛-還---釘] 718
214. 浪子回头金不换 [---頭---] 132

　　　劳民伤财 [勞-傷財] 220

215. 劳心者治人, 劳力者治于人 [勞----, 勞---於-] 503

　　　老好人 [-] 24

216. 老皇历 [--曆] 13

　　　老天不睁眼 [---睜-] 207
　　　老天瞎了眼 [-] 209
　　　老天显灵 [--顯靈] 208

217. 老天有眼 [-] 206
218. 礼乐射御书数 [禮樂--書數] 584
219. 李白斗酒诗百篇 [----詩--] 317
220. 历史悠久, 地大物博 [歷---, -] 100

　　　脸皮厚 [臉--] 494

221. 良药苦口利于病 [-藥-----] 731
222. 两耳不闻窗外事, 一心只读圣贤书 [---聞---, ---讀聖賢書] 242

　　　两小无猜 [--無-] 616

223. 了却君王天下事, 赢得生前身后名 [-, 贏----後-] 141
224. 烈女不嫁二夫 [-] 557

　　　烈女传 [--傳] 559

225. 林森入森林, 只见树木 [-, -見樹-] 482
226. 留得青山在, 不怕没柴烧 [-, ----燒] 645, 740
227. 留有余地 [--餘-] 35
228. 流言止于智者 [---於--] 459

　　　柳暗花明 [-] 659

229. 六月飞雪 [--飛-] 744
230. 龙生龙, 凤生凤, 老鼠的儿子会打洞 [龍-龍, 鳳-鳳, ---兒-會--] 553
231. 鲁班门前耍大斧 [魯-門----] 710
232. 麻三斤 [-] 212
233. 满朝朱紫贵, 尽是读书人 [滿---貴, 盡-讀書-] 603
234. 满口仁义道德, 一肚子男盗女娼 [滿--義--, ----盗--] 91
235. 毛主席万岁 [---萬歲] 416

　　　没富贵命 [--貴-] 355

236. 没什么问题, 有一定难度, 应该差不多: See in-text. 454
237. 美国梦 [-國夢] 339
238. 梦反 [夢-] 330

　　　绵里藏针 [綿裏-針] 715

124 *Alphabetical index of Chinese expressions in footnotes*

239. 面子是别人给的, 脸是自己丢的 [-----給-, 臉-----] 452
240. 民以食为天 [---為-] 303
241. 名不正则言不顺, 言不顺则事不行 [---則--順, --順則---] 229
242. 名垂青史[-] 136, 145, 217
243. 名缰利锁 [-繮-鎖] 85

名利场 [--場] 87

244. 名利双收 [-] 84
245. 命中注定 [-] 181
246. 莫说九族, 十族何妨 [-說--, -] 8
247. 莫须有 [-須-] 277, 467
248. 谋事在人, 成事在天 [謀---, -] 182
249. 木秀于林, 风必摧之 . . . 行高于人, 众必非之 [--於-, 風---. . .--於-, 眾---] 57

沐猴而冠 [-] 682

250. 哪边风硬哪边倒 [-邊風--邊-] 22
251. 男主外, 女主内 [-] 539

南朝鲜 [--鮮] 280

252. 难得糊涂 [難--塗] 119
253. 囊萤映雪 [-螢--] 595
254. 内斗内行, 外斗外行 [-鬥--, -鬥--] 637
255. 你耕田来我织布, 我挑水来你浇园 [---來-織-, ---來-澆園] 540
256. 你好自为之 [--- 為-] 734
257. 你看着办吧 [--著辦-] 735
258. 你说你公道, 我说我公道, 公道不公道, 只有天知道 [-說---, -說---, -, -] 187
259. 你算老几啊 [-] 51

拈花惹草 [-] 660

260. 鸟生鱼汤 [鳥--湯] 415
261. 宁教我负天下人, 休教天下人负我 [寧--負---, -----負-] 472
262. 宁落一群, 不落一人 [-] 399
263. 宁用奴才, 不用人才 [寧---, -] 408

佞幸列传 [---傳] 405

264. 女大十八变 [----變] 15
265. 女儿是父母贴心的小棉袄 [-兒---貼----襖] 555

女汉子 [-漢-] 580

266. 女人当家, 房倒屋塌 [--當-, -] 569
267. 女人能顶半边天 [---頂-邊-] 579
268. 女人心, 海底针 [-, --針] 713
269. 女子无才便是德 [--無----] 90, 563
270. 赔钱货 [賠錢貨] 562
271. 朋友妻, 不可欺 [-] 620
272. 捧臭脚 [-] 412
273. 贫居闹市无人问, 富在深山有远亲 [貧-鬧-無-問, -----遠親] 371

274. 贫穷不是社会主义, 更不是共产主义 [貧窮---會-義, ----產-義] 379

平常心 [-] 74
泼冷水 [潑--] 647
泼脏水 [潑髒-] 648

275. 破财免灾 [-財-災] 71

破四旧 〔--舊〕104

276. 破鞋 [-] 105, 572
277. 七十三, 八十四, 阎王不请自己去 [-, -, 閻--請---] 751

骑墙 〔騎墻〕20

278. 千军易得, 一将难求 [-軍--, -將難-] 407
279. 千里马常有, 而伯乐不常有 [--馬--, --樂---] 633
280. 千里姻缘一线牵 [---緣-綫牽] 536
281. 欠债的是大爷 [-債---爺] 385
282. 枪打出头鸟 [槍--頭鳥] 60
283. 强龙压不住地头蛇 [-龍壓---頭-] 232
284. 墙倒众人推 [墻-衆--] 728

墙花路草 〔墻---〕661

285. 墙里开花墙外香 [墻裏開-墻--] 726
286. 墙头草 [墻頭-] 21, 724
287. 巧妇难为无米之炊 [-婦難爲無---] 708
288. 巧言令色鲜矣仁 [----鮮--] 95
289. 亲君子, 远小人 [親--, 遠--] 401
290. 青出于蓝而胜于蓝 [--於藍-勝於藍] 608

青梅竹马 〔---馬〕615

291. 青山不老, 绿水长流 [-, 綠-長-] 644

穷光蛋 〔窮--〕369

292. 穷家富路 [窮---] 373
293. 穷人的孩子早当家 [窮-----當-] 377, 534

穷酸相 〔窮--〕374

294. 穷则变, 变则通, 通则久 [窮則變, 變則-, -則-] 11

穷则思变 〔窮則-變〕378

295. 求人不如求己 [-] 473

求天天不应, 求地地不语 〔----應, ----語〕476

296. 求爷爷, 告奶奶 [-爺爺, -] 475
297. 去食, . . . 民无信不立 [-,-無---] 305

燃眉之急 [-] 689
热锅上的蚂蚁 [熱鍋--螞蟻] 699

126 *Alphabetical index of Chinese expressions in footnotes*

298. 人不风流枉少年 [--風----] 366
299. 人不为己, 天诛地灭 [--爲-, -誅-滅] 42
300. 人多力量大 [-] 265
301. 人非草木, 孰能无情 [-] 664
302. 人非圣贤, 孰能无过 [--聖賢, --無過] 240
303. 人过留名, 雁过留声 [-過--, -過-聲] 137
304. 人皆可以为尧舜 [----為堯-] 241

人民的大救星 〔-〕 258

305. 人民英雄永垂不朽 [-] 143
306. 人怕出名猪怕壮 [-] 59

人情世故 〔-〕 489

307. 人穷志短 [-窮--] 375
308. 人上人 [-] 286, 502
309. 人生得一知己足矣, 斯世当以同怀视之 [-, --當--懷視-] 625
310. 人生得意须尽欢, 莫使金樽空对月 [-----盡歡, -----對-] 308
311. 人生苦短, 何不秉烛夜游 [-, ---燭--] 297
312. 人生在世, 吃喝二字 [-] 304
313. 人生自古谁无死, 留取丹心照汗青 [----誰無-, -] 138, 163
314. 人为财死, 鸟为食亡 [-為財-, -為--] 88, 162
315. 人为刀俎, 我为鱼肉 [-為--, -為魚-] 688

人小鬼大 〔-〕 193

316. 人心不足蛇吞象 [-] 127

人心险恶 [--險惡] 491
人有脸, 树有皮 [--臉, 樹--] 450

317. 人在江湖, 身不由己 [-] 492
318. 人在做, 天在看 [-] 175, 197
319. 仁者心动 [---動] 213
320. 入国而问俗 [-國-問-] 301

入世 [-] 290
软/硬/贱骨头 [軟/-/賤-頭] 700
软钉子 [軟釘-] 721

321. 撒泡尿照照自己 [-] 446
322. 三不足 [-] 269

三从 [-從] 566

323. 三代为官作宦, 方知穿衣吃饭 [--為---, -----飯] 364

三分像人, 七分像鬼 〔-〕 189

324. 三分药, 七分养 [--藥, --養] 730

三脚踢不出一个屁来 [------個-來] 117
三妻四妾 [-] 548

Alphabetical index of Chinese expressions in footnotes 127

325. 三人成虎 [-] 460

三十功名尘与土 ［----塵與-］83

326. 三十功名尘与土, 八千里路云和月[----塵與-, ----雲--] 139
327. 三十亩地一头牛, 老婆孩子热炕头 [----頭-, ----熱-頭] 531
328. 三世无犯法之男, 五世无再婚之女 [--無----, --無----] 530
329. 三岁看到老 [-歲---] 551
330. 杀父之仇, 不共戴天 [殺---, -] 432
331. 杀鸡骇猴 [殺鷄駭-] 684

山寨文化 ［-］638

332. 山中无老虎, 猴子称大王 [--無--, --稱--] 686

善财童子 ［-財--］351

333. 善恶到头终有报, 只争来早与来迟 [-惡-頭終-報, -爭來-與來遲] 200
334. 善有善报, 恶有恶报 [---報, 惡-惡報] 199

伤天害理 ［傷---］174

335. 上有所好, 下必甚焉 [-] 47
336. 舍己为人 [捨-爲-] 41
337. 身体发肤, 受之父母, 不敢毁伤, 孝之始也 [-體髮膚, -, --毁傷, -] 517

深仇大恨 ［-］434

338. 生的伟大, 死的光荣 [--偉-, ---榮] 157

生老病死 [-] 152
生离死别 [-離-別] 156
生死存亡 [-] 153

339. 生死有命, 富贵在天[-, -貴--] 154, 354

生死之交 ［-］155

340. 生要同衾, 死要同穴 [-] 561

生在帝王家 ［-］239

341. 圣人不死, 大盗不止 [聖---, -盜--] 244
342. 胜败乃兵家常事 [勝敗-----] 76
343. 胜不骄, 败不馁 [勝-驕, 敗-餒] 79

胜负手 ［勝負-］78

344. 胜者王侯败者贼 [勝---敗-賊] 44, 75, 282

师说 ［師説］609

345. 师徒如父子 [師----] 604
346. 虱子多了不咬, 账多了不愁 [-, 賬----] 386

十恶不赦 ［-惡--］319

128 *Alphabetical index of Chinese expressions in footnotes*

347. 十里不同风, 百里不同俗 [----風, -] 300

十里洋场 [---場] 643

348. 时势造英雄 [時势---] 30
349. 食色性也 [-] 302
350. 士农工商 [-農--] 497
351. 士为知己者死 [-] 628

世风日下 〔-風--〕478

352. 事不关己, 高高挂起 [--關-, -] 108

事了拂衣去, 深藏功与名 〔-, ---與-〕144

353. 是药三分毒 [-藥---] 729

受命于天 〔--於-〕178

354. 书读百遍, 其义自见/现 [書讀--, -義-見/現] 588
355. 书山有路勤为径, 学海无涯苦作舟 [書----為徑, 學-無----] 594
356. 书中自有黄金屋, 书中自有颜如玉 [書------, 書---顏--] 600
357. 熟读唐诗三百首, 不会作诗也会吟 [-讀-詩---, -會-詩-會] 590
358. 数风流人物, 还看今朝 [數風---, 還---] 368
359. 树挪死, 人挪活 [樹--, -] 12

甩手掌柜 〔---櫃〕533

360. 水很深 [-] 646

水火不容 [-] 650
水火无情 [--無-] 652
水深火热 [---熱] 651

361. 水土不服 [-] 653
362. 顺情说好话 [順-說-話] 66
363. 说风凉话 [說風涼話] 109

说句公道话 [說---話] 185
说梦话 [說夢話] 333

364. 说你行你就行, 不行也行; 说你不行你就不行, 行也不行 [說 . . ., 說 . . .] 56, 409
365. 死不瞑目 [-] 167
366. 死要面子活受罪 [-] 448
367. 死者为大 [--為-] 166
368. 死罪死罪 [-] 158

四大美女 〔-〕344

369. 四六不懂 [-] 750

四人帮 〔--幫〕261

370. 四世同堂 [-] 528

俗不可耐 〔-〕92

371. 虽千万人, 吾往矣 [雖-萬-, -] 27

372. 随便聊聊 [隨---] 457

随大流/溜 [隨--] 396

373. 岁月静好 [歲-靜-] 289
374. 碎碎平安 [-] 73

损人利己 [損---] 39

375. 贪嗔痴 [貪-癡] 318

贪得无厌 [貪-無厭] 123
唐诗宋词元曲 [-詩-詞--] 481

376. 韬光养晦 [韜-養-] 61
377. 天变不足畏, 祖宗不足法, 人言不足恤 [-變---, -, ----卹] 270
378. 天不变, 道亦不变 [--變, ---變] 10

天不怕, 地不怕, 就怕 . . . [-] 738

379. 天不生仲尼, 万古如长夜 [-, 萬--長-] 257
380. 天地君亲师 [---親師] 613

天干地支 [-] 748

381. 天理即人欲 [-] 172

天理难容 [--難-] 173

382. 天命不可违 [----違] 179
383. 天人合一 [-] 169

天下大治 [-] 234

384. 天下读书种子 [--讀書種-] 7
385. 天下无不是的父母 [--無-----] 522
386. 天下兴亡, 匹夫有责 [--興-, ---責] 293
387. 天圆地方 [-圓--] 184
388. 天之亡我, 非战之罪 [-, -戰--] 80

天子 [-] 177
铁哥们 [鐵-們] 618

389. 听天由命 [聽---] 180
390. 同甘共苦 [-] 151

童子鸡 [--鷄] 346

391. 童子尿 [-] 347
392. 童子烹茶 [-] 349

童子献茶 [--獻-] 350

393. 外国的月亮比中国的圆 [-國-----過--] 640
394. 晚节不保 [-節--] 146
395. 万般皆下品, 唯有读书高 [萬----, --讀書-] 602
396. 万变不离其宗 [萬變-離--] 9

万事不求人 [萬----] 474

130 *Alphabetical index of Chinese expressions in footnotes*

397. 万岁, 万岁, 万万岁 [萬歲, 萬歲, 萬萬歲] 249

    万岁爷 [萬歲爺] 250

398. 网开一面 [網開--] 32
399. 妄议中央 [-議--] 278
400. 望门寡 [-門-] 558
401. 为人师表 [爲-師-] 612
402. 唯恐天下不乱 [-----亂] 114
403. 唯女子与小人为难养也, 近之则不逊, 远之则怨 [---與--為難養-, --則--, 遠-則-]
    400, 570
404. 惟上是从 [---從] 53
405. 惟以一人治天下, 岂为天下奉一人 [-, -為-----] 252
406. 未嫁从父, 既嫁从夫, 夫死从子 [--從-, --從-, --從-] 567
407. 为朋友两肋插刀 [為------] 619
408. 文治武功 [-] 271

    我一个都不宽恕 [--個--寬-] 38

409. 我亦无他, 唯手熟耳 [--無-, -] 121
410. 无酒不成席 [無----] 307

    无为 [無爲] 274

411. 无债一身轻 [無債--輕] 383
412. 吾从周 [-從] 99
413. 五毒俱全 [-] 321
414. 物以类聚, 人以群分 [--類-, -] 96

    膝盖软 [-蓋軟] 50

415. 喜新厌旧 [--厭舊] 101
416. 先人后己 [--後-] 40

    享受生活 [-] 283

417. 萧规曹随 [蕭規-隨] 606
418. 小赌怡情, 大赌伤身 [-賭--, -賭傷-] 324
419. 小国寡民 [-國--] 294
420. 小人常戚戚 [-] 403
421. 小人得志 [-] 404

    孝经 [-經] 510
    笑面虎 [-] 440

422. 笑贫不笑娼 [-貧---] 45
423. 卸磨杀驴 [--殺驢] 68

    心黑 [-] 495
    心里有鬼 [-裏--] 191

424. 形势比人强 [-勢---] 31

    兴师动众 [興師動衆] 219

425. 兄弟如手足, 妻子如衣服 [-] 546

426. 兄弟阋于墙, 而外御其辱 [--閱於墻, --禦--] 723
427. 修桥补路瞎眼, 杀人放火儿多 [-橋補---, 殺---兒-] 3
428. 秀才造反, 三年不成 [-] 248

袖手旁观 〔---觀〕 107

429. 学而优则仕 [學-優則-] 292
430. 学好数理化, 不如有个好爸爸 [學-數--, ---個---] 587
431. 学我者生, 似我者死 [學---, -] 599
432. 血债血偿 [-債-償] 380
433. 崖山之后无中华 [---後無-華] 227

睚眦必报 〔-眥-報〕 37

434. 雅俗共赏 [---賞] 93
435. 严谨, 勤奋, 求实, 创新 [嚴謹, -奮, -實, 創-] 582
436. 严以律己, 宽以待人 [嚴---, 寬---] 33
437. 研究研究 [-] 455, 742
438. 眼中钉, 肉中刺 [--釘, -] 720
439. 阳盛阴衰 [陽-陰-] 194
440. 洋为中用 [-為--] 641
441. 仰天掉馅饼 [---餡餅] 122
442. 养儿方知父母恩 [養兒-----] 525

养育之恩 〔養---〕 423

443. 尧舜禹汤 [堯--湯] 414

遥遥领先的预言 〔遙遙領--預-〕 463

444. 要想富, 先修路 [-] 2
445. 一白遮百丑 [----醜] 343

一草一木 [-] 662
一场春梦 [-場-夢] 336

446. 一尘不染 [-塵--] 215
447. 一代不如一代 [-] 479
448. 一方水土养一方人 [----養---] 654

一锅端 [-鍋-] 695
一粒老鼠屎, 坏了一锅粥 [-, 壞--鍋-] 697

449. 一马勺坏一锅 [---壞-鍋] 696
450. 一默如雷 [-] 118
451. 一起同过窗不如一起扛过枪/分过赃/嫖过娼 [. . . 過槍/-過贓/-過-] 97

一人 [-] 253
一人千古, 千古一人 [-] 254

452. 一日为师, 终身为父 [--為師, 終-爲-] 605
453. 一失足成千古恨 [-] 131
454. 一死百了 [-] 164
455. 一笑泯恩仇 [-] 421
456. 一蟹不如一蟹 [-] 480

132 *Alphabetical index of Chinese expressions in footnotes*

457. 一叶浮萍归大海, 人生何处不相逢 [-葉--歸--, ---處---] 1

一针见血 [-針--] 714

458. 疑人不用, 用人不疑 [-] 471

疑神疑鬼 [-] 469
疑心生暗鬼 [-] 470

459. 以成败论英雄 [--敗論--] 43
460. 以人为镜, 可以知得失 [--為鏡, -] 445
461. 阴盛阳衰 [陰-陽-] 195

阴阳怪气 [陰陽-氣] 196
雍容华贵 [--華貴] 665

462. 友谊地久天长 [-誼---長] 623
463. 有便宜不占王八蛋 [-] 387
464. 有的人活着, 他已经死了; 有的人死了, 他还活着 142
465. 有面子 [-] 447
466. 有娘生, 没爹教 [-] 586
467. 有其父必有其子 [-] 552

余勇可贾 [餘--賈] 29

468. 与人为善 [與-爲-] 490
469. 与天斗, 其乐无穷, 与地斗, 其乐无穷, 与人斗, 其乐无穷 [與-鬥, -樂無窮, 與-鬥, -樂無窮, 與-鬥, -樂無窮] 272

欲壑难填 [--難-] 124

470. 欲加之罪, 何患无辞 [-, --無辭] 466
471. 鹬蚌相争, 渔翁得利 [鷸--爭, 漁---] 112
472. 冤仇宜解不宜结 [------結] 437
473. 愿赌服输 [-賭-輸] 326

月下老人 [] 537
越描越黑 [-] 464
砸锅卖铁 [-鍋賣鐵] 692
赞拜不名 [讚---] 231

474. 凿壁偷光 [鑿---] 596
475. 早死早超生 [-] 165

曾参杀人 [-參殺-] 462
占女人的便宜 [-] 391

476. 占小便宜吃大亏 [------虧] 389

站队 [-隊] 496

477. 站着说话不腰疼 [-著説話---] 110

丈山尺树, 寸马分人 [---樹-馬--] 487

478. 朝为田舍郎, 暮登天子堂 [-] 601

照猫画虎 [--畫-] 598

479. 这山望着那山高 [這--著---] 128

这是天意 [這---] 183

480. 贞洁牌坊 [貞潔--] 560
481. 真金不怕火炼 [-----煉] 736
482. 正大光明 [-] 228
483. 只见树木, 不见森林 [-見樹-, -見--] 483
484. 只要功夫深, 铁杵磨成针 [-, 鐵---針] 711
485. 知恩图报[--圖報] 417

知音 [-] 626
知音少, 弦断有谁听 [-, -斷-誰聽] 631

486. 指鹿为马 [--爲馬] 54
487. 治大国若烹小鲜 [--國---鮮] 224
488. 中共中央总书记, 国家主席, 中央军委主席 [----總書記, 國---, --軍---] 18

中国共产党 [-國-產黨] 260

489. 中国梦 [-國夢] 340

中国人民共和国 [-華----國] 16
中国人民解放军 [-國----軍] 19
中华人民共和国万岁, 世界人民大团结万岁 [-華----國萬歲, -----團結萬歲] 251

490. 中学为体, 西学为用 [-學為體, -學為-] 642
491. 中庸之道 [-] 393

中庸中庸, 屁股打得通红 [-, -----紅] 591

492. 终南捷径 [終--徑] 120
493. 众口铄金, 积毁销骨 [衆-鑠-, 積毀銷-] 461
494. 众人拾柴火焰高 [衆------] 264

众志成城 [衆---] 268
周恩来 [--來] 430
周公解梦 [---夢] 337

495. 猪狗不如 [-] 679

祝你好梦成真 [---夢--] 331
庄周梦蝶 [莊-夢-] 338

496. 自求多福 [-] 477

走狗 [-] 406, 669

497. 罪莫大于不孝 [---於--] 513
498. 醉翁之意不在酒 [-] 311

尊皇后为皇太后 [---為---] 223

499. 尊师重道 [-師--] 611
500. 坐山观虎斗 [--觀-鬥] 111

Appendix 4

Index of entries by their cultural value

10   Auditory impression of the Chinese language (汉语的听觉印象) #4
10   Beauty (美女) #127
10   Chinese language and culture: Negative tendency (中国语言的负面倾向) #1
10   Dream (梦) #126
10   Fame and fortune (名利) #31
10   Filial (孝) #168
10   Heavenly principles (天理) #58
10   Husband and wife: good (夫妻: 关系好) #173
10   Old or new (新与旧) #39
10   Parents (父母) #169
10   People, the (人民) #14
10   Poor (穷) #132
10   Purpose of life (生活的目的) #118
10   Retribution, karma (报应) #66
10   Social hierarchy (等级) #165
10   Three Immortal Deeds (三不朽) #97
10   Women and goods (女人与货) #181
 5   'Death penalty' and modesty (死罪死罪) #52
 5   Ancestors (祖宗) #167
 5   Antithetical couplets (对联) #161
 5   Change (改变) #12
 5   Children (孩子) #175
 5   Chinese characters and way of thinking (汉字与思维) #2
 5   Chinese emperors should thank historians. (中国皇帝应该感谢史官) #100
 5   Civilities (客套) #149
 5   Correctness of names (名正言顺) #82
 5   Courage (勇气) #16
 5   Custom (风俗) #121
 5   Die, death (死) #55
 5   Dogs (狗) #215
 5   Education: importance, content (教育: 重要性和内容) #190
 5   Emperors, kings, generals, ministers (帝王将相) #91
 5   Euphemisms for 'sexual intercourse' ('做爱'的委婉语) #263
 5   Euphemisms for 'to die' ('死'的委婉语) #262
 5   Face and dignity (脸, 面子) #148

Index of entries by their cultural value   135

5   Families: exemplary and satisfactory (家庭: 令人羡慕的和令人满意的) #171
5   Fawn (吹捧) #141
5   Find a happy medium (折中) #135
5   Fondness for children (恋童) #128
5   Food and drink (饮食) #122
5   Friends and friendship (朋友, 友谊) #196
5   Gain extra advantage and suffer losses (占便宜与吃亏) #134
5   Gamble (赌) #125
5   Gold and jade (金玉) #229
5   Good or bad (优劣) #36
5   Hatred (仇) #144
5   Heavenly Stems and Earthly Branches to compute time (天干地支纪年) #258
5   Human relations (人际关系) #164
5   Individual vs. group (一人与一群) #136
5   Juxtaposed antonyms meaning 'category' or 'scope' (并列反义词表范围) #249
5   Kick someone to the curb (卸磨杀驴) #28
5   Laws (法) #60
5   Legacy (功名) #47
5   Life and death (生死) #51
5   Liquor and drinking (酒, 喝酒) #123
5   Louis Cha Leung-yung (金庸, Jin Yong) #139
5   Lu Xun (鲁迅) #40
5   Lucky numbers (6和8) #287
5   Mandate of Heaven, or God's will (天命, 天意) #59
5   Mean person (小人) #137
5   Men vs. ghosts (人与鬼) #64
5   More bad guys (坏人多) #247
5   Mystic Dragon Cult Leader (神龙教主) #140
5   Naming taboo (避讳) #86
5   No principles (无原则) #25
5   North Korea and South Korea (北韩与南朝鲜) #116
5   Not flip flop (不折腾) #110
5   Not standing out (不出头) #26
5   Onlookers (看客) #41
5   Outstanding statecraft and brilliant military exploits (文治武功) #73
5   Parents and children (父母与子女) #170
5   Party, the (党) #106
5   Posthumous titles (谥号) #83
5   Respecting teachers (尊师) #195
5   Rich and powerful (富贵) #129
5   Rosy cheeks (红颜) #185
5   Same and different (同与异) #57
5   Soulmates (知己) #197
5   Spatial-temporal metaphors (时空比喻) #251
5   Speculative (投机) #22
5   Standpoint (立场) #15
5   Sub-ministerial level universities (副部级大学) #188

136 *Index of entries by their cultural value*

5 Success and failure (胜负, 成败) #30

5 Synonyms (近义词) #283

5 Teacher and student, master and apprentice (师生, 师徒) #194

5 Temporal sequence (时间顺序) #6

5 The battle of Chinese character forms: traditional, simplified or pinyin? (汉字之争) #3

5 The meaning of yisi ('意思'的意思) #254

5 The most heartbreaking vows (最让人心碎的誓言) #268

5 The verse that changed China the most (影响中国最大的一句话) #11

5 Tolerant (宽容) #18

5 Unrestrained (风流) #131

5 Utilitarianism (功利主义) #20

5 Value and joy of learning (读书的价值和快乐) #193

5 What was needed to rule China? (如何治理中国?) #75

5 Wives, housewives and brooms (妻子, 妇女与扫帚) #184

5 Women, regarding sex and marriage (忠, 贞, 烈的女人) #177

5 Women, unlucky (倒霉的女人) #178

5 Yin and yang (阴阳) #65

3 'And' vs. 和 (和与 'and') #253

3 Auspicious signs and the color white (祥瑞与白色) #61

3 Bad habits (恶习) #124

3 Benevolence and justice (仁与义) #33

3 Binomal words (连绵词) #284

3 Blessing and the unfortunate Song dynasty (宋朝年号与'祐') #78

3 Brothers' names and radicals (兄弟人名的汉字与部首) #274

3 Buddha and monks (佛与和尚/僧) #68

3 Change (化) #10

3 Change, in the wrong way (变坏) #13

3 Chinese literary works with the richest culture (富含中国文化的文艺作品) #160

3 Chinese ordinal numbers (汉语顺序号) #285

3 Classics (经) #257

3 Collectivism (集体主义) #108

3 Colors and culture (颜色与文化) #155

3 Discrimination of women (女人干坏事) #179

3 Discuss in an open manner (妄议) #113

3 Earthquakes and women (地震与女人) #183

3 Education: learning methods (教育: 学习方法) #191

3 Find fault (找借口) #151

3 Flunky vs. talent (奴才vs. 人才) #138

3 Four magnificent characters and the declination of the Northern Song ('丰亨豫大'与北宋的衰败) #77

3 Gifted scholars and beautiful women (才子佳人) #159

3 Gifts to avoid giving (不能送的礼物) #146

3 Given names: taboo and honor (改名) #87

3 Greedy (贪婪) #45

3 Homophonic puns (谐音双关) #264

3 Husband and wife: bad (夫妻: 关系差) #174

3 Idioms with 'heaven/earth' (带'天/地'的成语) #259

Index of entries by their cultural value 137

3 Idioms with markers of simile (带比喻词的成语) #7
3 Innovation and Chinese college mottos (大学校训与创新) #189
3 Integrity vs. ability (德与才) #32
3 Japanese era names feature common Chinese characters (日本年号中的汉字) #115
3 Kindness (恩) #143
3 Kindness and hatred (恩仇) #142
3 Long live (万岁) #102
3 Men's three treasures (农民的三宝) #54
3 Nonverbal love (无言的爱) #49
3 Not even recognize cows and goats (见牛羊亦不识) #93
3 Partial and impartial (公与私) #21
3 Prime ministers must be chosen from Confucian scholars (宰相须用读书人) #76
3 Rulers and the ruled, ancient and present (社会的两极) #166
3 Rumor (流言) #150
3 Sages and men of virtue (圣贤) #94
3 Share weal or woe? (同甘还是共苦) #50
3 Stay foolish (难得糊涂) #43
3 Stress the past, not the present (厚古薄今) #37
3 Temple names and achievements of emperors (庙号与成就) #85
3 Temple names of emperors (庙号) #84
3 The history and a young girl (历史与小姑娘) #117
3 The pride of a great empire and the reluctance to lose power (帝国不愿舍弃的荣光) #80
3 The worst curse word (贼) #245
3 Thoughtcrimes (思想罪) #112
3 Times and heroes (时势与英雄) #17
3 To one's face and in his back (当面与背后) #145
3 To speak eloquently (能说) #279
3 To survive by all possible means (活着) #53
3 Vast land and abundant natural resources (地大物博) #38
3 Wall (墙) #235
3 Water (水) #206
3 Women and their names in ancient China (女人的名字) #180
2 'Go drink tea' (吃茶去) #71
2 Attitude to life (生活态度) #120
2 Bats (蝙蝠) #220
2 Boldest proclamation of reform (三不足) #109
2 Bo Le (伯乐) #199
2 Boss (老板) #198
2 Buns or dumplings (包子) #226
2 Chinese characters composed of 人 (比, 从, 北, 化) #282
2 Chinese condolences (节哀顺变) #56
2 Chinese cooking methods (中国菜的做法) #225
2 Chinese equivalent of the English word 'do' (弄) #256
2 Choice of Chinese characters for foreign place names (外国地名中的汉字的选择) #269
2 Circle of. . . (*坛/界) #278

138 *Index of entries by their cultural value*

2 Classical translation of movie titles (电影片名经典翻译) #270
2 Common lengths of forms in Chinese literature (几种中国文学体裁的长度) #157
2 Copycatting culture (山寨文化) #202
2 Cousins (表亲) #176
2 Debt (债) #133
2 Difficulty levels of Chinese rhyme (韵脚的难易) #281
2 Dogs and chicken/pigs (鸡犬/猪狗) #216
2 Dusts and the human world (尘与世) #72
2 Electricity and Chinese idioms (成语中的电) #8
2 Experienced and inexperienced (内行与外行) #201
2 Fairness (公道) #63
2 Feudal (封建) #88
2 Flowers and unfaithfulness (花与不忠) #211
2 Flowers and willows (花柳) #209
2 Foreign and rustic (洋与土) #203
2 Foreign countries with '国' in their Chinese names (*国) #243
2 Forms of address: respectful, honorific and modest (尊称, 敬称, 谦称) #275
2 Four Noblemen (四君子) #213
2 Heroines (女英雄) #186
2 Humorous (幽默) #35
2 I'll think about it (研究研究) #255
2 Ignorant young ladies (无知少女) #107
2 Importance of tools (工具的重要性) #232
2 Keeping the emperor company (与大人物相处) #92
2 Language games (文字游戏) #260
2 Language play on internet (网络上的语言游戏) #261
2 Little * (*小*) #105
2 Locations of the four temples in Beijing (北京四坛的方位) #62
2 Loyal and martial (忠武) #98
2 Master (*子) #95
2 Medicine (药) #239
2 Mental balance (心理平衡) #29
2 Middlemen (中间人) #200
2 Model of all Chinese (中国人的楷模) #96
2 Monkeys (猴子) #219
2 More precious than gold (比金子还贵) #231
2 Nails (钉子) #234
2 One Belt One Road Initiative (一带一路) #114
2 One man (一人) #103
2 Oneself and others (人与己) #19
2 Open and aboveboard (光明正大) #81
2 Painting (画画) #163
2 Peaceful and chaotic (治与乱) #89
2 Penitential decrees and letters of self-criticism (罪己诏与检讨书) #90
2 Peonies and prosperous (牡丹和富贵) #212
2 Prostitutes, other names of (妓女的别称) #182
2 Quality and rice (质量与大米) #238

Index of entries by their cultural value   139

2 Refined and popular (雅俗) #34
2 Repent (回头) #46
2 Representatives of Chinese literature (中国文学的代表) #156
2 Seek others for help (求人) #153
2 Sharp-witted remarks (机锋) #70
2 Shortcuts (捷径) #44
2 Silence (沉默) #42
2 Sound and culture (语音与文化) #5
2 Suspicious (怀疑) #152
2 Symbolism of goats (羊的象征意义) #218
2 Things (东西不是南北) #248
2 Three and four (*三*四) #286
2 Tigers (老虎) #214
2 To take or decline the throne (劝进与固辞) #79
2 Warning inscription on a stone (戒石铭) #111
2 Water and fire/soil/wind (水火/水土/风水) #207
2 Wok (锅) #224
1 73 and 84 (七十三，八十四) #289
1 Blue mountains (青山) #205
1 Boats (舟和船) #236
1 Bone (骨头) #227
1 Buddhism and emperors with a posthumous title of 武 (佛教与'*武帝') #67
1 Buddhist texts and knife (佛经与刀) #69
1 Chinglish, updated (新中式英语) #273
1 Color and lust (色) #228
1 Confucius says (子曰) #158
1 Cows (牛) #217
1 Deterioration (变差) #154
1 Dilution of vulgar words (傻*) #267
1 East . . . west. . . (东/西) #240
1 Eyebrows and urgency (眉毛与紧急) #222
1 Fish and 'surplus' (鱼和余) #265
1 Fish and meat (鱼与肉) #221
1 Five buttons (五颗扣子) #288
1 Flowers, grass, trees (花草木) #210
1 Foreign and imported goods (洋货) #204
1 Forget-me-not (勿忘我) #271
1 Getting rich and building roads (致富与修路) #9
1 Hands and feet (手和脚) #223
1 I was here (到此一游) #242
1 Integrity in one's later years (晚节) #48
1 Juxtaposition of male and female (连绵词: 雌雄) #250
1 Learning methods (学习方法) #192
1 Metals, precious and non-precious (金银铜铁) #230
1 Ministry of Rites and its importance (礼部的地位) #99
1 Mirrors (镜子) #147
1 Modal verb serial (能愿动词的连用) #252

140 *Index of entries by their cultural value*

1 Music one gets to kneel down when listening (跪着听的音乐) #162
1 Needle (针) #233
1 Noble temperament (贵族气质) #130
1 Not afraid (不怕) #246
1 Ordinary Chinese people's dream, now and then (河清海晏与岁月静好) #119
1 Prosperity and prostitution (繁荣'娼'盛) #266
1 Roads and ways (道和路) #237
1 Rule the roost (当家) #172
1 Savior (救星) #104
1 Snobbish (势利眼) #24
1 Sophistication (灵活) #27
1 South . . . north. . . (南/北) #241
1 Southern Chinese names and 阿* (南方人名中的'阿') #276
1 Super 'wind' (超级风) #208
1 The first thing to do after a new emperor ascended the throne in ancient China (新皇继位后做的第一件事) #74
1 The last bit of an emperor's dignity (皇帝最后的尊严) #101
1 The true. . . (真 . . .) #187
1 Three hundred (三百) #290
1 To talk nonsense (胡说) #280
1 Vegetables introduced to China (传入中国的蔬菜) #272
1 Warning, mild (温和的警告) #244
1 White Bone Spirit (白骨精) #277
1 Who do you think you are? (你算老几啊?) #23

Appendix 5

A brief chronology of Chinese history (to 1912)

夏 Xia dynasty		c. 2100 BCE–c. 1600 BCE
商 Shang dynasty		c. 1600 BCE–c. 1100 BCE
西周 Western Zhou dynasty		c. 1100 BCE–c. 771 BCE
东周 Eastern Zhou dynasty	春秋 Spring and Autumn period	770 BCE–476 BCE
	战国 Warring States period	475 BCE–221 BCE
秦 Qin dynasty		221 BCE–206 BCE
汉 Han dynasty	西汉 Western Han	206 BCE–25 CE
	东汉 Eastern Han	25–220
三国 Three Kingdoms	魏 Wei	220–265
	蜀 Shu	221–263
	吴 Wu	222–280
晋 Jin dynasty	西晋 Western Jin	265–317
	东晋 Eastern Jin	317–420
南北朝 Southern and Northern dynasties	南朝 Southern dynasties	420–589
	北朝 Northern dynasties	386–581
隋 Sui dynasty		581–618
唐 Tang dynasty		618–907
五代十国 Five Dynasties and Ten Kingdoms period	五代 Five Dynasties	907–960
	十国 Ten Kingdoms	902–979
辽 Liao dynasty		907–1125
宋 Song dynasty	北宋 Northern Song	960–1127
	南宋 Southern Song	1127–1279
西夏 Western Xia (Tangut)		1038–1127
金 Great Jin		1115–1234
元 Yuan dynasty		1206–1368
明 Ming dynasty		1368–1644
清 Qing dynasty		1636–1912

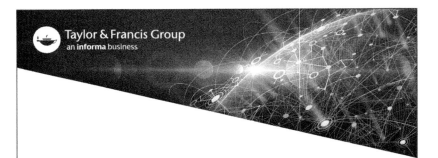